Planning in Cities

Urban Management Series

Series Editor: Nick Hall

Titles in the Urban Management Series:

Planning in Cities
Sustainability and Growth in the Developing World

Edited by

Roger Zetter and Rodney White

Assisted by

Lesley Downing

Practical ACTION PUBLISHING

Practical Action Publishing Ltd
25 Albert Street, Rugby, CV21 2SD, Warwickshire, UK
www.practicalactionpublishing.com

First published in 2002

ISBN 13 Paperback: 9781853395437
ISBN Library Ebook: 9781780441283
Book DOI: http://dx.doi.org/10.3362/9781780441283

A catalogue record for this book is available from the British Library.

Since 1974, Practical Action Publishing has published and disseminated
books and information in support of international development work
throughout the world. Practical Action Publishing is a trading name
of Practical Action Publishing Ltd (Company Reg. No. 1159018), the
wholly owned publishing company of Practical Action. Practical Action
Publishing trades only in support of its parent charity objectives and any
profits are covenanted back to Practical Action (Charity Reg. No. 247257,
Group VAT Registration No. 880 9924 76).

Index by Indexing Specialists (UK) Ltd, Hove, East Sussex
Typeset by J&L Composition, Filey, North Yorkshire

Contents

Foreword – Setting goals for development

Michael Mutter

Our world in the early twenty-first century is steadfastly urbanizing, the more so in the less developed countries. In many ways this is a product of world development and globalization. Our modern lifestyles are urban-biased. Cities can be seen as the engines of growth of our economies, offering many advantages for a gregarious way of life that can reap the benefits of economies of scale – more opportunities for education, healthcare, water supply, sanitation, electricity, transport, telecommunications – and the benefits of multiple opportunities for families, their work opportunities, welfare and livelihoods.

Unfortunately, these opportunities are not yet available universally. The urban poor in particular find themselves marginalized from too many of these opportunities, and instead tend to become caught in a 'poverty trap', a downward spiral of vulnerability where issues of gender, health and age become more acute; where poor urban environments limit health and life chances; where water supply is expensive and at best intermittent; where garbage too often remains uncollected and clogs the surface water drains; where there is little or no sanitation and people spend otherwise productive time disposing of wastes; where eviction from even the meanest of space can be a constant worry; where the law and regulation becomes an enemy rather than a friend.

So why do so many poor people migrate to towns and swell their numbers? Their former circumstances may well have been even worse. Even more likely, however, is that they have not migrated but are already part of the faster-growing urban population, born there, with little or no option to move away.

At the same time, the processes of urbanization affect everyone no matter where they live. The rural hinterland of the growing towns and cities are now more likely to be affected by them. The rural–urban linkages are important parts of the broad economic development of whole regions.

So how should the international development cooperation community relate to these problems? How can we best support processes which can improve the conditions and livelihood opportunities for the urban poor in ways that can benefit also the poor in rural areas? How should we set targets for development that can reverse the causes of poverty?

The broad objectives of all the international development goals can be seen to be relevant in dealing with the issues of urbanization and poverty.

The 1990s saw a decade of remarkable United Nations global conferences. These addressed a range of development aims from the positive inclusion of women in development to a greater respect for human rights, children and their education; from concepts of better health to a greater concern for environments; and from governance and settlement development to a demand for more equitable access to water and other basic human requirements. All of these aims contribute to the better well-being of the global population as a whole, and, in particular, to the eradication of the scourge of poverty.

This decade of global conferences led the partners in international development cooperation to define the future potential for a better world for humankind. The specific objectives include inclusiveness as a means to achieving development, and a recognition that there are physical and economic linkages in the dynamics of growth that have effects on broad groups of society, whether they are spatially lodged in 'urban' or 'rural' places.

At the beginning of a new millennium, this willingness to cooperate on global development issues is the hallmark of an emerging new global society. The objectives are to realize the ideals of the United Nations to act on behalf of 'We, the Peoples of the World' to work together in producing better environments and better opportunities for everybody in the quest for a just and equitable future. These ideals have been encapsulated in the Millennium Development Goals as the outcome agreed by all the member heads of state of the United Nations at the Millennium Summit in September 2000.

How can we now interpret these goals and objectives to ensure a better life for everyone in the future? An underplayed and yet critical part of the answer is to understand where people live and under what circumstances and how these circumstances may change in the future. We must help people to analyse the resources that are available for the future of their own development, no matter where they live, or want to live.

A specific international development goal set by the Commonwealth Consultative Group on Human Settlements reflects the specific aspects of the 1996 Istanbul Habitat II conference: *'to achieve demonstrated progress towards adequate shelter for all with secure tenure and access to essential services in every community by 2015'.*

This target implies that there will be sufficiently improved and inclusive governance that will enable this expression of development planning, progress and potential to be observable in all communities whether urban or rural, or, crucially, those caught in between in the 'no man's land' of the periphery – the so-called 'peri-urban' areas. The 'governance' issue is the second of Habitat's two campaigns. The first is security of tenure, the assurance that people need to invest their labour and hard-won materials in a home of their own – their most essential livelihood asset – without risk of eviction or demolition, so often a hallmark of slum-removal in the past.

The Millennium Development Goals represent the full range of development goals as they arose out of the UN conferences and their outcomes. The indicators of these are to be used to measure progress (normally reported on a country basis to the 5-yearly interval Conference Reviews). Within this large picture, a particular focus for local sustainable development is provided by Local Agenda 21, a chapter of the larger Agenda 21 outcome of the 1992 Rio Conference on Environment and Development. The tighter focus provided by the Habitat Agenda, with its particular stress on shelter, human settlements and urban development, will guide the development of future Department for International Development (DFID) strategy, but with reference to these larger development agendas.

In this respect, the goals of providing basic services to all neighbourhoods and settlements, for example, would include references to the achievement of other development targets for primary healthcare and education in these areas. Similarly, the strategies for managing urban development and change will have fundamental implications for achieving a reduction by one-half in the proportion of people living in poverty in both rural and urban areas (more particularly those rural areas that have close links with towns and cities). The targets that relate to reductions in mortality rates for children and maternal mortality rates will be substantially affected by public health improvements resulting from up-grading and providing essential services to informal low income urban settlements.

A further stress of the targets is on 'inclusiveness', largely through the Habitat Agenda objective of good urban governance. This has important implications for policies and mechanisms to ensure effective participation by communities in the development of their settlements, and the sustainability of their livelihoods. It is important to ensure that they are sufficiently well educated and fully informed, particularly in relation to the development goal of demonstrated progress towards gender equality and the empowerment of women.

What is clear is that the targets for international development goals will not be achieved unless they are applied equally in urban domains as well as rural circumstances, and they will not be pertinent if they do not integrate with one another. More importantly, they will not be achieved unless all targeted groups are involved in the detailed design and implementation of the antidotes, in practice, on the ground. The implication of the new stress on inclusiveness will, I think, guide new international development cooperation strategies in new ways of thinking and new ways of implementation, bringing far more resources directly to the field so that they can be used more efficiently.

This book explores a range of ways in which people can approach the achievement of development. It compares the conceptual basis of the economic advantage of having more sustainable approaches to development with methods for putting these ideals into practice. Such practice needs to become commonplace if the ideals are to be sustained in the future. The book argues a clear way towards such goals.

Michael Mutter
Department for International Development

The Urban Management Series

Nick Hall

The Urban Management Series focuses on the impacts of demographic and economic change in developing countries.

The series offers a platform for practical, in-depth analysis of the complex institutional, economic and social issues that have to be addressed in an increasingly urban and globalized world. One of the UN's Millennium Development Targets calls for significant improvement in the lives of at least 100 million slum-dwellers by 2020, but this is a very modest target.

By 2025 it is estimated that two-thirds of the poor in Latin America, and a third to almost half the poor in Africa and Asia, will live in cities or towns. An estimated 600 million people currently live in life and health threatening homes and neighbourhoods. The urban poor face different issues and livelihood choices in comparison to the rural poor. The reduction of urban poverty requires appropriate policies and approaches. The livelihoods and rights of the poor must be at the centre of any strategy to reduce poverty and develop an inclusive society. This is equally true in urban areas.

Cities and towns, and the industrial and commercial activities located in them, are a positive force for national economic growth. This is why cities are popular: where you find the mass of bees is where to look for honey. Urban areas provide consumer markets and services for agricultural producers. They are also gateways to larger national, regional and international markets. But the opportunities from urban development have not been maximized by poor people. Their rights are curtailed and they are often excluded from accessing secure land, shelter, services, employment and social welfare due to the discriminatory practices of government, the private sector and civil society.

This series of books addresses the many challenges facing urban management professionals. First and foremost, they aim to improve understanding of the impact of urbanization on the livelihoods and living conditions of poor people. With better understanding, the institutional and political conditions for poor people to participate and benefit from the urban development process may be improved. New knowledge from research and dialogue should show how best to involve the private sector and civil society in mobilizing the necessary resources for inclusive and sustainable development; how to mitigate the impact that poor environments and natural hazards have on the poor; how to enhance the economic synergy between rural and urban economies; and how to strengthen efforts by the international community to coordinate support for a positive urbanization process.

Planning in Cities tackles all these issues by focusing on the changing role of planners and on the challenges facing the planning profession. Whereas in the past, attention seemed to centre on the physical shape of cities and the relationships between residential, commercial and industrial uses of land, now and in the future planners are expected to be able to manage complex and often conflicting environmental, social, economic, cultural and political pressures.

This book is about equity and inequity. It highlights the fact that increasing levels of poverty for the majority are a consequence of the way global resources are selfishly controlled to protect the interests of a wealthy minority. Environmentally unsustainable western lifestyles are seen as the cause of socially, politically and economically unsustainable 'southern' lifestyles. Poverty, in effect is the product of wealth, and this is all too evident in the cities of the world's poorer countries. The way land is managed and allocated is just one example of the inequitable and unsustainable use of public resources. Another is the way water resources are managed so that a minority in low-density areas are able to keep their lawns green, while millions in high-density slums are thirsty for clean water.

The challenge for the next millennium presented in this book is that new ways must be found to encourage and ensure public engagement in the way we run our communities and cities.

Acknowledgements

Globalization and the neoliberal economic development paradigm are the driving forces of urbanization in the developing world in the twenty-first century. These processes question the extent to which the increasingly rapid scale and speed of city growth is sustainable: they present profound challenges to the design of effective urban planning policies and management strategies. *Planning in Cities: Growth and Sustainability in the Developing World* is an innovative book which bridges theory and practice to explore these conflicting challenges.

The origins of this book lie in a conference entitled 'Sustainable Cities: Sustainable Development – the Urban Agenda in the Developing World', organized by one of the authors – Roger Zetter – and held in Spring 2000, at the School of Planning at Oxford Brookes University, UK. Drawing on the perspectives of both researchers and professionals, we have taken a selection of papers delivered at that conference. These papers have been rewritten for this book and supplemented by some new chapters commissioned from other authors working in the field.

We owe gratitude to many people involved in the taxing task of translating conference papers into a book. For the original conference, Roger Zetter would like to record his thanks to two colleagues in the School of Planning. Silva Ferretti used her prodigious C&IT skills to turn nearly 30 disparate papers into a cohesive and publishable set of conference proceedings. This ensured that we had a valuable base on which to start the task of constructing this book. That the conference itself was so successful is due to the organizational skills and assistance of Karen Hughes.

We have had excellent support and cooperation from ITDG Publishing from the moment they agreed to publish this book. We thank Nick Hall, the series editor, for his timely, effective and objective advice. His suggestions for improving the overall structure of the book, as well as the individual contributions, have been invaluable. Similarly we want to thank Helen Marsden, Publisher, ITDG Publishing. Her support for the project, as well as her indulgence of hard-pressed academics needing to extend publisher's deadlines, has been appreciated.

Finally, but most importantly, we owe a huge debt of thanks to Lesley Downing, the book's desk editor. Only those who have edited books and journals know the logistical, stylistic and temporal challenges of keeping a project like this under control. With clarity, good humour, patience and organizational skills, Lesley has ensured that there is now a book, rather than a portfolio of valuable papers lodged in a PC.

The publishers would like to thank Chris Stowers/Panos Pictures for permission to use the cover image.

Figures

Tables

Boxes

Acronyms and abbreviations

AVAUME	*Asociación de Asentamientos de Vecinos Unidos de El Mezquital* (Association of United Residents of El Mezquital), Guatemala City
BCIE	Central American Bank for Economic Integration, Costa Rica
CDP	Community Development Programme, UNHCS
CEOSS	Coptic Evangelical Organization for Social Services (Egyptian NGO)
COINAP	Inter-institutional Committee for Vulnerable Areas, Guatemala City
COIVIEES	*Cooperativa Integral de Vivienda Esfuerzo y Esperanza* (Integrated Cooperative of Housing Esfuerzo and Experanza), Guatemala
DAPD	District Administrative Department of Planning, Bogotá
DFID	Department for International Development, UK
DLHUD	Directorate of Lands, Housing and Urban Development, Lesotho
EAJP	Executive Agency for Joint Projects, Housing Ministry, Egypt
EIA	environmental impact assessment
EPSA	Water and Sanitation Provider, Bolivia
FONAVI	National Housing Fund, Costa Rica
FUNDAESPRO	*Fundación Esfuerzo y Prosperidad* (Foundation of Courage and Prosperity), Guatemala
FUNDESCO	*Fundación para el Desarrollo Comunitario* (Foundation for Community Development), Guatemala
FUPROVI	*Fundación Promotora de Vivienda* (Foundation for the Promotion of Housing), Costa Rica
GoL	Government of Lesotho
GOPP	General Organization for Physical Planning, Housing Ministry, Egypt
GOSD	General Organization for Sanitary Drainage, Egypt
HLS	household livelihoods strategy
IAURIF	Institut d'Aménagement et d'Urbanisme de la Région d'Ile-de-France (Paris planning agency)

ICLEI	International Council for Local Environmental Initiatives
IDB	Inter-American Development Bank
ILCS	Integrated Low Cost Sanitation Programme, Government of India
IMF	International Monetary Fund
IPTU	*Imposto Predial e Territorial Urbano*, Urban land and property taxation, Brazil
ISS	*Imposto sobre Serviços*, Service land uses taxation, Brazil
ITBI	*Imposto sobre a Transmissão de Bens Imóveis*, Real estate transactions tax, Brazil
IVVC	*Imposto sobre Veiculos combustiveis*, Vehicles and fuel tax, Brazil
MSF	*Médicos son Fronteras* (Doctors without Borders), Guatemala
NEF	New East Foundation (Egyptian NGO)
OECD	Organisation for Economic Cooperation and Development
PHED	Public Health Engineering Department, Rajasthan, India
PROFAC	Project for the Strengthening of Community Self-management in the Development and Operation of Human Settlements, Costa Rica
PROUME	*Programa de Urbanización de El Mezquital* (Programme for the Urbanization of El Mezquital), Guatemala City
REPROINSAS	*Representantes del Programa Integrado de Salud* (Representatives of the Integrated Health Programme), Guatemala City
SPARC	Society of the Promotion of Area Resource Centres, India
SSA	Strategic Sanitation Approach, UNDP/World Bank
UMP	Urban Management Programme, UNHCS
UNCHS	United Nations Centre for Human Settlements (Habitat)
UNEP	United Nations Environment Programme
UNICEF	United Nations Children's Fund
UPAVIM	*Unidas para Vivir Mejor* (Women United for a Better Life), Guatemala
USAID	US Agency for International Development
WCED	World Commission on Environment and Development
WEDC	Water, Engineering and Development Centre, Loughborough University, UK
WSP	Water and Sanitation Programme, UNDP/World Bank
WSP-SA	Water and Sanitation Programme, South Asia division

Introduction

Roger Zetter and Rodney White

URBANIZATION AND THE CHANGING ENVIRONMENTAL AGENDA

Sustainability has often been conceived in specifically environmental terms. More recently, the relevance of sustainability to the urban sector – city building, urban policy and urban governance – has gained currency. *Planning Cities: Sustainability and Growth in the Developing World* brings these two discrete discourses into closer conjuncture. It reviews the conceptual issues that underpin sustainability in the context of the urban sector. And it explores the experience of translating these concepts to the field through case studies which assess the challenges and limitations to urban sector capacity-building.

As the world population surpasses 6 billion people, we are also crossing another statistical threshold as more than half of that population have become urbanized. No form of government has been able to reverse, or even slow down, this trend towards urbanization, although that has been the objective of a great many planning initiatives in both market economies and centrally planned economies. As demographic growth is mainly a feature of the developing world, it is there that cities grow the fastest, a dynamic fuelled by natural increase and by rural–urban migration, and accelerated, in the past decade, by processes of economic globalization and market enablement. The combined pressures of urban growth and economic development are reflected in eroded living standards, degraded environmental conditions and depleted environmental resources. Cities are in an era of great social, environmental and economic turbulence.

Conditions in the poorest of these cities, and in the poorer quarters of richer cities, remain static, and in many cases have declined as development proceeds. Despite being leading sectors of economic growth, their productive base is fragile: they lack adequate food supplies and employment, are poorly resourced, and lack effective waste management, clean water supplies and satisfactory air quality. Yet high birth rates and the irreversible influx of new migrants sustain the continued growth of such urban areas. In this context, what does the term 'sustainable cities' mean?

There are at least two quite different responses to this question, and the interplay between these two interpretations forms an important theme for this book – especially in the first part. Perhaps the dominant interpretation is that sustainable cities must be based on the sustainable livelihoods of their inhabitants. This approach builds on the established theme of 'basic needs' which dominated development theory until the last decade. This notion of sustainability is rooted in the attainment of an acceptable quality of life for all, including the poor. It answers the question 'sustainable for whom?' with an inclusive 'for all'. This emphasis on satisfying basic needs is similar to the notion of a brown agenda for development.

However, the term 'sustainable development' did not spring from these grassroots concerns at all. The term was popularized by the publication of *Our Common Future* by the Bruntland Commission (WCED, 1987). That report was written in response to a concern for humanity's future at the global scale, where the pressure derived from growing wealth, not the persistence of poverty. The Bruntland Commission was a travelling forum that represented all types of country – rich and poor, capitalist and communist – and received inputs from many varied sources. Its mandate was to assess the state of the planet from the perspective of a growing human population which, as it moved from poverty to wealth, required more and more resources and filled up more and more of the world's 'sinks' with its waste. The global extent of acid deposition had been recognized, as had the thinning of the stratospheric ozone shield that protected the Earth from ultraviolet radiation. Thirty years of monitoring confirmed that build-up of greenhouse gases in the atmosphere that was expected to lead to global warming. These atmospheric problems were added to existing concerns with loss of biodiversity and the depletion of water resources, soils, fisheries and forests.

The Commission was directed to address the problems of all humanity, poor as well as rich. However, what distinguished the Bruntland Commission from earlier assessments was that, this time, the rich were worried for their own future. Inevitably it was this novelty that caught the attention of the western press and public. The persistence of poverty was recognized by the Bruntland Commission, but it was implied that the western development process could be reconstructed in a sustainable mode. Bilateral and multilateral development agencies hastened to label all their inspirations and activities as 'sustainable', and thus the term was coined without a fundamental reappraisal of the global situation.

This somewhat guileless retreat did not impress people working at grassroots level. Many felt that the output from the Commission was more a public relations exercise than a serious attempt to examine alternative development models. The atmospheric and resource depletion problems were labelled somewhat dismissively as the 'green agenda', the selfish preoccupation of the wealthy in the West who had no interest in the problems of the poor in the developing world. This lack of engagement between the grassroots or brown agenda and the green agenda leads to a number of problems, both theoretical and empirical, that are taken up in the chapters of this book.

First, both agendas are real and urgent, and require attention now. It will not suffice to address the brown agenda first, and the green agenda later. Later will be too late. A model is urgently required that will alleviate poverty *and* reduce the planetary impact of the rich. Second, although the problems of the green agenda are primarily the result of the activities of the rich, they also – through their global reach – have potentially dire consequences for the poor. Thus the poor countries have a very strong motive to become involved in dealing with the green agenda – from global warming to the loss of biodiversity. Third, although physical indicators, such as litres of water and tonnes of greenhouse gases, measure the items on both agendas, the problems on the agenda are the result of political and social choices. Thus they can be addressed only through the political process. If the political process cannot be changed, then none of these physical trends, which chart the physical impoverishment of the planet, will be affected.

Poverty is not a technical problem. It is an outcome, or side-effect, of human choice. Even 6 billion people could live on planet Earth at a reasonable standard of of living if resources were allocated differently. They could not live in the way people of the West currently live, each emitting 4 tons of carbon into the atmosphere every year and using several hundred of litres of water every day. In other words, 6 billion people cannot be supported under the current western mode of production and consumption. In the West there is a slowly growing realization that the current lifestyle will have to change in almost every way, although so far, the changes adopted (such as metered water supply and recycling of solid waste) have been small.

The big question is whether or not changes in the western lifestyle can be used beneficially to alleviate the worst conditions in the developing world. Can cities, for example, be redeveloped both to provide a financial surplus for poverty reduction and to provide a better, more sustainable model for the cities evolving in the developing world? In other words, can the green agenda be used to fund the brown agenda? One reason for exploring this possibility with some optimism is that the western model of development is exceptionally wasteful. Environmental impacts, such as resources depletion and pollution, are largely externalized from the western economic system. At most, some of the recurrent costs of waste are recovered, for example through charges for waste disposal and water rates. But such charges fail to reflect the wider costs and the irreversibility of some of the impacts, such as climate change and loss of biodiversity. Developing countries that followed the western model have largely adopted the same approach to resource use. People squander resources as soon as they become rich enough to do so.

Thus we face both sets of problems simultaneously. The rich waste resources, while the poor cannot access enough. What is obviously needed is a development model that encourages wise use of resources and the minimization of waste. Until such a model is available, sustainable development is unattainable.

URBANIZATION, THE ENVIRONMENT AND PLANNING

Within the context of this malleable agenda of environmentalism, and against the backcloth of economic development and urbanization, this book explores the challenge of accommodating both sustainability and growth in urban planning.

In recent years there has been a profound reconceptualization of the role of the urban sector, and the significance of urbanization to the broader framework of development aspirations. Premised on the macro-economic forces of globalization and structural adjustment, underpinned by new approaches to urban governance, and complemented by the challenge of sustainability outlined above, this paradigm shift has had equally profound impacts on the nature of planning policies, strategies and instruments, and on the institutional and governmental structures that regulate them. However, at the core of this reappraisal of how cities might be planned, governed and managed, the status of urban sustainability remains highly ambivalent. One of the book's main themes addressed the extent to which the 'new' praxis of urban planning and management successfully engages concepts of sustainability alongside the economic imperative of growth. This is addressed principally in the second part.

In a period of rapid globalization of economic activity, and the increasingly unfettered mobility of finance capital, manufacturing enterprise locates where costs are lower and the regulation of production (through e.g. environmental and planning controls) is less restrictive. This is where cities in the developing world have challenged the comparative advantage of developed economies. Combined with the imperative of rapid economic growth, many developing countries (sub-Saharan Africa is a notable exception) have acceded to the pragmatic demands of internationally mobile finance. This has placed great pressure on the spatial structure and physical infrastructure of cities, and has challenged the concept of sustainability.

In the developing world, city survival in a globalizing economy is critical because these cities constitute the vital leading sector, the main contributors to the economic output of these countries. Consolidating this comparative advantage, and expanding new economic activity in profit-maximizing, externally traded activities, has significant implications for urbanization and urban planning. Reshaping the role of cities sets the agenda for urban development, changes the economic and spatial composition of urban areas, and induces further rapid growth and physical change. On one hand, the transformation of the 'formal' city continues unchallenged. Traditional domestic industries intensify and expand production into heavily export-oriented production for a global market. Meanwhile, footloose high-tech and service industries, largely financed by foreign investment, locate randomly on the urban periphery. Formal sector residential land use also becomes increasingly disaggregated from a coherent city structure, further accentuating a haphazard and unsustainable city form. On the other hand, the formal city remains globally competitive only by sustaining low internal costs of labour, development and infrastructure for the mass of city-dwellers – the urban poor. These imperatives ensure that the formal economy can be sustained only by the burgeoning but marginal 'informal' city, on which the survival strategies of the mass of impoverished urban dwellers are increasingly dependent. These conditions intensify their physical, economic and social vulnerability.

Simultaneously, structural adjustment and lending policies over the past decade have radically reshaped domestic economies to fit the new economic order. Deregulation and macro-economic reform programmes are the necessary instruments of global economic integration and mobile capital, and have confirmed the salience of market processes. Alongside globalization, structural adjustment and lending policies have important implications for the processes of urbanization, urban sustainability and city planning. Reinforcing cities in the developing world as centres of production has required policies that reduce public costs derived from the regulation of urban development and production (e.g. relaxing planning controls, limiting the impact of brown and green environmental strategies, reducing infrastructure and servicing costs and standards). These policies have a negative impact on environmental quality, intensify formal and informal urban growth, and are unsustainable.

Clearly, global redistribution of economic activity constitutes the dynamic which is restructuring cities in the developing world – not simply national demographic growth and population redistribution, the major dynamics for urbanization in the past. Economic and spatial disaggregation and restructuring of cities also reinforces the complexity of managing and planning these processes of urban change at the macro-level. The fundamental challenge is to mediate contradictory short- and long-term economic and environmental impacts. Increasingly, though, whether informal or formal, most urban growth takes place largely outside strategic planning objectives and regulation. Environmental conditions deteriorate; congestion and pollution intensify.

These themes and the concepts which underpin them are addressed principally in the first part of the book. This forms the necessary backcloth to the second part, which elaborates, in the case studies, the impacts of the changing paradigm and responses to it.

The critical question, which the second part of the book addresses, is the susceptibility to intervention of these processes of urban change and their consequent environmental impacts. In short, who plans and manages cities in this new development paradigm? The normative assumptions, that it is a combination of conventional national and municipal government machinery, and orthodox planning instruments, are no longer tenable.

New urban interests compete for power and responsibility for the future shape and structure of the city. In addition to the public sector authorities and agencies, business associations, trade unions, non-governmental organizations (NGOs), community-based organizations (CBOs) – not to mention aid donors and international consultants – all exist in the turbulent arena of urban governance. Although by no means unique to the developing world, this new configuration is particularly evident here because it forms part of the wider restructuring of the development paradigm discussed above. Internationally funded reform programmes and market enablement are contingent on conditionally: the reform of government structures combined with a reduction in the state's primacy through privatization, increased channelling of aid through NGOs, democratic reform, and the promotion of civil society. This fundamental restructuring of governance is most pronounced at the urban level.

As the book shows, the crucial challenge lies in promoting sustainable urban planning strategies and tools where the majority of city dwellers and activities are informal and remain largely outside the emerging power structures, and where competing interests make consensus and partnership over spatial and environmental goals difficult to achieve. Ironically, urban institutional reform appears to have replicated, in social and governance structures, the spatial disaggregation of the city produced by economic reform programmes. The ability of private capital and urban élites to secure short-term gains is enhanced. And privatization of urban services tends to reduce not only public expenditure, but also the scope of urban administrations to coordinate the development and phasing of infrastructure – key instruments in managing the spatial structure of cities in a sustainable way. Unregulated urbanization by the poor, and poorly regulated development undertaken by private capital, are not easily amenable to long-term effective strategic planning and policy-making. These structural challenges inhibit the production of innovative planning policies and instruments to coordinate development city-wide.

PLANNING CITIES: SUSTAINABILITY AND GROWTH IN THE DEVELOPING WORLD

In two parts comprising 14 chapters, this book explores these complex and challenging themes. The first part sets the scene, exploring the discourse on sustainability within the context of the urban sector. It provides a bridge between theory and practice. It reviews, elaborates and debates the main conceptual issues and conflicts that underpin planning for sustainable urban growth, and shows how these issues and conflicts have become embedded in the wider discourse on economic development within which cities play a crucial role.

The opening chapter (Al-Moataz Hassan and Zetter) sets the scene for the book. They demonstrate how the evolution of the paradigms of economic development, urbanization and sustainability has proceeded on parallel trajectories, rather than in an interactive and coordinated fashion. The chapter highlights the centrally significant role of both developmental and environmental policies in processes of urbanization, but concludes that policies for urban sustainability can be achieved only by reconceptualizing the relationship and tensions between needs and environmental imperatives.

Zetter (Chapter 2) reflects on these themes with a more specific focus on the impact of the current development paradigm – market enablement – on prospects for more sustainable processes of urbanization. Premised on the role of cities as a leading sector of the economies of most, if not all, developing countries, the chapter argues that neoliberal economic policies, combined with shifts in urban governance and the promotion of private land market interests, inevitably constrain the potential for producing environmentally sustainable cities.

McGranahan and Satterthwaite (Chapter 3) describe the conflicts that occur between those who prioritize environmental health issues (often called the brown agenda) and those who prioritize ecological sustainability (often called the green agenda). Areas of agreement between these two agendas are outlined, and the measures that help encourage the simultaneous achievement of improved environmental health and more ecologically sustainable urban development are discussed.

White (Chapter 4) links the local challenge of developing sustainable urban conditions for the mass of the urban poor with the global need to reduce greenhouse gas emissions. He argues that these links could provide the momentum for design-makers in the international agencies and richer countries to confront the challenge of Africa's urban future by seriously addressing the policy of carbon credits. African countries, he argues, should make a commitment to gas emission reduction conditional on rich countries first implementing domestic low-carbon technology.

Linking discourse to practice, the second part of the book explores, through case studies, the experience of translating these concepts to the field. The case studies assess the successes and failures of different planning interventions, and the challenges and limitations to urban sector capacity-building. Lessons for sustainability, learned from different approaches to planning, governance and institution-building, are demonstrated and critiqued. The cases presented come from a variety of countries and different urban policy sectors. Encompassing both national-level perspectives and community-based grassroots experiences, a consistent theme is the need to bridge the gap between these complementary levels if planning policies for the rapidly urbanizing developing world are successfully to accommodate both sustainability and growth.

Ortiz-Gomez (Chapter 5) bridges the two parts of the book, showing how macro-level explanations are necessary to account for the profound micro-level spatial reconfiguration of the city of Bogotà. He argues that market enablement policies, by encouraging the privatization of planning and social responsibilities and an entrepreneurial approach to urban development, have produced an essentially unsustainable spatial structure. Taking the examples of housing, retailing and educational provision, he shows how simultaneous processes of atomization and fusion have destroyed the functional base and community structures traditionally found at the inter-mediate level (the neighbourhood). He argues that new planning initiatives which are more pragmatic and flexible are necessary to counter these forces.

The theme of innovative planning tools and institutional capacity-building is taken up by Davey (Chapter 6) in his study of urban policy change in Lesotho. Assessing the effectiveness of international assistance, he identifies a number of critical factors and lessons. He suggests that polit-ical will, public sector accountability and engagement with a wider con-stituency of stakeholders are critical to facilitating sustainable change. Similarly, piloting a multi-stakeholder approach to urban land develop-ment provides a fertile method for encouraging dialogue on policy change.

Lima (Chapter 7) introduces another critical dimension: public finances. His study is based in Belém, Brazil. The capacity of municipal authorities to generate revenue by property taxation, on the one hand, and the deploy-ment of taxation systems to regulate urban development patterns and the quality of urban environments, on the other, are important factors in deter-mining the extent to which sustainable urban forms can be established. He shows how the relationship between property valorization and the larger portfolio or urban planning instruments is often neglected; consequently, significant opportunities to plan and regulate more sustainable patterns of spatial development are neglected.

Sanderson (Chapter 8) takes as his theme the fact that it is almost always the poorest – those living on dangerous land with few resources – who are worst affected by natural disasters, despite their predictability. Resources invested to improve the capacity of national disaster organizations have generally not been effective, and urban planning strategies rarely consider the threat of disasters in development programmes. The chapter shows how the methodology of livelihoods analysis, by helping to interpret the complexities of urban poverty, demonstrates that households are less vulnerable when they are able to build up a range of physical and non-physical 'assets' to withstand disasters. Beginning with vulnerable house-holds, livelihoods analysis offers an approach which unifies understanding of disaster management with development planning. Such an approach has major policy implications for decision-makers aiming to make cities truly sustainable for all.

Jenkins and Smith (Chapter 9) review the experience of implementing United Nations and World Bank shelter sector policies at the end of the 1980s and early 1990s. The chapter takes Mozambique and Costa Rica as examples which, despite significant differences between them, display similarities with respect to the institutional form of action and relation-ships between the three main sectors: state, private sector and civil society. The authors show, on the other hand, how the call to support a strength-ened role for civil society in shelter provision has had limited impact. By contrast, macro-economic forces have reduced state roles and capacity, while not necessarily attracting sufficient effective private sector investment. The authors argue the need to strengthen the role of civil society in shelter policy and practice to enhance sustainability by opening spaces for negotiation with 'horizontal' actors as well as permitting more traditional 'vertical' forms of political negotiation.

Judson Dorman (Chapter 10) considers the effects of the Egyptian state's quasi-rentier political economy on the urban development of Cairo. Drawing on examples of western-backed shelter, upgrading, infrastructure and technical assistance programmes, his analysis shows how these projects either were not implemented, or suffered from problems of replicability and sustainability. These shortcomings fundamentally challenge the state's distributive governance of Egyptian society. The tangled history of urban interventions embodied in the case studies is one of Egyptian government agencies maximizing their access to international assistance, while resisting donor efforts to foster sustainable development through increased state intervention and social mobilization.

Based on fieldwork in El Mezquital, an informal settlement in Guatemala City, Grant (Chapter 11) identifies positive and negative experiences of the 'development process' that took place in this large settlement over a 15-year-period. Considering both the acquisition of basic services and social infrastructure on the one hand, and empowerment and community mobilization on the other, she explores the sustainability of these different initiatives. The chapter shows how the intervention of government and international agencies in the community appears to have been the least significant of factors bringing about change, and is often motivated by clientelism. Conversely, an evaluation of the sustainability of the poverty reduction initiatives taken through community organizations shows how these have generated a process of community empowerment to provide for firmly established community-managed projects with limited external support.

Mchunu (Chapter 12) draws on his research in South Africa to explore the concept of the compact city and sustainability. The chapter argues that the concept has a particular salience in post-apartheid South Africa, not only offering the potential for improving environmental quality, but also in terms of promoting political stability by reference to an ideal form of living and a common sense of destiny. However, in the current situation three issues – the legacy of the apartheid planning framework; the multicultural context; and economic factors – undermine the adaptability and the application of the compact city approach for the potentially novel conditions in South Africa.

Two chapters follow which explore the relationship between sustainable planning and urban infrastructure. Flores' review (Chapter 13) links both conceptual and operational perspectives in assessing the consequences of urban water supply privatization in Bolivia under conditions of structural adjustment. Like Ortiz-Gomez, Flores shows how these global macroeconomic policy frameworks impact with particular force on poor urban communities, reproducing conditions of poverty and inequality. New hierachical management systems to support privatized interests replaced and conflicted with social organizations in the so-called Cochabamba Water Wars, undermining the access of the urban poor to water and the traditional consensus-building mechanisms of governance.

Kevin Tayler (Chapter 14) uses the example of urban sanitation to examine the ways in which planning and development theories need to be critically examined and modified in the light of experience. Sanitation provision has generally failed to keep pace with urban growth in the developing world, but he explores a 'new' approach proposed by the UNDP–World Bank Water and Sanitation Program, the Strategic Sanitation Approach. Using a pilot lesson-learning project in Bharatpur, Tayler shows how many of the concepts underpinning the Strategic Sanitation Approach, such as a demand-based approach to service provision, institutional capacity and funding models, needs rethinking. He argues for a more balanced approach incorporating supply-side factors and the need for improved links between different stakeholders as much as the unbundling and devolution of responsibilities to individual agencies.

These chapters provide the concepts, and illustrate a range of practices for planning the growth of cities in the developing world, while accommodating the principle of sustainability. Taking the structural context of economic growth and market enablement as a given, the role of planning outlined in this book is to provide innovative policies, instruments and modes of intervention that link national spatial strategies through to community-based capacities. At the same time, the effectiveness of urban planning initiatives in guiding rapid urban growth is contingent on the extent to which they coexist with, and are embedded in, appropriate institutional and management frameworks.

This book shows how current thinking and practice provide a platform for reconciling growth and sustainability. The challenge is demanding.

PART I

ISSUES AND DISCOURSES: DEVELOPMENT, URBANIZATION AND SUSTAINABILITY

Sustainable development: between development and environment agendas in the developing world

Al-Moataz Hassan and Roger Zetter

INTRODUCTION

During the twentieth century the world experienced a major shift of population and resources from rural to urban areas. Over 50 per cent of the world's population now live in urban areas, and by the year 2010 it is expected that approximately three-quarters of the population of the developing world will be living in urban areas (UNDP, 1991). Despite the potential benefits of urbanization, cities of developing countries are rarely able to meet the costs that this process imposes (Zetter and Hamza, 1998). Urbanization increases the pressure on limited resources and available services, and threatens health, the environment and urban productivity.

These conflicts highlight the central and significant role of both development and environmental strategies in the production of sustainable forms of urbanization. However, while the evolution of the development paradigm is well established, the development of environmental concepts is less clear-cut, especially in the developing world, and the struggle to achieve economic growth and material prosperity has continually overshadowed the relationship between people and biosphere.

This chapter considers the relationship between the evolution of development strategies and environmental concerns within the urban context during the past four decades. It discusses this interaction in order to explore the impacts on policy formulation for sustainable urban development and the effects on the urban environment in the developing countries.

ECONOMIC GROWTH, MODERNIZATION AND THE ENVIRONMENT

The development paradigm – modernization

The dominant approach to development during the 1950s and 1960s was 'modernization'. The concept of development was defined largely as an economic process (UNEP, 1999) in which wealth and economic growth would improve living conditions and safeguard the environment (Drakakis-Smith, 1986; Webster, 1990). Consequently the 1950s and 1960s was a period of rapid industrialization in many developing countries, based on import substitution.

However, despite the high growth levels among some low and middle economies during this period (Hewitt, 1992), the expected flow of resources to enhance savings and to accumulate surplus did not materialize. Instead, the outflow of private capital from foreign direct investments; insufficient investment in building up national capacity; a decline in the terms of trade of primary products; and endemic difficulties in the balance of payments all inhibited economic take-off.

It had become clear towards the end of the 1960s that the expected trickle-down of economic development was not taking place, and that growth on its own was not a sufficient condition to initiate socio-economic change and development.

From the perspective of this chapter, the key outcome at this stage was the inception of the process of urbanization, and the profound environmental consequences this entailed. Cities expanded, and growing metropolitan areas connected to global and national economies.

The urbanization process was haphazard and chaotic in developing countries (Smith and Lee, 1993). It resulted in increasing demand for land, shelter and service provision, and rapid peripheral growth in squatter settlements or in slums in the already built-up areas of the city: both settlement forms lacked basic living standards and perpetuated conditions and processes that slum clearance and forced displacement policies failed to counteract (UNDP, 1991; Brennan, 1993). Despite the potential benefits of urbanization, its rapid pace has led to well documented economic, social and physical problems, including rising urban poverty; growing demand for urban services and infrastructure; and environmental degradation (UNDP, 1991). The process of increased urban dominance was undermined by the growing deterioration of urban conditions.

The emergence of environmental concerns

Urbanization and industrialization during this period brought about high levels of environmental pollution which contributed to deteriorating conditions for the mass of poor people living in cities. In many of the developing countries, government institutional capacity to deal with these emerging problems was very weak. Responsibility for environmental matters was often distributed across various government ministries; environmental policy based on clear objectives, guiding strategies and monitoring did not exist. Tolba and El-Khouly (1992) argue that the increasing concern in developed countries about the capacity of the world environmental system to support its human population, and the recognition in the 1960s of the unforeseen environmental impacts of industrial pollution, began to reach developing countries only a decade later, by the time of the Stockholm Conference in 1972. The developing world was more preoccupied with the pollution of poverty and the failure of economic growth. As this chapter unfolds, it will become clear that at this time the stage was already being set for the conflicting environmental agendas between developed and developing countries.

For developed countries, in retrospect, the 1950s–1960s constitutes a period of remarkable growth. In general, these countries experienced high levels of employment and low levels of inflation (Hewitt, 1992). Despite warnings of the adverse consequences of the misuse of technologies, overstressed ecosystems, wasted resources and contaminated environments, there was little impact on public attitudes and governmental policies.

In the late 1950s, however, unprecedented economic growth was accompanied by a growing awareness of environmental deterioration and a demand for higher standards of environmental quality and awareness (Caldwell, 1996). National environmental concerns first appeared in the industrialized countries and spread, albeit slowly at first, to the rest of the world. The emerging themes of environmental pollution and limits of growth demonstrated two main concerns.

First, it was increasingly recognized that high rates of industrial growth and production threatened rapidly to deplete the earth's limited stock of natural resources, the consequence being severe social and economic impacts (Tolba and El-Khouly, 1992; Caldwell, 1996). By the late 1960s there was deep concern about the declining level of natural resources, and their capacity to support current consumption patterns. The ability of technological advances to 'rescue' the planet from environmental destruction was questioned.

Second, the environmental agenda reflected the changing characteristics of environmental problems – principally the production of new substances such as plastics and radioactive material, and the challenge of disposing of waste in a consumer-based society (Yearley, 1996). Caldwell's (1996) seminal work argues that, in some respects, environmental conditions were better in the 1960s than for earlier generations. However, the new generation of environmental problems – massive destruction of the natural ecosystem, smog and radiation – seemed critically to challenge the ability of the ecosystem to absorb and reverse the destructive impacts.

Consequently, by the end of the 1960s many developed countries had put in place policies and institutional structures to tackle the environmental agenda. These covered matters such as environmental management (agriculture, fisheries, forestry); nature conservation; town and country planning; and industrial development.

Public environmental awareness expanded internationally, and it became clear that national action alone would be neither sufficient nor successful in addressing environmental problems. The national basis for international cooperation thus commenced because of the inability of national governments to protect environmental resources unilaterally beyond their boundaries.

In response to the popular interest, the Biosphere Conference in 1968 represented the first international meeting concerned with the global environment (Caldwell, 1996). The conference highlighted: (i) the need to change patterns of natural resource consumption and to recognize the biosphere as a system; (ii) the strong relationship between people and the biosphere and the need to consider wider social goals; and (iii) the inadequacy of natural sciences and technology alone to address these challenges.

These themes were an early sign of a shift to a broader conception of the environment that emphasizes the interplay between the natural environment and the human situation. This prepared the ground for the landmark United Nations Conference on Human Environment in Stockholm in 1972.

In summary, as between the developed and the developing world, a divergent approach emerged to development and the environment. In the developed world, the environmental consequences of economic development were acknowledged and absorbed into the policy frameworks of these countries, which increasingly mediated the impacts of development on the environment. In the developing world, the imperatives of rapid urbanization, industrialization and a huge growth in commercial exploitation of natural resources proceeded largely untouched by both the increasingly intractable environmental impacts which they created, and the emerging environmental consciousness of the North. Reconciling these conflicting agendas between North and South, and within the South, came to dominate the succeeding development paradigms.

PARADIGM SHIFT: GROWTH WITH EQUITY, BASIC NEEDS AND HUMAN ENVIRONMENT

Urbanization

During the 1960s and 1970s, urban growth in developing countries not only continued to expand rapidly, but for the first time produced huge cities – the mega-cities – which were much larger than in developed regions. The number of cities of over 4 million jumped from only one city in 1950 (greater Buenos Aires) to eight cities by 1960, and to 22 cities by 1980. The features of contemporary urbanization in developing countries differed from those experienced in the developed world. Whereas urbanization in the industrialized countries took many decades, permitting a gradual emergence of economic, social and political institutions to deal with the problems of transformation, the process in developing countries was very rapid, against a background of higher population growth rates and lower incomes. The pattern of urbanization in a large proportion of developing countries became characterized by a heavy concentration of economic activities and wealth in few large urban centres (Holdgate et al., 1982). It outstripped the developing countries' abilities to provide housing, services and environmentally satisfactory conditions.

Growth with equity – a new development paradigm

By the early 1970s, a paradigm shift in economic development thinking had occurred in response to the shortcomings of the economic growth modernization model. The shift was targeted at three main issues: (i) mass poverty caused by the failure of assumed trickle-down mechanisms; (ii) the impoverished living conditions of the mass of the population in the developing world, especially in urban areas; and (iii) environmental threats, pollution and pressure on natural resources. Three strategic approaches appeared to deal with the failure of modernization: redistribution with growth; basic needs; and ecologically sound development (Holdgate et al., 1982; Webster, 1990; Oman and Wignaraja, 1991; Caldwell, 1996).

Despite differences, the three approaches have common themes, and laid important foundations for subsequent environmental policies and agendas in the developing world. There was an emerging recognition that economic growth, urbanization and the environment are interactive components requiring interactive policy responses. Thus national development plans and strategies were directed to social aspects and the quality of life of low-income groups (including environmental conditions), alongside economic needs, in order to achieve more equitable distributional outcomes. The concept of human settlements policies – from Habitat I in Vancouver in 1972 – embraced quality of life and environmental priorities as primary aims of economic development. This was another important landmark in trying to reconcile the competing aspirations of urbanization, development and the environment. Increasingly, while accepting the inevitability of economic development, the principle of strong governmental intervention to enhance the market, ensure redistribution and mediate environmental conflicts was gaining some ground.

Environmental aspects of urbanization

Despite the conceptual challenges that the growth-with-equity paradigm offered to an unfettered economic growth model of modernization, the condition of human settlements and poor people in the less-developed countries continued to deteriorate. The negative social and economic impacts on the environments of cities in the developing world, and on urban dwellers, grew significantly (Holdgate et al., 1982). Maurice Strong[1], in his statement to the Stockholm 10th anniversary commemorative session in Nairobi, 1982, stated that:

> Cities in developing countries continue to grow faster than measures to make them habitable. The result is that more people than ever face the devastating consequences of the breakdown of cities which are overwhelmed by populations for which they cannot provide the most basic services.

> *(cited by Tolba, 1988).*

Three main negative environmental aspects of urbanization can be identified at this stage: (i) characteristics of dwellings (living space, ventilation, sanitation, water supply, waste disposal, recreation space, domestic energy); (ii) ambient environment quality (air pollution, water pollution, environmental risk, hazards, noise, stress and crime); and (iii) the peri-urban environment (deforestation, soil erosion, changes in micro-climate). These are considered in turn.

In terms of housing conditions, the development model was targeted towards the provision of so-called basic needs (Streeten, 1984; Brennan, 1993) with the expectation that, if satisfied, improved living conditions would be reflected in improved housing environments and economic productivity. The practical means to improve shelter environments – upgrading and sites-and-services – did not reach the majority of low-income people, and failed to satisfy the criteria of affordability, cost recovery and replicability (UNDP, 1991; Burgess et al., 1997) for a variety of economic, fiscal, technical and political pressures.

Consequently, the period of the 1970s–1980s saw the rapid growth of unconventional or informal cities, reflecting the inability of governments and aid donors to implement human settlement policies to house rapidly expanding urban populations. For example, informal housing in Cairo was estimated to account for 84 per cent of all housing units built in the city between 1970 and 1981 (Brennan, 1993).

The environmental conditions of shelter in most cities of the developing world continued to deteriorate: densities were excessive, so that residents suffered health problems mainly related to the poor environmental quality and the deficit of primary urban services such as water and sewage disposal. Insecurity of land tenure, and low household investment priorities accorded to housing, exacerbated the poverty of the residential environments. Subsequently, by the 1980s governments in most developing countries had come to accept the reality, if not the legitimacy, of informal settlements as the driving force of urbanization. Faced with no credible alternative, the outcome of this policy switch was to intensify the need for strongly interventionist environmental policies to remedy the declining conditions. But this was constrained by the inadequacy of national resources and lack of political will to implement, on a sufficiently large scale, the necessary enabling policies (UNDP, 1991).

As regards ambient environmental quality, the excessive concentration of urban-based industry and commerce in developing countries led, on the one hand, to the concentration of people, settlements, and employment. On the other hand, it led to the concentration of polluting activities in urban areas: air and water pollution; congestion and accidents; increasing vulnerability of poor people through occupation of hazard-prone areas (such as steep slopes, flood plains, land adjacent to polluting industries or waste disposal sites); and loss of cultural resources and open spaces (Kreimer et al., 1992; Smith and Lee, 1993; Barton et al., 1994; Burgess et al., 1997; Hamza and Zetter, 1998).

In contrast to the degraded environmental quality of housing, the impacts of the declining quality of the ambient environment affected the entire urban area, including rich and poor, although not necessarily in equal measure. Low-income groups were more vulnerable and more likely to be affected by proximity to sources of pollution in the workplace and residential locations, and by the lack of regulation and enforcement of environmental standards (Tolba, 1988; UNDP, 1991). Conversely, middle- and upper-income groups increasingly began to trade-off negative impacts such as travel time against environmental preferences for less polluted, peripheral residential locations – a process which market enablement dramatically accentuated (Zetter and Hassan, 2002)

However, ambient environmental conditions in many cities of the developing world also continued to worsen as a result of increased industrialization and the consequential impacts on factors such as increased power generation. Arguably, the negative consequence of development was the acceptable price of increasing economic growth (Tolba, 1988; Yearley, 1996). Many developing countries could not afford to contemplate the diversion of scarce economic resources to environmental protection. This 'willingness' to tolerate the pollution consequences of development coincided with the increasing globalization of Northern capital, which ensured that the negative externalities of industrial production were increasingly transferred to developing countries. Because they inevitably placed lower social value on, and incurred higher social costs from, adopting environmental protection (Faber, 1996), it was difficult not only to persuade them to join the international environmental agreements, but also to enforce environmental protection standards at national level as well.

Finally, the spread of urban agglomerations placed mounting pressure on the ecosystem and natural resource base surrounding the expanding cities. This resulted in the loss of agricultural land; deforestation; loss of biodiversity; and, in some cases, environmental refugees.

Several conclusions can be drawn from the shift in development thinking and the environmental aspects of urbanization between the 1970s and early 1980s.

First, the environmental living conditions of low-income people were scarcely better in the mid–1980s than they had been during the 1960s and 1970s. The economic pressures (including market recession, deteriorating terms of trade in primary products, oil crisis, debt servicing), constrained the ability of less-developed countries to invest in environmental protection and to intervene effectively to improve the quality of life.

Second, urban development policies were broadly framed in socio-economic terms aimed at improving living conditions in order to underpin economic growth. While the focus of this approach was on basic needs (including problems of the brown agenda), environmental aspects (problems associated with the green agenda) – in terms of the carrying capacity of the biosphere – were overlooked. For example, while safe drinking water and sanitation were considered as basic needs, inadequate waste-water treatment and disposal facilities were ignored. Increasing job opportunities via industrialization was a priority; meanwhile, industrial hazardous waste and emissions were left untreated.

Third, it can be argued that, while the 1972 Stockholm Conference increased awareness of environmental problems, the shift in the development model failed to provide a clear framework that integrated the environment as an essential component of the development process. Lack of commitment and binding agreements pre- and post-Stockholm prevented the implementation of effective protection measures.

ENABLEMENT: REFORM AND ADJUSTMENT

Towards the end of the 1980s and the beginning of the 1990s, a new development policy framework was elaborated, partly as a response to the failure of state intervention associated with the growth with equity paradigm. Based on neoliberal economic principles, and subsequently termed market enablement, the main objectives of the new model were the elimination of supply and demand constraints; the withdrawal of the state; reduction in regulatory frameworks; and privatization. Environmental considerations are conspicuous by their absence.

Based on the neoliberal approach, poverty was redefined away from households that earned low income to those with poor employment opportunities and low labour productivity (World Bank, 1991; Drakakis-Smith, 1996). Consequently, the key policy challenge in tackling urban poverty and environmental degradation was conceived to be the enhancement of urban efficiency and productivity. Correcting environmental externalities, it was argued, would raise returns for capital, and environmental problems themselves would be corrected by policy measures to increase urban efficiency. From this perspective, there appears to be no conflict between attempts to increase productivity (growth), and attempts to improve environmental conditions and prevent degradation. From a neoclassical economic perspective, the argument goes further. Desirable environmental policies would be: to improve urban infrastructure and urban environmental management; to adjust taxes and infrastructure pricing to reflect social costs; to issue tradable permits for polluting industries; and to restrict only the location of certain types of heavy industries (Burgess et al., 1997).

Such an approach has marginalized environmental and ecologically sustainable growth, while giving precedence to economic sustainability. To the extent that an environmental agenda was embraced at all by market enablement, this appears to have been expressed in terms of sectorally based approaches, rather than an overall policy framework that coordinated and guided other policy areas. Just as the assumption that prosperity and economic growth would bring environmental protection dominated development thinking over the preceding four decades, so market enablement continued this trend.

Despite the claims, it seems clear that the speed at which market enable-ment has been engaged, compared to political and community enable-ment, has inevitably rendered environmental objectives far less compatible with development priorities. As Zetter argues in Chapter 2 (this volume), while cities are the vehicle of economic growth, structural adjustment poli-cies have had considerable impacts on rates of growth and the spatial structure of cities, promoting an unprecedentedly rapid urban transforma-tion in developing countries. The priority to maintain and improve pro-ductivity and competitiveness contradicts a wider agenda, where environmental aspects are of limited significance in decision-making and planning processes.

FROM ECO-DEVELOPMENT TO ENVIRONMENTALISM AND SUSTAINABLE DEVELOPMENT

A consistent theme in the process of urbanization over the preceding decades, almost irrespective of the development paradigm, is the disjunc-ture between economic development objectives, environmental priorities and urbanization. This chapter now turns to investigate in more detail the conceptual challenges which this disjuncture poses, particularly with respect to the impact of market enablement. In the final section, we attempt to define how environmentalism and sustainability principles might be better linked to provide an effective policy framework to manage urban growth.

Fundamentally, the conceptual challenge lies in reconciling the conflict between the world as a reservoir supplying unfettered human needs to support economic development (Hettne, 1990), and the alternative ecologic-al view in which human beings are only part of a vaster, but ultimately limited, natural environmental order. The three economic development paradigms have been largely antagonistic to claims of resource scarcity. But in the late 1960s, human domination over the natural environment and faith in technological advance were challenged, effectively for the first time, by growing environmental concerns. It became clear that scarce natural resources and environmental conditions were increasingly threatened, and that the orthodox view of unlimited growth as a 'natural law' would need to be replaced. As a result, the notion of 'eco-development' appeared at the Stockholm Conference in 1972.

The eco-development approach constituted a radical challenge to the modernization paradigm. Propositions about the finitude of the planet demanded, in principle, extensive intervention in established economic and social institutions, and a new political ideology of environmental sustainability which could not easily be accommodated within the in-herited capitalist or state socialist regimes (Pugh, 1996). Eco-development was styled as an approach to development, calling for specific solutions to regionally based problems in the light of cultural as well as ecological constraints, and long-term as well as immediate needs (Hettne, 1990). As opposed to the conventional economic inputs of capital, labour and land leading to development in terms of rising GNP, the main elements of the eco-model were the satisfaction of needs contingent on available natural resources. There are some parallels between eco-development and economic development thinking which appeared early in the 1970s. Growth with equity, redistribution and basic needs defined an approach to development that encouraged self-reliance as a fundamental principle: this implicitly mirrored the concept of development as ecologically self-reliant or sustainable. However, ecologically sound development remained more an ideal to be realized than a process to be readily adopted and implemented (Hettne, 1990; Caldwell, 1996). In practice, too, the optimism attached to the growth-with-equity model, which would both alleviate poverty and subsequently improve the environment, was dissipated. The achievements were limited in scale, could not be replicated, and continued to ignore natural resource scarcity and the pressures of unrestrained economic growth on the environmental functions of the ecosystem. Moreover, although some developing countries also attempted to tackle institutional incapacity by establishing environmental agencies and regulations, little happened to improve policy formulation and implementation.

Despite the potential of eco-development thinking and the failure of the growth and modernization models, they continued to represent two irreconcilable extremes. While it was difficult to abandon the economic growth model and replace it with radically different approaches, at the same time it was not possible to ignore deteriorating environmental conditions and growing resource scarcities.

By the 1980s, therefore, a growing need was expressed to find new ways of reconciling economic growth with ecocentric priorities. The concept of sustainable development was introduced in 1980 by the International Union for Conservation of Nature (IUCN) and UNEP's 'World Conservation Strategy', and began to acquire status as an official policy among governments, particularly as a consequence of adoption by the World Commission on Environment and Development (WCED), established in 1983 by the UN General Assembly, and its publication in 1987 of the report *Our Common Future* (WCED, 1987). The term sustainable development had now become widely used to express the need for the simultaneous achievement of development and environmental goals. While the WCED report was not the first attempt to address the global environmental issues in a development context, the achievement of this report was its ability to convey, in ways that had not been presented before, the vital link between the state of our natural environment and economic growth, and to establish the principle that one could not be sustainable without the other (Koenig, 1995).

Controversy has of course surrounded what, on the face it, was an appealing simple concept of sustainable development, most frequently defined as 'development which meets the needs of the present without compromising the ability of future generations to meet their needs' (WCED, 1987). For some, the environmentalism of the 1980s compromised the eco-development principles of Stockholm. Thus Sage (1996) argues that the Brundtland report, on which the WECD report was based, effectively still called for conventional developmentalism through more economic growth, and that there was no clear distinction between 'sustainable economic growth' and unsustainable current practices. While more growth may be necessary for developing countries to improve the living standards of poor people, there was no clear justification for the need for continued growth in Northern, developed countries, bearing in mind the existing disparities and patterns of consumption.

Indeed, in support of Sage's contention and to this end, we can detect the ascendancy of market enablement in the following:

> If large parts of the developing world are to avert economic social and environmental catastrophes, it is essential that global economics be revitalized. In particular terms, this means more rapid economic growth in both industrial and developing countries, *freer market access for the products of developing countries, lower interest rates, greater technology transfer and significantly larger capital flows and both concessional and commercial.*

> (WECD, 1987, p. 89; our emphasis)

Five years after publishing the Brundtland report, the UN organized the United Nations Conference on Environment and Development (UNCED) in 1992 at Rio de Janeiro. The overall purpose was to attempt, yet again, the reconciliation of environmental and development priorities by agreeing operational objectives for national and international policy making. Much was achieved at Rio – notably the twin-track, national-to-local approach of environmental policy and practice. There was acceptance, in principle, that overall national development aspirations must be mediated by environmental policies – the two could no longer be separated. This principle was balanced by linking environmental aspirations to local capacities and community engagement. Agenda 21 was strongly oriented towards bottom-up, participatory, community-based approaches. The implementation of this comprehensive agenda required an openness and breadth of input in policy making that would, if adopted in practice, change the responsibilities of policy makers and encourage participation.

Both the national and local agendas of the action plan had clear implications for urban policies and strategies to tackle the continuing process of urbanization in a more sustainable way. They indicated the acceptance of market processes but, in principle at least, within appropriate environmental regulatory frameworks. These located urban planning strategies within a wider framework of environmental priorities, while at the same time engaging local communities in articulating environmentally sensitive responses to their needs (Sage, 1996).

As the 1972 Stockholm Conference witnessed the emergence of an ecocentric development approach, it can be argued that, 20 years later, the 1992 Earth Summit was dominated by environmentalists' insights. While the former approach was described by some scholars as a Utopian, radical approach, the later is pragmatically reformist, able to co-exist with the existing political ideology, but calling for reform and adjustment for existing policies and institutions. This approach to environmentalism suggests that reconciliation between sustainability and patterns of economic growth is achievable, which will have progressive impacts on the society.

The advocates of this approach argue that the presumed incompatibility between economic growth and environmental protection is exaggerated (Pugh, 1996; Garner, 2000). As evidence, they stress the shift from orthodox economic principles, which have often regarded environmental resources as given, to the new environmental economics, which considers the feedback loops connecting the economic system and natural environmental systems. Environmentalists sought to reach a compromise between sustainability and economic growth. The neoliberal concept of enablement (including economic, political and social enablement) was expanded to include the environment as a fourth essential input alongside the three classic inputs of land, labour and capital (Pugh, 2000).

Nevertheless, bearing in mind the environmental deterioration that accompanied the introduction of neoliberal policies from the late 1980s, the assumption of a fourth dimension to enablement and a fourth input into economic balance sheets still seems to leave an unresolved conflict with the concept of market enablement and emergence of the sustainable development concept.

On the other hand, the Rio Conference did agree, in theory at least, the concept of sustainable development, as a balance between human needs and environmental protection, and an ultimate goal of an environmentalist agenda.

Agenda 21 contained a relevant statement on human settlements. According to Pugh (1996), the agenda argued that all countries had reason to address their urban development needs within a framework that embraced environmental criteria within their policies, programmes and institutions. Additionally, there was clear recognition of the relevance of the multiple objectives and multi-institutional character of human settlements. Of the total estimated costs of implementing Agenda 21 (US$561 500 million), the human settlements' share was US$218 000 million, about 40 per cent of the total cost (Bryner, 1999).

In 1997, the UN General Assembly organized a special session to review the implementation of Agenda 21. The review showed that, while some countries have reduced emissions of pollutants and resource use, and population growth rates have declined in most areas, the overall, global environmental conditions have worsened and significant environmental problems remain deeply embedded in the socio-economic fabric of countries in all regions. In addition, persistent poverty contributes to ecological decline.

Contrasting views have emerged regarding the success of Agenda 21. These assessments depend on how the Agenda is perceived. From one perspective, it is a catalogue of policies that can be adopted by different countries to produce more sustainable development. To this end, Agenda 21 did activate some policy innovations. The success of the Agenda depends on its ability to influence the local context and to provide a policy framework directed to desirable political, economic and social objectives. From an alternative viewpoint, the Agenda represents a national commitment to a new set of policies that local pressure groups can use to persuade their governments to take concrete steps towards sustainable development. However, although governments signed up to the Agenda, a large proportion failed to demonstrate practical commitment. A third perspective is to view the Agenda as an attempt to make profound changes in the way we think about economic growth. To this extent, also, the Agenda has yet to generate a totally convincing rethink about the current approaches to development (Bryner, 1999).

SUSTAINABLE DEVELOPMENT, ENVIRONMENTAL POLICY AND URBANIZATION

The previous section explored the changing conceptualization of the links between environmentalism and sustainable development. There are differing perceptions of sustainability and thus different balances between the four key variables – political, economic, social and environmental. This section highlights the distinctive characteristics of the main contending perspectives, setting the context for the final part of this chapter, which examines the links between environmental policy making and urban planning.

Between strong and weak sustainability

Sustainable development is concerned with the continued existence and well-being of humankind, and that of the environment. However, in seeking harmony between these two requirements there remains a gulf between environmentalists, whose aim is to protect the natural environment from destruction or deterioration, and those whose concerns include reducing environmental hazards for human populations and promoting environmental justice for those lacking healthy environments and an adequate natural resource base for their livelihood (Figure 1.1; Mitlin and Satterthwaite, 1996). These contrasting perceptions can be characterized as strong (ecologically oriented) sustainability; and weak (economically oriented) sustainability (Haughton and Hunter, 1994; Latesteijn and Schoonenboom, 1996; Pugh, 1996).

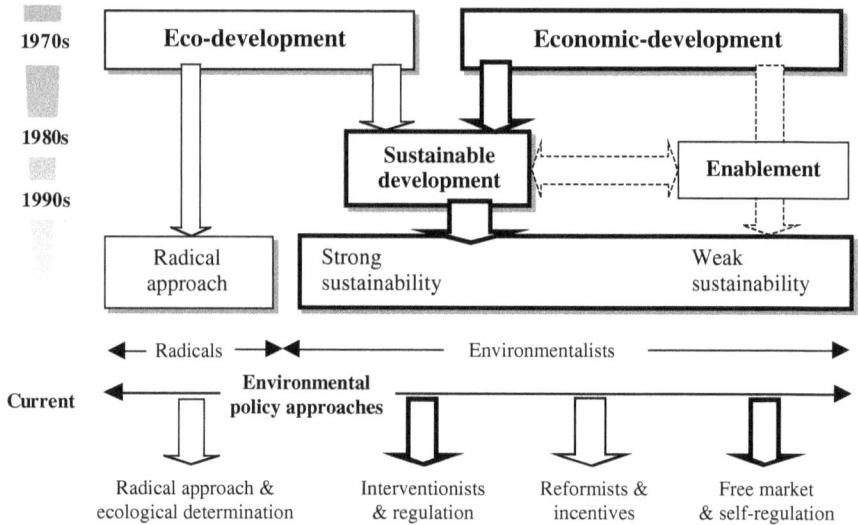

Figure 1.1   Development paradigms and environmental policy approaches

Weak sustainability regards natural environmental capital as potentially commensurate with man-made capital. Activities are evaluated against the background of social needs, and the satisfaction of these needs is given primacy. This perspective emphasizes the retention of the status quo. Reforms implied by this approach include: re-regulation of economic activity; use of taxes and incentives to modify production and consumption patterns; attention to property rights to achieve some measure of conservation and protection; and the introduction of impact assessment where development might have an adverse impact on environmental capacity. Haughton and Hunter (1994) argue that, based on such an approach, achieving economic development is compatible with environmental protection, provided society's response mechanisms are sufficient, appropriate and timely.

On the other hand, a stronger interpretation of sustainability gives greater priority to environmental criteria (environmentalism as fundamentalism) than to human needs. This approach challenges the status quo, requiring a break in the economic growth paradigm, and would impose well defined limits within which human activities must take place if they are to be sustainable. It also requires the reduction of current demands and a fundamental reformulation of production and consumption involving investments in new substitute technologies that are capable of reversing negative environmental impacts. Extremist supporters of strong sustainability suggest far-reaching policy change to relieve the burden imposed on the environment, including population control and adjustment of material welfare through a reduction in per capita income.

The debate between the two approaches revolves around the notion of carrying capacity. While the strong sustainability position argues the urgency of rapid action to ensure that we live within the world's carrying capacity, the weak position adopts an incremental shift over a longer period, accompanied by technological innovations to curb the likely negative impacts on the environment. The latter is directed towards the concept of carrying capacity as a long-term objective.[2]

Towards local sustainability: urban environmental planning

What are the implications for developing more environmentally sustainable approaches to rapid urbanization? Are there appropriate tools and instruments that might provide effective ways forward? This section completes the analysis by relating the foregoing discussion to modes of intervention in the urban environment, and outlining the options for urban planning and management that are locally sustainable.

It is fair to say that neither of the two polarized perspectives of sustainability discussed above provides a convincing or acceptable resolution of the tension. However, summarizing Welford's (1996) analysis, it is possible to elaborate a potentially more viable spectrum of environmental policy approaches between the extremities of strong and weak positions. He proposes the following typology: (i) the free market and self-regulation (weak sustainability); (ii) the reformist and incentives; (iii) the interventionist and legislation; (iv) the radical (strong sustainability) (Box 1.1).

Box 1.1   Environmental policy approaches

The market approach relies on fully accessible information. It assumes that consumers have perfect information about products and services and all alternatives, and that firms have full information about the activities of other competitors in order to make informed decisions about needs versus the environment.

The reformist approach emphasizes the use of market forces to influence the behaviour of both consumers and firms, accompanied by incentives to encourage the shift towards more environmentally friendly production and consumption. The reformist approach is targeted to incremental shifts towards environmental protection.

The interventionist approach challenges the reformists' trust in market mechanisms, and calls for increased legislation. Its advocates argue that the harmful impacts of consumption and production can be prevented only by the introduction and enforcement of direct regulation.

The radical approach argues that, no matter how we try to integrate the environmental costs, the system is largely unsustainable. While the three previous approaches accept, to differing degrees, the existing form of capitalism and the objective of influencing current practices and organizations towards environmental protection and sustainability, the radical approach argues that the dominant ideology of capitalism based on the exploitation of valuable resources needs to be fundamentally readdressed.

These four positions, highlighting the different approaches to sustainable environmental policy formulation, have a bearing on what might be possible in the urban setting in the developing world. Discounting the extreme positions at both ends of the spectrum, the argument we put is that an interim position, built around reformist and interventionist urban sector strategies to support environmental needs, resonates with the more structured approach to localized planning strategies envisaged in Agenda 21.

The modalities for sustainable urbanization depend on localization. As we have seen, the Earth Summit in 1992 called on governments to mobilize their communities for localization of Agenda 21. The conference's thematic guidance favoured community-led participation as an approach to environmental improvement, emphasizing bottom-up participation, rather than top-down approaches, as the core of planning practices – although not neglecting this level (Dahiya and Pugh, 2000). Arguably, the local level is the more effective level at which to intervene in order to generate an enduring commitment to environmental responsibility by individuals (Selman, 1996).

Localism as an effective level of intervention is not new. It can be traced back to the ecocentric style of development (mentioned above), which calls for specific solutions to particular problems in each region in the context of locally specific cultural and ecological conditions.

However, while both eco-developmentalists and environmentalists stress the effectiveness of local-level intervention, they have different views in terms of local sustainability. While the strategy of the eco-model of development is directed to sustainability for specific contexts in order to accomplish a higher degree of needs satisfaction, the localization approach of environmentalists attempts a compromise between human needs satisfaction (development) and environmental protection.

Ecocentric reformists pose an alternative view of development consonant solely with the interests of local communities (however defined), who identify their problems, propose solutions, and work alongside those who can provide external technological and financial support.

In contrast, environmentalists accept various possible routes to sustainability: such a compromise is not accepted by the ecocentric approach. The former perspective points to the success of key programmes initiated to support the reform process and localize Agenda 21, including the Sustainable Cities Programme and Local Agenda 21 initiatives introduced in many cities and municipalities around the world. It could be argued that, in the developing world, the outcome of these reformist/interventionist projects, to use Welford's typology, has been to commence the process of bridging the gap between the dominant top-down master planning approaches, and an environmental planning and management system that is more localized in content and direction.

Taking the argument a stage further, we can begin to test the appropriateness of different kinds of instruments which tackle the lacuna between top-down and bottom-up approaches. What is needed are modes of intervention that integrate environmental concerns into the planning and management of urban areas. Much debate remains, but to this end Leitmann (1999) usefully describes three main styles of urban environmental planning that address this challenge: reactive; relatively strategic; and strategic environmental planning (Box 1.2).

In this threefold conceptualization, environmental and urban priorities are harmonized under three complementary approaches to policy-making. The three models respond to different conditions, from the specific and localized to the increasingly generic. Yet, in each case, bridging the lacuna is achieved by linking the local to the strategic. These approaches are given momentum by necessary preconditions for the success of locally sustainable development planning: (i) multi-level participation in the planning process; (ii) consultation with various groups; (iii) participatory assessment; (iv) target-setting through negotiations; and (v) monitoring and reporting procedures, including local indicators and progress measures (Leitmann, 1999).

Box 1.2   Main styles of urban environmental planning

Reactive approaches include post-disaster and project-specific environmental impact assessments. In this approach, plans are made to correct what has already happened (post-disaster needs), or to avoid re-occurrence by deploying environmental impact assessment (EIA) to identify the potential environmental impacts of project, programme and policy proposals, and the mitigation measures for likely negative impacts in an early stage of project development. The main limitations of this approach lie in the fact that the EIA process usually takes place only after the project has been proposed for review, and is unable effectively to address the cumulative impacts.

Relatively strategic approaches respond to the limitations of project-specific assessment. They include: regional environmental assessment; sectoral assessments; and environmental guidance criteria to help project designers consider environmental issues at an early design stage. In addition, a strategic environmental assessment process has been developed that can cover regional/sectoral assessment as well as policies, programmes and plans. It can also be used for preparation of environmental action plans.

Strategic local environmental planning is a framework for urban environmental planning that can be used to formulate an integrated set of policies, programmes and projects to tackle priority problems and support strategic objectives, instead of (or in addition to) EIA. The main advantages of this approach, in comparison with the two former approaches, include: addressing a city's priority problems and future needs; the capacity to deal with cumulative and interactive impacts; proper consideration of stakeholder participation; a more accountable and democratic approach; building local management capacity; and creation of a baseline information system.

In summary, while the notion of sustainable locality is partially valid, localism provides insufficient understanding of environmental problems, which in most instances transcend the local administrative boundaries. Thus, in the end communities are unlikely to be able to set themselves targets of sustainable development in the narrow sense of self-sufficiency, at the level of either settlements or regions (Selman, 1996; Leitmann, 1999). At the same time, while international and national regulation encourages a shift – albeit slow – towards new forms of production and consumption cycles that minimize the environmental impacts, and stresses the importance of the role of individual, national and global relations, such relations must also be captured with the new localist agenda (Marvin and Guy, 1999).

CONCLUSIONS

This chapter demonstrates that, in the evolution of development strategies and the growth of environmental concerns, no matter what the prevailing paradigm of development, economic growth (and unfettered urbanization) is the dominant concept in the developing world. Despite the adverse environmental impacts of rapid industrialization, urbanization and deteriorating quality of life for the mass of the poor population in developing countries (which may threaten the sustainability of economic growth), innovative development concepts do not easily challenge the ascendancy of economic priorities and market determinants. Even under the paradigm of growth with equity, the attractiveness of explicit socio-economic objectives, environmental aspects (in terms of the carrying capacity of the biosphere) were overlooked in favour of sustaining economic growth priorities. Despite firm evidence that more environmentally sustainable concepts of development were needed, the inherent ambiguity of the concept, combined with the power of the new global neoliberal economic order, has reinforced the developmental agenda and the process of urbanization in the developing world. Adverse impacts on low-income people and their urban environments produced by market enablement strategies have raised the need for mitigation measures; but these have been far too small compared with the magnitude of adjustment programme impacts. In any case, declining provision for public sector intervention and regulation has reduced the capacity and scope for mitigation policies.

In this sense we close on a pessimistic note, with the two agendas – development and the environment – some considerable way from harmonized interaction within the urban setting. Arguably, the stage is set for improved collaboration by newly emerging ways of bridging the top-down and bottom-up lacuna. It is by bridging this gap both conceptually and – more importantly – operationally, that a more sustainable approach to urbanization might be accomplished in the developing world.

CHAPTER TWO

Market enablement or sustainable development: the conflicting paradigms of urbanization

Roger Zetter

THE PROBLEM STATED

Currently two major paradigms of sustainable development are being pro-moted globally. My argument in this chapter is that these two paradigms are in competition with each other, and consequently environmentally or socially sustainable urban development under conditions of rapid urban-ization is unsustainable. The underlying trends and processes of contempor-ary urbanization and the macro-economic policies associated with those processes are irreconcilable with objectives of environmentally sustainable urban development. In other words, there are countervailing aspirations and disjunctive objectives. The factors that drive urbanization in the devel-oping world – economic sustainability or, more popularly, market enable-ment – are incompatible with a broader conceptualization of sustainability in terms of environmental aspirations and objectives.

Each of the conceptualizations of sustainability is operationalized through a variety of global frameworks, institutions, national interests and needs. But the paradigm of maximizing economic development, set within a global market place and dependent on the productivity of cities, especially in the developing world, currently prevails at the expense of the alternative and broader environmental conceptualization. Macro-economic impera-tives present a formidable challenge to the UNCHS Global Plan of Action and the ambitious programme, set out at Habitat II (UNCHS, 1996b), to build environmentally sustainable cities (UNCHS, 1991; Badash, 1996).

Because of the limitations of time and space, four dimensions are selected to argue this case. These examples illustrate the challenges and barriers that must be confronted at an operational level, in order to develop the capacity to manage sustainable urban development.

CONTEXT – THE RATE AND SCALE OF URBANIZATION

At the beginning of the twentieth century, just over 10 per cent of the world's population lived in cities. Estimates vary, but approximately 13 per cent of the world's population lived in cities in 1900. Yet, barely 100 years later, early in the new millennium half the world's population will be living in cities: the 50 per cent threshold will be passed sometime around 2005.

Despite the drive to urbanization in this century, half the world – that half with the steepest demographic curve – has yet to experience that process. Thus within 25 years, if currently accelerating trends towards urbanization continue, over 60 per cent of the world population (or about 5.2 billion people) will be living in cities. In the year 2000, there now exist 28 mega-cities with more than 8 million inhabitants in each. The population of the mega-cities alone almost equates to the total urban population of the world at the beginning of the twentieth century. The phenomenon of urbanization is perhaps one of the most profound and significant changes of the past century.

A second, and perhaps even more striking, characteristic is the changing distribution of the world's urban population. Whereas in the developed world both the overall population level and the very high proportion living in urban areas is relatively stable, by far the largest proportion of the growth of urban population has taken place in developing countries, and will continue to do so.

In the past 50 years, to the turn of the century, the urban population in the developing world will have increased from about 300 million to nearly 2.0 billion. This figure will double again by 2025, when nearly three-quarters of the world's 5.2 billion urban dwellers will be living in the developing world. Whereas there were only 31 millionaire cities in the developing world in 1951, in 2000 there are nearly 500. Of the 28 mega-cities in 2000, 22 are in the developing world. By 2010, 21 of the 26 cities of 10 million plus will be in the developing world, and 21 of the 33 cities with populations in excess of 5 million plus will be in the developing world. While it is easy to overemphasize the phenomenon of mega-cities, they do illustrate the tendency towards high degrees of urban primacy as another problematic characteristic of the distribution of urban population in developing countries.

With some cities doubling their size perhaps every 10–12 years, and some evidence to suggest that, until recently, the secondary cities (which were often low on the development agenda) were expanding at an even faster rate, urbanization is perhaps the most problematic outcome of the development process.

But if there is a dynamic *of* cities, there is also the dynamic *in* cities. In the developing world we continue to build our cities essentially in a back-to-front mode, building first and servicing last, developing first and then creating planning instruments and strategies second. Contemporary urbanization processes raise important questions about efficiency and externalities. Yet, despite all the attendant problems this produces, it remains all but impossible to restrain this mode of city-building. Questions of equity are also significant. Highly skewed patterns in the distribution of poverty and wealth, despite two decades of poverty alleviation programmes, means that poverty levels remain very high, and are deteriorating further in many cities. Cities in the developing world are unequal places.

There is little evidence that intervention at any level has done much to manage this process in a more equitable way, or achieve development that satisfies broader conceptions of efficiency, equity or sustainability. Conversely, there is some limited evidence from Latin America that conditions for the urban poor have not always become worse: perhaps paradoxically, in Latin American mega-cities the quality of life (in terms of employment, physical and social infrastructure) may be better than in smaller cities (Gilbert, 1996). Nonetheless, it seems likely that many of these processes will continue, irrespective of planning or political intervention. Current market enablement models of economic development require spontaneous, unplanned growth of cities at the unprecedented scale outlined above.

Thus the countries anticipating the greatest growth in urban population, and at unprecedented scales and rates, are those countries where the tensions between the different conceptualizations of sustainability are most dramatic.

STRUCTURAL ADJUSTMENT, GLOBALIZATION AND ECONOMIC SUSTAINABILITY

Cities as the leading sector

It is the problematic outcomes of rapid and uncontrolled urban growth that are always emphasized – consuming disproportionately high volumes of imported goods; distorting political power, spatial strategies and investment patterns away from rural areas (where, until now, the majority of the population of developing countries have lived).

At the same time, if developing countries are to sustain (albeit fragile) levels of economic growth, and as these countries are further integrated into an export-led global economy, the role of cities and city-building as leading sectors of most developing countries will continue to be actively promoted. Cities provide high levels of latent and actual demand and internal resources, good access to services and labour, and the base for efficient use of nationally scarce resources.

Urban housing, in particular, is a major contributor to the leading sector role. Typically, housing investment may account for between 8 (UNCHS, 1993) and 20 per cent of GNP (Malpezzi et al., 1990), representing up to 50 per cent in some situations. Whether in the formal or the informal sector, housing is a significant multiplier for employment and the building materials industry, with substantial forward and backward linkages. Estimates suggest that it achieves a multiplier of up to 2.5 (income created per unit of capital invested). Housing absorbs labour with low opportunity costs, both in the formal and (especially) the informal sector. Between seven and 14 jobs per US$10 000 are created by housing investment (examples in Korea, Pakistan, Mexico, Colombia; UNCHS,

1993). Housing investment stimulates small-scale enterprises and increases in inter-household income transfers (Spence et al., 1993), and adds signifi-cantly to capital formation in the national economy by as much as 30 per cent (UNCHS, 1984; 1987, 209–211; 1993; World Bank, 1993, 62–64).

But the role goes further than this. The corollary to rapid urbanization is that cities offer large markets and are a spur to industrial capacity-building and productivity. For example, Sao Paulo already contributes 40 per cent of Brazil's GDP. While data are scarce, it seems a reasonable assumption that other cities, especially where there are high levels of pri-macy, offer similar concentrations of economic productivity. World Bank estimates suggest that in 2000, 80 per cent of the GDP of countries in the developing world is generated in cities. Employment in the formal and informal sectors of the urban economy grow at substantially faster rates than in other sectors. Not surprisingly, average household incomes are higher in cities than in rural areas; more significantly, in the context of the present chapter, average size of household income is positively associated with city size.

All this is not to say that multi-dimensional characteristics of urban poverty are not also expanding (Harriss, 1989), nor that longer-term, en-vironmentally sustainable policies for employment and development strategies are not needed. Rather, in the short term the leading sector role of cities will remain ascendant in the struggle for development. The wealth-generating role of cities is an imperative in the development process.

Structural adjustment, globalization and the economic competitiveness of cities

Cities have always been the engine of economic growth. This conclusion is not new. What is new in the continuing drive to enhance the productivity of cities is the changing macro-economic context in which the development of urban economies is taking place. Globalization and structural adjust-ment have marked impacts on the rates of growth and spatial structures of cities of the developing world. These forces have introduced a new and powerful dynamic to the conditions of unprecedented rapid urban-ization already being experienced. They further reinforce the imperative of economic sustainability at the expense of a wider conceptualization of sustainability.

Within this new paradigm, city growth is more than the primary source of and outcome of economic development. Perhaps the most significant of contemporary challenges to the sustainability of cities is not that eco-nomic processes exert such a crucial impact on the scale and pace of urbanization, but rather that these processes and functions underpinning rapid urbanization are directly and actively premised on a range of macro-economic policies. Structural adjustment on the one hand, and policies for the liberalization of the world economy through globalization of trade, labour division and capital on the other, are the major driving forces of urbanization. They introduce new dynamics into the process.

There is considerable evidence demonstrating the profound impacts of structural adjustment on developing countries. While some of this is contested, such as evidence about changing levels of poverty, the implications of structural adjustment and reform packages for city systems and the patterns and processes of urban development are clearer. Structural adjustment is radically reinforcing and reshaping domestic economies to fit the new economic order. The intentions of improved efficiency and productivity have a marked effect on cities which, as already demonstrated, are the leading sectors and the main contributors to the economic output of these countries.

With respect to globalization of production and trade, here again there is equally profound evidence for the impact on cities. This points to a marked differential effect between the cities of the developed and developing worlds.

Counterbalancing the decline in the comparative advantage of the urban–industrial base in developed countries is the expansion and diversification of the manufacturing base in cities of the developing world. The shift from import substitution to export orientation is reformulating the role of cities in the developing world, and restructuring the spatial distribution of activity. Low labour costs, fewer and less regulatory frameworks, low land and infrastructure costs, and sometimes tax and import and export advantages, are some of the main factors underpinning these changes.

The future of the city in a globalizing economy depends on these economic imperatives, and especially on the new division of labour in which cities of the developing world offer highly competitive advantages. These advantages are experienced not just in manufacturing, but also in provision of higher-level service industries that can be delivered through global electronic communication. Higher levels of productivity enhance the competitiveness of cities in the developing world, and thus their attractiveness to multinational corporations within this policy framework of global trade.

Consequently, city managers are now reassessing more closely the comparative advantages of cities within a global frame (Harris, 1994). The priority to maintain economic productivity and competitiveness contradicts a wider agenda, in which environmental considerations are of only limited significance in decision-making and planning.

The implications

Some of the most striking effects of these changes are felt in the labour markets of cities of the developing world. However, more relevant from our point of view, these transformations in urban systems have, in turn, led to the revision of planning processes and methodologies on one hand, and the spatial restructuring of cities on the other.

Reshaping the spatial structure; reshaping the management strategies

Market enablement and structural adjustment policies impose potentially profound impacts on the spatial structure of cities and on shifting activities between sectors. Equity considerations apart, it is difficult to predict precisely the spatial consequences of these process and policies for cities in the developing world. In any case, conditions will vary considerably. There are obvious contrasts between countries in Latin America, already highly urbanized and relatively high-income, but still offering comparative advantages in the global economy; and countries and cities in Africa and South-East Asia, where the process of urbanization is still very rapid. These differ again from cities on the Pacific Rim.

There is little doubt that a reshaped landscape of production is emerging in the developing world. It has some similarities with contemporary experiences in the developed world, particularly in relation to industrial and residential decentralization (Gilbert, 1993). But this new landscape is developing within a very different context. First, urbanization is still proceeding rapidly; second, the instruments to manage and regulate spatial development processes are severely limited.

So far as housing is concerned, the implications suggest accelerated peripheralization (Burgess et al., 1997) as demand is expressed in terms of seeking lower land costs. On the supply side, owners either constrain land delivery to reap speculative profits (in the absence of any financial controls) or, themselves, increase activity on the periphery to capture high profits with limited external costs. The diseconomies and unsustainability of this process are obvious.

With regard to commercial uses, evidence from Dakha, for example, suggests that in their response to global markets, export-oriented industries display two tendencies (Hassan, 1998). First, existing industries such as textile production and garment manufacturing are securing growth within global production by a dramatic intensification of land and buildings use. This increasing density, often taking place in poor, downtown locations, places additional burdens on the limited infrastructure, and very high plot ratios have a variety of negative impacts. Running counter to the view that global production necessarily demands new technology in new peripheral locations, this evidence suggests resistance to decentralization. Sectoral clustering and reinforcing networks of production appear to be equally important locational factors among these labour-intensive industries. On the other hand, there is some peripheralization of industrial development. Added to the influx of new, high-tech industries, the peripheralization of cities and the tendency away from a sustainable, compact city form seems the inevitable consequence of the market enablement agenda. Here again, the evidence is confusing. There is certainly no large-scale flight of industrial production from the existing city. Paradoxically, not only labour-intensive firms, but also information-intensive firms, are also competing for inner-city locations. There is a suggestion that environmental strategies may destroy the important synergies that have enabled traditional industries such as textiles to reconstruct themselves as part of the global production network.

Thus concentration and deconcentration co-exist (Gilbert, 1993; Townroe, 1996), and the map of the disaggregated city as a pattern of localized pockets of unplanned commercial/industrial may be particularly characteristic of cities in the developing world. Evidence from Mumbai partly confirms these tendencies (Harris, 1995), indicating that medium- to large-scale industries have been shifting to highway locations outside the city boundaries. Of greater concern is that the population rapidly followed this relocation, with some peripheral areas showing remarkably high levels of demographic change. As manufacturing industries moved out, new, skill-intensive and innovative service industries moved in, thus creating a wave of in-migration as in the case of Dhaka.

Again, the point is that the factors driving the spatial restructuring of cities are, themselves, the result of the drive for urban economic sustainability. To the extent that market enablement policies have such potentially enormous spatial impacts, the fact that little attention has been given to these potential spatial impacts raises particular concern.

Structural adjustment and globalization are paralleled, at the urban policy-making level of the developing world, with spatial and management strategy policies, which themselves reinforce a market-enablement approach by enhancing the power of private sector investment, service providers and the short-term interests of continuing high levels of urban productivity; this is discussed below.

With regard to planning processes, arguably, political and especially economic forces in a global context have taken precedence over technical, environmental and social priorities. The package of macro-economic reforms places maximum strain on the environment and the physical and social fabric of cities – which are already highly unstable. Rapid urbanization, combined with pressure to sustain increasingly high levels of economic performance, suggest that the spatial and economic structure of cities is changing at a rate that is further outstripping the capacity of the physical fabric to respond (Harris and Fabricus, 1996; Townroe, 1996). The implication is a potentially negative trade-off between production, competition and efficiency on the one hand, and environmental and social sustainability on the other. Such negative trade-offs, it is argued, are the only ones affordable in most cities in the developing world; the negative balance is bound to dominate.

LAND MARKETS

The third contemporary trend in urbanization in the developing world, militating against the broader interests of sustainability, concerns the behaviour of urban land markets. Sustainable urban development requires coherent land policies that can:

- deliver an affordable supply of land, especially for the mass of the urban poor
- provide a framework for the orderly supply of land within a strategic planning framework
- retain private use rights consistent with public needs and interests
- offer long-term investment stability without the negative impacts of speculation or windfall gains.

These are major challenges confronted in every city of the developing world. Many innovative attempts to address these needs have been made. Instruments such as land readjustment in Asia; certification of occupancy in a number of African countries; valorization in some Latin American countries; and a variety of attempts to develop cross-subsidy financing of low-income group housing. But these are exceptions; there have been few systematic or structural attempts to address the urban land market crisis. More usually, approaches have been project- rather than programme-driven, and replicability is limited. Often they have addressed the consequences of land market failure, rather than the root causes. The key here is the extent to which state intervention and regulatory tools to manage land market behaviour are acceptable.

Significant in this context, Habitat II made only one very generalized recommendation on land policies, in marked contrast to the radical provisions in Habitat I. This may reflect more realistic attitudes to the intractable problem of managing the dynamic and volatile land markets that characterize most cities in the developing world. But what this contrast signifies is the profound change in the wider framework of the current development agenda. Consistent with market enablement, current policies to address the urban land crisis, promoted by the World Bank and all the frontline bilateral and multilateral donor agencies, seek to remove supply-side blockages in order to enhance private sector development objectives. By removing what are thought to be the barriers to market efficiency, this supports the self-maximizing interests of private landowners, whether corporate or individual. Furthermore, it is argued that the turbulence engendered by market enablement is accentuating investment uncertainty in cities in the developing world, and thus encouraging the search for short-term investment returns (Townroe, 1996). As land speculation already generates supranormal profits for investors in most cities in the developing world, given the lack of competing rates of return on other investments, it seems reasonable to assume that market enablement policies will further intensify urban land price inflation and speculation.

Many of the new land policy instruments of the urban management programme – improved tenure and titling, developing land information and registration systems, privatization funding initiatives for infrastructure provision – are interventionist only in the sense of facilitating improved land delivery through private means. Reforms to improve the functioning of land markets are undoubtedly needed. However, the role of strategic land-use planning as the main mechanism to ensure the orderly delivery of urban land, dependent as it is on regulatory procedures, is now likely to become an even less effective instrument to manage urban growth than it was in the past.

Set within the broader context of neoliberal reforms affecting the urban sector – improving access to credit facilities for housing and land development, increasing the supply of goods and services such as building materials and construction labour, privatizing urban service delivery – it seems likely that short-term speculative land development is likely to expand, as a result of market enablement, at the expense of longer-term and more orderly land supply and development. This is precisely in the rapidly urbanizing cities of the developing world, where planned sustainable urban development is essential. Especially bearing in mind the impacts of globalization and structural adjustment, which favour the already high levels of competitiveness offered in cities in the developing world, these policies will only exacerbate the increasing demand for developable urban land in these cities.

COMMUNITARIANISM AND GOVERNANCE

The economic fragmentation and restructuring of cities increases the complexity of urban government and management. New formulae for the government of cities are appearing, in which governance and civil society are the cornerstones. Donor-driven reforms are explicitly reshaping the power and policy-making structures governing the development of cities in the developing world. Thus the last contemporary trend in urbanization constraining sustainability is the changing institutional framework within which macro-economic policies are implemented.

There are several dimensions as to why urban governance is a key issue and why reforms are producing problematic outcomes. Not surprisingly, there are many parallels, at the level of urban government, with the broader context of macro-economic reform. Institutional change at the local level serves to reinforce the already dominant economic paradigm at the macro level.

In many cities, old coalitions persist and new coalitions of urban interests are emerging and assuming responsibilities and power for the future city. On the one hand, elite groups continue to appropriate and consolidate power, as they always have, through formal and informal structures at the urban level, as our work in Egypt illustrates (Zetter and Hamza, 1998). Benefiting from twin opportunities provided by macro-economic reform policies and the deregulation of development and service provision at the micro-level in fast-growing cities, these groups are able to reinforce their interests and legitimize control. The process of urban development is facilitated by deregulation in planning instruments, and investment in potentially lucrative urban services is opened up.

On the other hand, the reform of urban administration in the developing world is driven by explicit policies for power sharing with other stakeholders. Promoted by donors, and combining the agendas of aid conditionality and deregulation, new groups are empowered by these reforms in the governmental structure of cities designed to decentralize administration, improve management of cities, and embed the culture of governance (Edralin, 1997; Hoshino, 1997).

One most significant and novel feature of this emerging pattern of new stakeholders is the promotion of communitarian interests. This is reflected by the proliferation of urban-based non-governmental organizations (NGOs) involved in the urban sector. Approximately one quarter of Organisation for Economic Cooperation and Development (OECD) development aid is now channelled though NGOs (not all of it in the urban sector) in a new community of transnational development organizations – another dimension of globalization, incidentally. Working with local partners, northern NGOs command much of this resource, and at the local level community-based organizations have burgeoned in cities of the developing world. The promotion of local networks of community-based organizations (CBOs) and NGOs has enabled the consolidation of new institutional structures. This has reinforced new partnerships in urban development and management in which CBOs and NGOs are complementary partners to more conventional forms of local government. The reasons for this rapid growth are complex. The development discourses that seek to explain this growth in terms of donor subordination, or a new political economy of development, or patron–client relationships are outside the present context.

The outcome, however, has been to release the innovative energies of low-income communities. Recent work in Mexico City, for example, has illustrated how local communities with contrasting forms of organization have built local partnerships and obtained public sector resources. They have successfully accomplished a variety of physical development priorities, consolidated their informal settlements, cooperatively built housing, and resisted the invasion of commercial development interests seeking to extend a nearby business quarter (de la Macorra, 1998).

However, when set in the broader context of the changing role of the city in the developing world and the economic reform package, this shift of power from the state to diverse groups of stakeholders in city governance highlights the tensions between economic and environmental sustainability.

The evidence suggests two outcomes. The first outcome, and the difficult challenge for urban governance, is how to reconcile fundamentally contradictory tendencies. How can economic transformation, derived from the international agenda of trade liberalization, globalization and structural adjustment and contingent on deregulated urban growth, be accommodated simultaneously with the continuing need to manage the excessive pressures for growth imposed by rapid urbanization? (World Bank, 1991, 1993; Pugh, 1995a). In other words, the dilemma for urban authorities in the developing world is: how to produce spatial strategies and regulatory frameworks that consolidate their comparative advantages in raising productivity, yet defend the entitlements of low-income urban poor to reasonable living space, improved access to service provision and reduced environmental degradation? The shift from a centralized state-governed regulatory planning framework to a more flexible, market-oriented model of development planning barely leaves open the question of whether economically sustainable cities of the developing world can also be environmentally sustainable.

The second outcome of changing models of governance suggests that, as in the case of Mexico City, while individual communities may benefit from empowerment and can achieve definable gains in their physical and social surroundings, local innovation heightens the organized competition for scarce urban resources. The outcome, in this case, was further disaggregation of decision-making, resource allocation and service delivery, militating against strategic provision and strategic planning processes. Micro-level sustainable development was accomplished at the expense of making macro-level urban strategy far less sustainable. The paradox here is that power-sharing seems to intensify problems of governance and management by institutionalizing competing claims.

It appears that, beyond the attractiveness of the concept of governance, there exist neither the methodologies nor the instruments to reconcile the competing claims and fragmentation this presents.

CONCLUSIONS

To sum up: I have argued that there is an irreconcilable tension between two competing development discourses – economic and environmental. The economic and spatial fragmentation of the global economy and its reconstruction within a new global economic order, underpinned by structural readjustment packages, accentuates the need to enhance the productivity of cities and to ensure their role as leading sectors. In this context, cities in the developing world offer two primary comparative advantages over cities in the developed world. Economically, they provide potentially high-productivity, low-production-cost locations in conjunction with weaker and (under reform packages) weakening regulatory controls over spatial development processes.

Simultaneously, these trends accentuate both the need for and also the complexity of urban management and planning processes which might satisfy a broader conceptualization of sustainability. However, the resources and methodologies to support these needs are not keeping pace either with the pressures that economic restructuring is imposing, or with the rapidity of urbanization which continues to take place. Indeed, the standard contemporary package of urban administrative reform measures, while enlarging the concept of how cities might be managed and governed, is in effect paradoxically reducing the capacity for strategic spatial planning. In countries where spatial planning has always been rudimentary and limited in its impact, the formal incorporation of new sets of stakeholders is disaggregating further the structures for providing comprehensive, strategic-level guidance of development.

The issue is not just one of the scale and rate of urbanization, which has been the preoccupation of urban planners and researchers until the start of this decade. On to the process of rapid urbanization, engendered from within, have been imposed the external imperatives of global economic reform and restructuring. Combined, these processes accentuate the scope for functional and spatial restructuring of cities, and will induce further growth and more rapid transformation in an already dynamic situation.

Thus the processes reshaping the structure and role of cities and the scale of urban development in the developing world create the circumstances in which sustainability can be achieved only in its relatively narrow configuration – economic growth, productivity and market-driven urban development. Even if poor countries in the developing world had the freedom to choose different development paradigms, only within a neoliberal and market-driven paradigm are they likely to continue to provide the meagre gains of development. At best, the factors outlined in this chapter indicate the scale of the challenge to adopt a different paradigm for building sustainable cities.

Environmental health or ecological sustainability? Reconciling the brown and green agendas in urban development

Gordon McGranahan and David Satterthwaite

Urban environmental problems can be divided into two sets of issues or two agendas. First, there are the sanitary and environmental health issues familiar to urbanists, which are the motivation for what has recently been labelled the 'brown' agenda (Barton et al., 1994; Leitmann, 1994). These include unsanitary living conditions, hazardous pollutants in the urban air and waterways, and accumulations of solid waste. Such problems have many immediate environmental health impacts which tend to fall especially heavily on low-income groups (Bradley et al., 1991; McGranahan, 1991; Hardoy et al., 1992a). Second, there are the items within the more recent 'green' agenda promoted by environmentalists (mostly from high-income countries): the contribution of urban-based production, consumption and waste generation to ecosystem disruptions, resource depletion, and global climate change. Most such problems have impacts that are more dispersed and delayed, and often threaten long-term ecological sustainability.

Conflicts arise between the proponents of these two agendas in regard to which environmental problems should receive priority.[1] The conflicts can be especially acute in the urban areas of Africa and much of Asia and Latin America, where environmental health problems are particularly serious, and where the capacity for environmental management is generally weak. However, provided both agendas are taken seriously, these conflicts can be minimized.

This chapter[2] is based on several contentions. First, many of the approaches traditionally used to improve urban environmental health – such as subsidizing piped water, water-borne sewerage systems and conventional solid waste collection systems – can undermine sustainability and often fail to reach those whose health is most at risk. Second, some of the new approaches promoted by those concerned with ecological sustainability, such as restrictive water-use regimes, can undermine the environmental health of the poor. Finally, there are approaches and frameworks more directly supportive of the needs and priorities of low-income urban dwellers that can improve environmental health while also achieving progress within the green agenda. There is also some practical evidence that these can work – as discussed in the final section.

THE BROWN AND GREEN AGENDAS

Table 3.1 highlights some of the contrasts between these two agendas. From a radically green perspective, a focus on the brown agenda is short-sighted: what about future generations? What about the impact of city-based consumption on rural resources and ecosystems? And might not a focus on improving environmental health conditions in cities encourage more people to move there? From a radically brown perspective, empha-sizing the new concerns on the green agenda is elitist: what about the needs and priorities of the poor? What about the very high environmental health burdens suffered by those lacking adequate provision for piped water, sanitation, drainage and garbage collection? Environmental hazards remain among the main causes of ill health, injury and premature death among lower-income groups in most urban centres in Africa, Asia and Latin America; in urban centres with the least adequate provision for basic infrastructure and services, they remain among the main causes of ill health, injury and premature death for the whole urban population (Bradley et al., 1991; Hardoy et al., 1992a; WHO, 1992, 1996).

Although there are very real conflicts between the proponents of the brown and green agendas as to what problems should receive priority, it is important not to create a false dichotomy. Some environmental improve-ments serve both agendas. Equally important, a concern for greater equity is central to both agendas – it is just that each chooses to emphasize different aspects of this equity.

EQUITY

Haughton (1999) has identified five interconnected equity principles that can apply to environmental problems in urban areas, and these help to clarify the different perspectives from which the proponents of the brown and green agendas work.

For proponents of the brown agenda, the main priorities are:

- intragenerational equity, as all urban dwellers have needs for healthy and safe living and working environments and the infrastructure and services these require
- procedural equity to ensure that all persons' legal rights to (among other things) a safe and healthy living and work environment are respected, that they are fairly treated, and that they can engage in democratic decision-making processes about the management of the urban centre in which they live.

For proponents of the green agenda, the priorities are:

- intergenerational equity, which includes a concern that urban devel-opment does not draw on finite resource bases and degrade ecological

Table 3.1 Stereotyping the brown and green agendas for urban environmental improvement

	Brown environmental health agenda	Green sustainability agenda
Characteristic features of problems high on the agenda:		
– key impact	Human health	Ecosystem health
– timing	Immediate	Delayed
– scale	Local	Regional and global
– worst affected	Lower-income groups	Future generations
Characteristic attitude to:		
– nature	Manipulate to serve human needs	Protect and work with nature
– people	Work with	Educate
– environmental services	Provide more	Use less
Aspects emphasized in relation to:		
– water	Inadequate access and poor quality	Overuse; need to protect water sources
– air	High human exposure to hazardous pollutants	Acid precipitation and greenhouse gas emissions
– solid waste	Inadequate provision for collection and removal	Excessive generation
– land	Inadequate access for low-income groups for housing	Loss of natural habitats and agricultural land to urban development
– human wastes	Inadequate provision for safely removing faecal material (and waste water) from living environment	Loss of nutrients in sewage and damage to water bodies from release of sewage into waterways
Typical proponent	Urbanist	Environmentalist

Note: the entries in this table are only indicative. In practice, neither the agendas nor the issues they address are so clearly delimited. For example, while the table refers to lower-income groups as the worst affected by brown environmental problems, in most urban centres there is considerable variation even within lower-income groups in the extent and nature of environmental health risks in the shelters and neighbourhoods in which they live. Each person or household makes their own trade-off between, for instance, cost, locations with good access to employment or income-earning possibilities, space, tenure (including possibility of home ownership), and the factors that influence environmental health (e.g. quality and size of accommodation and extent of basic infrastructure and services).

systems in ways that compromise the ability of future generations to meet their own needs

▓ transfrontier equity to prevent urban consumers or producers transferring their environmental costs to other people or other ecosystems – for instance, disposing of wastes in the region around the city

▓ interspecies equity, with the rights of other species recognized.

Working from this recognition of the different aspects of equity that the two agendas prioritize allows a better understanding of how progress on both brown and green agendas can proceed, and how potential conflicts can be minimized. It provides a common language for addressing both sets of concerns, and potentially a common goal of reducing inequity. It helps identify the conditions under which pursuing one agenda is likely to undermine the other – if, for example, the needs of low-income groups are ignored, they are likely to bear a disproportionate burden of any efforts to protect future generations, and vice versa. Moreover, by framing the problem in terms of equity, it is easier to see why in some cities, where intragenerational and procedural inequities dominate, the brown agenda deserves more attention; while in others, where other inequities predominate, the green agenda should prevail.

CONTRASTING BROWN AND GREEN PRIORITIES

Both green and brown proponents have reason to criticize many existing approaches to urban environmental management, even if their priorities differ. At a superficial level, the brown and green agendas are in direct opposition to each other. For example, the brown agenda would seem to call for more water use, more sewerage connections, more waste collection, more urban residential land, and more fossil fuel use to replace smoky bio-fuels. In contrast, the green agenda appears to call for water conservation, less water-borne sewerage, less waste generation, less urban expansion, and less fossil fuel use. While these potential contradictions should not be ignored, a review of existing policy problems indicates that the trade-offs need not be as sharp as such generalizations seem to imply.

Water

Urban water supply planning has historically been preoccupied with how to increase supplies to meet growing demand, given the physical and financial constraints of the city. By and large, demand has been assumed to be beyond the influence of water sector policies. For those households and businesses connected to piped water systems, water is generally provided far below its full cost. There is little incentive for users to conserve, or to give encouragement to the industries that are the largest water users to, for example, recycle waste water or seek less water-intensive systems of production.

In some of the wealthier cities, subsidized water-supply systems have brought major benefits to most of their populations, including a high proportion of their lower-income populations. For instance, there has been a considerable expansion in the proportion of the population with piped water supplies in many of the wealthier Latin American cities. In cities such as Sao Paulo, Belo Horizonte, Curitiba and Porto Alegre, most of the population receive piped water supplies to their homes (Jacobi, 1994; Mueller, 1995).

However, the proponents of the green agenda can rightly point to the serious consequences this often brings. The emphasis on increasing supply and keeping the price of water affordable has resulted in major cities throughout Africa, Asia and Latin America overexploiting local water resources. For instance, for many coastal cities local aquifers have been over-pumped, resulting in salt-water intrusion. Overexploitation of undergroundwater has also caused serious problems of subsidence for many buildings and sewage and drainage pipes in many cities (Damián, 1992; Postel, 1992). As local ground and surface water sources are overused or polluted, meeting rising city demands generally means having to draw on ever more distant and expensive water resources. This can be to the detriment of the populations and, often, the ecosystems in the areas from which the water is drawn. Often these high costs are not reflected in the water prices faced by large and affluent urban users.

Proponents of the brown agenda often share this green agenda concern for unrealistically low water prices, but for different reasons. They can point to how the discrepancy between water utilities' costs and revenues from water sales and public subsidies often inhibit expansion to low-income areas, and help ensure that high proportions of the population in most cities remain unconnected to piped water systems. Indeed, a combination of price controls and very limited public funds is a recipe for intragenerational inequities, with the subsidies that do exist flowing, along with the water, to those who least need them. Even for those low-income groups who have access to connections, water supplies are often irregular, or of poor quality, or difficult to access, for instance as dozens of households share each standpipe. At least 300 million urban dwellers in Africa, Asia and Latin America remain without piped water supplies (WHO/UNICEF, 1993), and tens of millions of those who governments include in their statistics as having access to piped supplies still face inadequate, irregular or unsafe supplies that are often difficult to obtain (Satterthwaite, 1995; WHO, 1996).

While the water-related priorities of the green and brown agendas are different, their goals are not inherently incompatible. The (often unmet) minimum daily needs for health (about 30 litres per capita) amount to about two flushes of a conventional toilet or one slowly dripping faucet. Providing sufficient water for health needs is not the reason that many cities are overtaxing their water supplies; indeed, in many cities, programmes encouraging water conservation and ensuring better management and repair of piped water systems can often free up sufficient 'new' supplies to allow regular piped water supplies to be extended to unserved households with no overall increase in water use (Connolly, 1999). Intra-generational water inequities need not be solved by creating intergenerational or transboundary water inequities, or vice versa. It is politics and policy instruments, not physical imperatives, that create a stark trade-off between environmental health and ecological sustainability. Moreover, for most cities it is relatively clear whether environmental health or ecological sustainability ought to be the more pressing concern.

Sanitation

Proponents of the green and brown agendas can also point to problems in provision for sanitation, although, as in water supplies, they emphasize different problems. Here the conventional approach has been to promote water-borne sanitation systems, or steps in that direction, with the ultimate aim of providing all households with a flush toilet connected to a sewer. Again, households obtaining connections receive considerable benefits, often at subsidized prices. But in most urban centres, sewerage systems are characterized by significant inequities, relevant to both brown and green agendas.

There are some cities in Latin America, Asia and parts of Africa where most of the population is adequately served by sewers. These are also generally the cities with low infant mortality rates and high life expectancies. However, the generally high unit costs of such systems also means that these cities are in the minority, and very few cities have sewer systems that serve most of their residents. In many cities, sewers serve only a small proportion of the population, generally in the more centrally located and wealthier areas. Most small urban centres have no sewer system at all. Estimates suggest that close to half the urban population of Africa, Asia and Latin America lack adequate provision for sanitation. Tens of millions of urban dwellers have no access to any form of sanitation, or have only such poor-quality, overcrowded public facilities that they have to resort to defecation in the open.

Proponents of the green agenda point to the environmental costs that conventional sewer systems can bring – especially the large volumes of water used to flush toilets and the problem of disposing of large volumes of sewage. In Latin America, Asia and Africa, only a small proportion of sewage is treated before disposal (WHO/UNICEF, 1993; Barton et al., 1994; WHO, 1996). Untreated sewage is a major contributor to highly polluted water bodies in most cities, although it is generally difficult to determine its contribution relative to that of untreated industrial wastes and storm and surface run-off. Fisheries are often damaged or destroyed by liquid effluents arising from cities. Thousands of people may lose their livelihood as a result, as some of the largest cities are close to some of the world's most productive fishing grounds (see Hardoy et al., 1992a for summaries of case studies). Sewage systems also require large volumes of water to function –

and help build high water demands into city sanitation systems. And although there are many examples of cities where some of the sewage is used for crop or fish production, the proportion of sewage used in such a way is limited by the sheer volume of such wastes, and the difficulties (and costs) of transporting them to areas where they can be productively used. Proponents of the green agenda often point to alternative sanitation systems which do not require sewers. These include many that bring ecological advantages, such as requiring no water at all, and some that are designed to allow the conversion of human wastes into safe fertilizers, allowing the recycling of nutrients in the food system. These limit water demand and remove the problem of sewage disposal. Simple, sewerless sanitation systems are also generally much cheaper than sewered systems, especially when account is taken of the cost of sewage treatment.

But here there is a serious potential conflict between the brown and green agendas. Proponents of the brown agenda can point to the hundreds of millions of urban dwellers who currently rely on sanitation systems that do not use water – for instance, pit latrines – which bring serious health risks and often contaminate groundwater. The inadequate maintenance of the piped water network means that there are often many cracks and leaks that can lead to contamination of piped water supplies. Water pressure is also not constant, as many city water-supply systems have irregular supplies with water available in many districts for only a few hours a day, and sewage can seep into the pipes. Pit latrines can be particularly hazardous in areas that regularly face floods, as the pits become flooded and spread human excreta. There is also a problem in many cities with the lack of services to empty them (or the high price that has to be paid for doing so; Muller, 1997), while space constraints inhibit provision for solutions to limit this problem such as twin-vault systems or larger pits. There is also the question of cost. In many cities, even a good-quality pit latrine within their home or plot is an unattainable luxury for many low-income households. This includes the large proportion of low-income groups who rent accommodation, and for whom there is no affordable rented accommodation with adequate sanitation. A stress on sewerless latrines may mean the importance of adequate water supplies is forgotten. These latrines may need no water, but the households that use them certainly do, including the water needed for washing and personal hygiene. A stress on dry latrines may also mean that the problem of removing waste water is forgotten; one of the key advantages of a sewer system is that it also conveniently and hygienically removes waste water other than sewerage after its use for cooking, laundry or washing. Brown agenda proponents can also point to instances where the unit cost of installing sewers was brought down to the point where they were no longer far beyond the price that low-income households could pay (Orangi Pilot Project, 1995), to community-level sewer systems that do not require high levels of water use, and to local treatment which greatly reduces the ecological impact of effluents on water bodies (Gaye and

Diallo, 1997; Schusterman and Hardoy, 1997). In assuming that all water-borne sanitation systems have unacceptable ecological impacts, there is a danger of promoting 'alternative sanitation systems' which bring inconvenience, higher maintenance costs and greater environmental risks to the users – or of simply producing latrines that the population do not use.

In short, an excessive reliance on conventional water-borne sewerage intensifies the discrepancies between the brown and green agenda: as a tool of urban environmental management it can reduce intragenerational inequities, but typically at the cost of transboundary and intergenerational inequities. There are undoubtedly many instances where extending water-borne sewerage systems is justified, especially in high-density residential areas. There are also measures that can be taken to reduce the ecological disadvantages of such systems, as noted above. However, proponents of both brown and green agendas can take issue with measures that subsidize sewer systems for relatively affluent urban dwellers, diverting public funds from low-income dwellers and imposing environmental costs on those living downstream, and on future generations.

Other urban environmental issues

In most other areas of urban environmental management, it is possible to identify conflicts between brown and green priorities. As with water and sanitation, the extent of the conflict depends as much on the socio-economic context and the policy instruments applied as on any underlying physical trade-offs.

For the solid wastes that households generate, a priority of improving environmental health includes ensuring regular and efficient collection of such wastes. In most urban centres, 30 to 50 per cent of the solid wastes generated are not collected – although this percentage is over 90 per cent for some urban centres (Cointreau, 1982; Grieg-Gran, 1998). Many households that, in theory, are served by garbage collection systems, in practice have no more than a communal skip or collection point at some distance from their home, with unreliable and irregular collection from these communal collection points. Uncollected wastes bring serious environmental health problems as they accumulate on open spaces, waste land and streets. These include smells; disease vectors and pests attracted by garbage (rats, mosquitoes, flies, etc.); and overflowing drainage channels clogged with garbage (Cointreau, 1982; Hardoy et al., 1992a). Leachate from decomposing and putrefying garbage can contaminate water sources (Cointreau, 1982; UNCHS, 1988; Hardoy et al., 1992a). In urban districts with the least adequate provision for sanitation, the uncollected solid wastes usually include a significant proportion of faecal matter.

But from an ecological perspective the critical concerns are the promotion of waste reduction, waste reuse or recycling, and addressing the environmental impacts of waste dumps. Most solid wastes that are collected are deposited in open dumps, many of them unauthorized. Even for those that are authorized, there is rarely careful environmental management as in a well-managed sanitary landfill site. This gives rise to many environmental problems, including the contamination of ground and surface water, methane generation, and air pollution from uncontrolled burning. Simultaneously, valuable materials are being lost. Indeed, from an ecological point of view, much of 'waste' reflects a twofold disruption of natural cycles, with materials once part of closed ecological circuits first lost to their original ecologies, then damaging the ecologies into which they are introduced.

Crude measures to reduce the ecological burden of waste can create an environmental health burden, and vice versa. Moreover, policies appropriate to one city may be entirely inappropriate in another. In affluent cities, for example, higher waste disposal fees are often an effective means of reducing waste generation, and have no adverse environmental health impacts. In a low-income city where environmental controls are lax and large sections of the population have inadequate incomes, these same waste disposal fees are likely to encourage illicit dumping, burying and burning of waste in residential neighbourhoods, creating environmental health problems without reducing ecological burdens.

Even air pollution priorities vary from brown and green perspectives, and between cities. Some of the worst environmental health problems are related to the residential use of smoky, but potentially renewable fuels such as fuelwood and charcoal. Green agenda proponents may object to the transition to cleaner fuels because they increase fossil fuel use – but this can bring major health benefits, especially to those who spend most time in the smoky environments, typically women and girls cooking and undertaking other household tasks (WHO, 1992). Some measures to reduce air pollution exposure, such as chimneys for households using smoky fuels, can reduce indoor air pollution but increase outdoor air pollution. Higher chimneys for industrial polluters can reduce air pollution within the city, but create transboundary environmental burdens even as they improve local environmental health. Alternatively, some measures to reduce greenhouse gas emission, acid precipitation and other ecological damage can exacerbate local environmental health problems. This even applies to interventions in low-income neighbourhoods where, for example, efforts to improve the efficiency of biofuel stoves are likely to increase the emissions of health-threatening pollutants. All measures that seek to reduce air pollution or, more generally, greenhouse gas emissions, need to be assessed for their effects on intragenerational as well as intergenerational equity. For instance, recent measures in Mexico City to allow the newest automobiles, which meet higher standards in terms of polluting emissions, to be exempt from restrictions on their use obviously advantage higher-income groups and disadvantage those unable to afford such automobiles (Connolly, 1999).

A final example of potential conflict between brown and green agendas is over land-use management. Proponents of the green agenda rightly point to the way in which most growing urban centres encroach on high-quality agricultural land and damage or disrupt rural ecosystems. Peri-urban forests, wetlands and other ecologically important sites are often lost to urban developments or to recreational facilities, such as golf courses, generally serving high-income urban dwellers. Other urban demands can also mean the loss of land with valuable ecological functions – for instance from the demand for building materials, fuelwood and landfill.

While proponents of the brown agenda share a concern for the impacts of such developments, they will highlight the extent to which low-income households need cheap, well-located land to allow them to develop better quality homes. Or, from a city-wide perspective, the extent to which increasing the supply and keeping down the cost of well-located land for housing helps to improve housing conditions, and provides many lower-income households with more secure and better serviced alternatives to illegal subdivisions or illegal land occupation. Allocating large areas of land around a city to parks or ecological belts can restrict the supply and increase the cost of land for housing (Barton et al., 1994) and undermine the livelihoods of those who depend on agricultural or forest lands for their livelihoods (Douglass, 1989; Kelly, 1998). Middle- and upper-income groups often claim to be promoting the green agenda to defend the maintenance of large green areas in or around their homes, when their real priorities are maintaining their privileged access to open space and ensuring no lower-income residential developments take place in their vicinity.

DRAWING TOGETHER THE BROWN AND GREEN AGENDAS

The discussion above concentrates on potential disagreements between proponents of the brown and green agendas. But there are also many areas where there is more agreement, and where both brown and green agenda proponents work together, for instance in the movement against what is generally termed 'environmental racism' (the location of dangerous or unsightly factories and waste management facilities in low-income areas), and in the campaigns by citizens, community organizations and NGOs against industrial pollution and its effects (for instance the destruction or damage of local fisheries) or, more generally, against air pollution.

Reconciling the brown and green agendas means recognizing that different cities and even different neighbourhoods within cities should have different priorities. Quite clearly, for example, the environmental agenda of affluent cities, where everyone has water piped into their home, good sanitation, door-to-door waste collection and clean fuels, ought not to be the same as that of a city where a sizable share of the population lack these basic services.

In any given city, however, the overlap between brown and green concerns is likely to be substantial. For instance, a brown agenda concern for the needs of low-income groups for health, air quality and good public transport can overlap with a green agenda concern to reduce fossil fuel use (and thus also greenhouse gas emissions) and the air pollution that can contribute to ecological damage downwind of the city, for instance through acid precipitation or ozone plumes. Both concerns are likely to be served by high-quality public transport, good traffic management (including appropriate provision for pedestrians and cyclists), land-use management that encourages public transport-oriented city expansion, and controls or financial disincentives on excessive private automobile use.

Similarly, a recognition of the importance of urban agriculture for the livelihoods of significant sections of low-income populations in many urban centres can combine a brown agenda perspective through supporting low-income groups' access to land with green agenda perspectives regarding the ecological advantages of increased local production (Smit et al., 1996). A commitment to improved solid waste collection and management can combine green and brown perspectives – for instance, in waste management systems that support waste reduction and the reclamation and reuse or recycling of materials from waste streams, which also generate many jobs. Improved provision for water supply and sanitation, which is so central to the brown agenda, can be done within a framework that recognizes green concerns – for instance, through water tariffs that ensure the price per litre rises with per capita consumption, or community sewer systems that reduce the volume of water needed and have local treatment systems allowing the nutrients in waste waters to be used for fish farming or crops (Smit et al., 1996; Gaye and Diallo, 1997).

There are also many complementarities that tend to be overlooked. For example, hygiene education is central to improved environmental health, and demand management is central to water conservation, but there have been few, if any, attempts to combine hygiene education with improved demand management. There is a serious danger that one agenda will come to be manipulated in the interests of the other: that an ostensible concern for health will mask a drive for conservation, or vice versa. But both health and, in the long run, water resources would benefit if people knew how to use water more effectively to protect themselves from disease. The tools of demand management could easily be adapted to serve both ends, as described in the following section. This serves as one example of a tool that can promote greater complementarity between green and brown agendas. Following this section, some of the broader institutional issues about how to reconcile the two agendas are discussed.

The example of demand management

In essence, demand management advocates a shift away from the 'supply-fix' approach to water, energy and urban infrastructure provision generally. Instead, attention is paid to 'providing the same services with less' by enabling improvements on the demand side – traditionally considered beyond the purview of the institutions that provide infrastructure and services. In many instances, it has proved less expensive for utilities to promote energy and water conservation through, for example, more efficient lighting, low flush toilets, or time-of-day metering than to engage in costly supply expansion. Moreover, the environmental benefits can be considerable.

The almost exclusive focus on resource conservation is inappropriate in many southern cities, where environmental health issues are more pressing. Indeed, there is a serious danger that resource-oriented demand management will leave many environmentally deprived urban households even worse off than with the conventional supply-fix approach. But many of the same insights apply to situations where the priority problems involve environmental health. Here, too, there is a bias towards supply-fix – put in more pipes and fill them with water; extend the electricity grid in the hope that people will switch from smoky fuels; etc.

Water demand management need not focus only on conservation. It is also a problem for health that water utilities cease to be concerned once the water has left the pipes, at least until it becomes a drainage problem. They do not pay sufficient attention to how the water is used; how the quality of water declines between tap and mouth, especially where water has to be collected from communal taps and stored in households; how an understanding of the demand side could increase access for the groups that need water most; and so on. Hygiene education is, in effect, a form of demand management, and many argue that it should accompany supply provision. So is finding connection arrangements that low-income groups can afford, for example, exploring the potential to shift the often high cost of connection to a piped water supply or sewers on to a monthly bill, providing cheap bulk supplies to a neighbourhood for a single payment. The inhabitants can organize the collection of individual household payments, negotiating with resident groups to find the best means of providing water, helping to develop in-house storage systems that will not allow dengue-bearing mosquitoes to breed there, or the water to become faecally contaminated.

In the energy sector, too, demand management need not be restricted to conservation. It could include offering consumers or settlements a wider range of demand-side electricity options, including, for example, pre-payment meters, boards containing the circuitry for households for whom house-wiring would be prohibitive, or the possibility of paying capital costs (potentially for electric stoves) through electricity charges. To the extent that urban consumers switch from smoky fuels, both environmental health and, depending on the local energy system, the broader environmental impacts should be improved.

In relation to solid waste, comparable possibilities range from improved storage systems, both for households and communities, to systems to promote recycling. Again, some of these measures could improve health by reducing pollution from waste burning, reducing pest infestation, and reducing the mixing of recyclable waste and faecal material. In this case, it is generation rather than demand that is being managed, but many of the principles remain the same.

WHAT BROADER INSTITUTIONAL PROCESSES HELP RECONCILE THE BROWN AND GREEN AGENDAS?

Reconciling the brown and green agendas in urban development requires institutions and processes that:

- reduce the inequities that are of concern to both brown and green agendas
- enable collective and democratic responses to the public aspects of both brown and green environmental problems
- provide a better understanding of the environmental issues different cities face.

There are at least three important areas where action is needed. Participatory processes within each city need development to allow environmental problems to be discussed, and agreements to be reached over priorities for action and investment. It is worth noting how green and brown agenda components have been integrated in various cities. These include the environmental action plans modelled on Local Agenda 21s, as recommended by the UN Earth Summit in 1992, developed in cities such as Manizales in Colombia (Vélasquez, 1998) and Ilo (Díaz et al., 1996; López Follegatti, 1999) and Chimbote in Peru (Forondo, 1998). These Local Agenda 21s were developed by a variety of groups, including community organizations, environmental NGOs, local academics and government agencies – and, in the cases of Manizales and Ilo, with strong support from municipal government. Porto Alegre in Brazil, which is well known for its successful brown agenda and its pioneering role in developing more transparent and participatory government structures, has a strong green component to its environmental policy. All these examples are from countries with democratic local governments and with decentralization programmes that had allowed city authorities more scope for environmental investment and management. The commitment to green issues can be seen in the major investment programme in ecological tourism and sewage treatment, and the extensive programme of environmental education which includes the production and dissemination in schools of a very detailed environmental atlas of the city and its surrounds (Menegat, 1998). In effect, the governance systems allowed citizens and their community organizations and NGOs to have more influence on development plans and investment priorities, and this increased the incorporation of green and brown agenda priorities. Most of the innovations also took place soon after decentralization and democratic reforms, and they need to be understood in the context of these broader, national-level reforms (Vélasquez, 1998; Miranda and Hordijk, 1998; Forondo, 1998).[3]

This highlights the second area where action is needed. National policies dealing with urban development deserve support that takes into account ecological sustainability and an understanding of potential conflicts with brown agenda priorities and other social and economic priorities. This is, in effect, the legislative, fiscal and managerial framework that allows 'good' city and municipal governance which, in turn, includes green and brown agenda priorities. For green agenda issues to be included within urban development, national governments need to support and respect appropriate international agreements that seek to protect sites of particular ecological importance and limit the generation of greenhouse gas emissions and stratospheric ozone-depleting chemicals, or to limit the generation of toxic or otherwise hazardous wastes (or their inappropriate disposal). Elected city governments are accountable to the populations living within their boundaries, not to those living in distant ecosystems on whose productivity the city producers or consumers may draw. It is difficult to ensure that the needs and rights of future generations and of other species receive adequate attention in urban policy and practice without the appropriate framework and support from higher levels of government. For instance, it is difficult for local authorities systematically to include concern for protecting biodiversity or for keeping down greenhouse gas emissions without a clear national policy. Although there are examples of cities whose Local Agenda 21s or other environmental action plans have included components to reduce the transfer of environmental costs outside city boundaries or into the future, the scope for such action will be limited by the need for all cities to be competitive in attracting new investments. For instance, no city can promote large reductions in greenhouse gas emissions if this encourages many enterprises to move to another city where no such measures are taken. Without supportive national policies and international agreements, it is difficult to realize fully the potential that cities have for combining safe and healthy living environments with resource conservation and waste reduction.

The third area where action is needed is a stronger basis for mutual understanding between brown and green agenda proponents, and this depends on a good knowledge of the environmental issues in and around each urban centre. Developing 'state of the environment' reports that draw on the knowledge and resources of citizens' groups, NGOs, private business and local educational institutions are often valuable underpinnings for this. Involving all such groups in developing reports can also be a valuable way of allowing each group to understand better the priorities of other groups. It is also worth noting the strong commitment by the different groups developing the Local Agenda 21 within Manizales, and the municipal government in Porto Alegre, to environmental education as a key part of their environmental policies. A well informed public debate about environmental priorities, backed up with good documentation of local and regional ecology, also provides the best defence against the misuse of brown or green agenda arguments by powerful commercial, industrial and real-estate concerns. New developments that primarily benefit middle- and upper-income groups or major industrial or commercial concerns often use green or brown agenda arguments to justify public support and even subsidy.

The cities and regions that are pioneering more ecologically sound, pro-poor and democratic development models deserve international as well as local attention. Historically, the most successful urban environmental initiatives, from sanitary reform to cleaner technology, have drawn on international experience and support. The inequities underlying both green and brown agendas have international dimensions. Allowing international priorities to dominate local environmental initiatives would further reinforce some of these inequities. But better, rather than less, international engagement can help to encourage innovative solutions.

CHAPTER FOUR

African cities and climate change: the global context for sustainable development

Rodney R. White

TENSIONS BETWEEN GREEN AND BROWN AGENDAS

For several years we have lived with an apparent conflict of priorities between researchers and practitioners in the field of development and those working on the challenge posed by climate change, sometimes referred to as the brown and green agendas (Gilbert et al., 1996: 13). The former focuses on issues of local environmental quality (such as water supply, sewage, solid waste, air quality); while the latter is most concerned with global issues such as climate change, loss of biodiversity, stratospheric ozone depletion, and the vulnerability of potentially renewable resources such as fresh water, soils, forests and fisheries.

I have always challenged this dichotomy because there are strong linkages between all these issues that require a holistic vision if any progress is to be made toward their resolution (White, 1997). Yet climate change and development still appear to be working on parallel tracks with little cooperation and cross-fertilization between them. That is not to deny that there is a very active body of researchers working on climate change issues in developing countries, nor to suggest that the development agencies are not actively engaged in issues on the green agenda (Downing, 1999; Downing et al., 1999; World Bank, 2000a).

Circumstances have already demonstrated the necessity for an integrated view of these issues as the manifestations of climate change (together with the other issues on the green agenda) bear down with a significantly higher impact on the poor than on the rich. Nowhere is this more evident that in the impact of tropical cyclones. In the North we measure the impact in economic damage and insured losses; in the South we estimate the number of dead. The power of these extreme weather events to reinforce the grip of poverty was forcefully demonstrated by the massive impact of a cyclone on Mozambique and Madagascar in February 2000. As the floodwaters subsided, it could be seen that the people had lost what little they had – the crops in the ground, their livestock and access to drinkable water.

The intensity of this new predicament is particularly notable in Africa, because Africa has not joined in the race toward material enrichment in the same way as many countries in Asia or Latin America. In Africa, there is no equivalent of Mexico (which joined with Canada and the USA in the North American Free Trade Agreement), or China, which has invented its own modernization paradigm for a transition to a socialist market economy.

The argument is made in this chapter that the challenge of climate change offers a unique opportunity for the poorest countries of the world – most of which are in Africa – to derive immediate benefits from the richer countries. Africa is offered as an example because it is the continent where poverty is most pervasive.

THE WESTERN MODEL OF DEVELOPMENT IS A DEAD END

There is a growing awareness that the western model of modernization – despite its ability to raise material standards of living – contains at least one fatal flaw. That flaw lies in what used to be seen as the technological foundation of its strength: the combustion of fossil fuels. The energy derived from fossil fuels provided the means to escape from our Malthusian dependence on land and labour. With the release of energy from the ground, the modern economy could leave agriculture in the hands of only 1 or 2 per cent of the working population, while the rest were free to produce a seemingly endless array of goods. When Walter Rostow heralded the age of 'high mass consumption' in the 1960s, no one predicted that life could be this rich.

The most serious flaw of the western model – as the world is slowly coming to understand – is that the combustion of fossil fuels releases greenhouse gases, such as carbon dioxide, methane and nitrous oxide, at a faster rate than the oceans are absorbing them. These accumulate in the atmosphere where they enhance the natural warming effect produced by trace gases and water vapour (Houghton, 1994; Harvey, 2000). Some of these gases will remain in the atmosphere for more than 100 years and thus they will destabilize the climate for a long time, even if our surplus emissions could be stopped today. We are committed to climate change, which will include higher temperatures, rising sea level, a more intense hydrological cycle and more extreme weather events, perhaps including tropical cyclones of greater frequency and intensity. As has been argued elsewhere, this is bad news for nearly everybody, but especially for the poor, who are more vulnerable to climatic variability such as floods and droughts (White, 1993).

It has been recognized for some time that this particular flaw, and other associated features affecting both resources and sinks for residuals, means that the western model cannot be employed to reduce world poverty to the point where the world population will achieve stability. As I and others have insisted, this means that 'you can't get here from there' (White, 1994). Even if some marvellous technological fix were found (such as a cheap means of carbon sequestration underground), the resource demands of the western style of living are too high for general distribution to *even the present world population.* That – as Wackernagel and Rees have calculated – would require approximately three planet Earths (Wackernagel and Rees, 1996: 15).

THE KYOTO PROTOCOL

Some appreciation of the magnitude of our predicament led to the signing of the Kyoto Protocol to the UN Framework Convention on Climate Change in December 1997, at the Third Meeting of the Conference of the Parties to the Convention. This required the industrialized countries to reduce their greenhouse gas emissions by at least 5 per cent below the 1990 level in the period 2008–12, as a first step toward climate stabilization (Grubb et al., 1999: 283). This is only a first step, because a typical western consumer emits about 4 tons of carbon per year. Stabilization – even at the present population level of 6 billion people – would allow only about half a ton per person per year. The annual emissions from 6 billion people – at half a ton of carbon per capita – are approximately equal to the amount that the atmosphere deposits in the oceans. This is the maximum under which we must learn to live if we wish to stabilize atmospheric concentrations of carbon dioxide. This challenge offers an opportunity to fashion a development path that could produce worldwide benefits.

Among the people in western industrialized countries who have heard of climate change and its possible implications, there is a widespread belief that we shall find an easy way out, preferably a technological fix that will leave everything on the surface pretty much the same. If this cannot be done, then it is possible that we can improve the capacity of the sinks for greenhouse gases. The most obvious solution would be to grow more trees and thus sequester carbon. Unfortunately, although such an initiative would help, the magnitude of our excess carbon emissions dwarfs our sequestration potential. Recently attention has been shifted to cultivation techniques, such as ploughing, which release carbon from the overturned soil. If we all practised minimum tillage then this too would help, but that would still be insufficient to balance the excess carbon dioxide that we emit. The argument concerning our sequestration potential was championed by the Americans and their allies at the Hague Conference of the Parties to the Kyoto Protocol in November 2000.

While the discussions continue, nearly every country in the world has been steadily increasing its per capita emissions, except in those ex-communist economies that imploded as they made their transition to a market system. Fuel efficiency has certainly become an important objective for forward-looking companies, but the fact remains that – based on the current technology – as people become richer they emit more carbon dioxide. Any savings we might garner from fuel efficiency we, as individual consumers, tend to spend on additional carbon dioxide-emitting activities. There is a very deep unwillingness to face up to the implications of this situation.

For those observers who have accepted the position as stated above (no technological quick fix, no easy salvation through carbon sequestration or energy efficiency), the next line of defence is to point out that if we must make cuts in emissions, it makes sense to do so where it can be done at the lowest cost. 'Market solutions' are in fashion throughout the world, so we should follow the logic of the market. This line of argument leads logically to the assumption that the most efficient emitters should be left alone and the inefficient emitters should be the target for reductions. This assumption, in turn, leads to the mechanisms proposed as vehicles for this market-driven solution to the greenhouse gas problem.

The first of these mechanisms was Joint Implementation, under which rich countries would team up with poor country partners to produce energy-efficient activities, such as power generation, in poor countries. The original thought was that the carbon avoided (by not continuing with the current, polluting technology) would then be 'credited' as part of the rich country's contribution to cuts. It would cost the rich country something in terms of loans or grants, but this would be less than the cost of reducing the same amount of carbon at home. Although a number of these projects were implemented on a trial basis, they have run into the ground for predictable political reasons (Grubb et al., 1999: 97). It smacks all too obviously of environmental colonialism, with the changes being made in the poor country under the direction of the rich, who receive the carbon credit and continue to pollute at home just as before. Joint Implementation is still on the agenda, but its future is not very bright.

A slightly subtler approach was launched with the Clean Development Mechanism, whereby clean technology would be transferred from rich countries to the poor with funding provided by the rich (Grubb et al., 1999: 133). Unlike Joint Implementation, this 'mechanism' would be under multilateral control, not a bilateral agreement. It also included provision for payment for administrative costs in the host country. The poor countries would have more control over the management of funds, and the amount of money channelled from rich to poor would be additional to existing aid commitments. The argument could still be made that the rich would continue to pollute as before while the poor made the adjustment to climate change, but the pot has been sweetened and further development of the Clean Development Mechanism is expected.

The third market-based mechanism was the proposal to trade carbon reductions among the signatories to the Kyoto Protocol, the countries listed in Annex 1 to the Protocol. The logic was same as that for Joint Implementation and the Clean Development Mechanism CDM – reductions should proceed in the most cost-effective way. Again, the greatest reductions could be made among the least efficient polluters, which for the Annex 1 group meant the ex-communist countries of central and eastern Europe, especially Russia and the Ukraine. The rich would pay the polluted for their 'reductions' and leave their own relatively 'efficient' societies alone. One of the grave defects of this proposal was that the baseline for the Kyoto Protocol's proposed reductions was 1990. Since that date, the collapse of the former communist economies had dramatically reduced emissions anyway. The 'reductions' they would sell to the West would be spurious; predictably, these reductions became known as 'hot air'. Despite the suspicion that this trading 'solution' is yet another attempt by the rich to dodge their responsibilities, there is considerable interest in the private sector for the development of the carbon market (Sandor, 1999; Cooper, 1999, 2000).

It is not yet known what role these mechanisms will play in implementing the Kyoto Protocol. For example, there is still no agreement on how much of a rich country's reduction can be credited from any of these mechanisms. Clearly, this is a very critical point. If these alternative mechanisms are unlimited in scope, they could be used to make up 100 per cent of a signatory's 'reduction' commitment. This is the first issue on which African countries must develop a firm position if their own emancipation from poverty is to take place. The issue must also be resolved in such a way that genuine emission reductions do take place in order to reduce the threat from climate change. It will do an African city little good to enjoy 100 per cent water and sewerage connection if torrential rainfall and rising sea level overwhelm the city's water supply and treatment system.

THERE MAY BE LIGHT AT THE END OF THE TUNNEL

Four encouraging points can be drawn from the climate change negotiations, despite the predictably sorry tale of national prevarication and international hostility. First, the most vocal source of opposition to the Climate Change Convention is losing strength. Many of the companies that founded the Global Climate Coalition have withdrawn their support, including BP–Amoco, Shell, Dow Chemical, Ford Motor Company, Daimler–Chrysler, and – most recently – Texaco. Denial is breaking down. Major pieces of the global corporate web are thinking of preparing for a post-fossil fuel world.

Second, all the alternative mechanisms proposed before and during Kyoto indicated that the rich countries were willing to pay for the privilege of continuing to emit greenhouse gases. This 'willingness-to-pay' can be turned to advantage, as was demonstrated by the Clean Development Mechanism's improved offer over Joint Implementation.

Third, there was a parallel conference going on in Japan at the same time as the Kyoto negotiations. This was the Fourth Local Government Leaders' Summit on Climate Change held at Nagoya, sponsored by the International Council for Local Environmental Initiatives (ICLEI, www.iclei.org). It is very significant that among the 140 delegations a number came from developing countries, and these delegations were already participating in ICLEI's Cities for Climate Protection Programme. At the city level there is already a working model of cooperation to share information on preparing for climate change. In contrast, one of the major stumbling blocks to the implementation of the Kyoto Protocol is the American insistence that developing countries make a 'meaningful' commitment to emission reduction. This is what the developing countries (led by China and the Group of 77) resolutely refuse to do, on the grounds that the carbon dioxide excess in the atmosphere is largely due to rich country emissions, and that those rich countries must take *the first 'meaningful' steps* towards emission reduction. A dispassionate observer would probably agree with both positions. At some point the developing countries must make a commitment, otherwise the exercise is a waste of time. It is equally important for the rich countries to take the first steps for many technical and political reasons, some of which are outlined below. My point is that, at the level of municipal cooperation, the Nagoya delegates have already got beyond this impasse and moved on to the practical challenge of working together on the climate change challenge. Of ICLEI's approximately 350 members, nearly 20 per cent are from developing countries, including more than 20 from Africa.

Fourth, the process has produced the beginning of a dialogue on rights, such as the rights of future generations, and the rights of rich and poor countries. Ultimately, these are not national but individual rights (Engelman, 1998: 3). It is completely arbitrary to assign 1990 emission levels to countries as a right, although a start had to be made somewhere just to begin this very novel global dialogue. Ultimately, this dialogue must converge on the notion that emission rights can be fairly assigned only on a per capita basis. This would be a radical step for global politics, but it is essential if we are to emerge from the climate change tunnel in any shape that resembles the present power structure – which is, presumably, what the countries that dominate that structure today would like to see.

A BRIEF LOOK AT SCENARIOS

At this stage, no one knows what the future might hold for the human race and our fellow occupants of the biosphere. We do not fully understand the science of climate change. There could be 'surprises in the greenhouse'. However, on the assumption that we do know roughly what might happen, the biggest unknown factor is ourselves. How are we most likely to comprehend, and act upon, the situation as described in the reports of the Intergovernmental Panel on Climate Change (Houghton et al., 1990, 1992, 1996; Houghton, 1994)?

Many scenarios have been generated, and every participant in the debate can imagine his or her own. I shall summarize the possibilities as simply best case, worst case and middle case.

Best case means that human beings finally understand what the better elements in all societies have been saying since the dawn of human history. People have the capacity to live in harmony with the Earth once they learn to live in harmony with one another.

Worst case means that we fail to resolve our differences at the international level. The Kyoto Protocol is subverted by carbon trading for hot air, spurious credits for Joint Implementation, and so on. The climate runs out of control. The future becomes utterly unpredictable. Crops fail. Famine returns. What happened in Mozambique and Madagascar comes home to roost in Japan and Florida.

Middle Case is what I call 'mankind muddles on'. We do some of the right things, but as we go one step forward, some other part of the system goes one step back. The carbon reductions of a more efficient power station are cancelled out by the carbon emissions of another million cars and trucks on the road.

I think it is imperative for the sustainability of all society, including African cities, that we expose the fatal weaknesses of 'muddling through' and go for the potential salvation of the best case scenario.

WHY THE RICH COUNTRIES MUST MOVE FIRST

There are two main reasons why the rich countries must move first to reduce greenhouse gas emissions. First, if they do not move first they may never move at all. Citizens and decision makers in those countries may cling to the belief that various Kyoto 'mechanisms', such as those mentioned above (Joint Implementation, Clean Development Mechanism, carbon trading), will provide sufficient momentum to deal with the problem of climate change without recourse to fundamental changes in their lifestyle. This is a vain hope.

Second, if they do not move first, then the poorer countries (non-Annex 1) will not move either. They may be prepared to emulate a shift of the richer countries toward a more sustainable lifestyle, but they will not move alone. Why should they? If it is not a serious problem for the richer countries, how can the poorer countries think it is a serious problem for them? (I believe it is still a problem for them, but this argument will not carry any political weight.) The expectation that poorer countries will embrace a low-carbon technology and 'leap-frog' their way to a novel technological future, while the rich countries continue to emit four tons of carbon per capita per year, is pure fantasy.

Western economists and politicians might produce all kinds of ingenious rationales to explain why the most cost-effective way to reduce carbon dioxide is to start in developing countries. However, they must recognize that the hypocrisy of this type of argument is transparent to all. This is a situation where both moral and pragmatic reason dictates that the rich countries should lead by example.

A STRATEGY FOR AFRICAN CITIES

Two factors are required as a basis for action. First, the various mechanisms that are being promoted to avoid real emission reductions in the rich countries must be limited in their applicability. At this stage we do not know what that limit may be. For the sake of argument, let us put it at 50 per cent on an annual basis, with no end-loading of domestic cuts to some distant time frame. Second, we need global agreement on the need to move towards a new environmental paradigm based on a low-carbon lifestyle (meaning greatly reduced emissions of all greenhouse gases, not only carbon dioxide). The second condition would have sounded like a Greenpeace dream even two or three years ago. Now it is a serious topic of discussion in the boardrooms of major corporations. One day the Age of Fossil Fuel may sound as remote as the Stone Age. Society will move on. The question for the poorer countries of the world is: can they benefit from this unusual moment in world history to break the deadlock of poverty?

Africa is already highly vulnerable to flood and drought. Both these phenomena are predicted to increase with climate change. African cities are already very poorly serviced, overcrowded, and still growing rapidly (Stren and White, 1989). Many of the major cities are located on the coast, on sites that are extremely vulnerable to sea-level rise (Timmerman and White, 1997). Some lie in the tropical cyclone belt. These coastal sites were carefully chosen by the colonial powers, all of whom arrived by sea and linked the African hinterland to their maritime empires.

Each African city needs to prepare a contingency list for responding to climate change in the expectation that funding will be provided under one Kyoto mechanism or another. For coastal cities, flood protection and water supply and treatment are the most critical infrastructure issues. Cities that occupy highly unsuitable sites will have to consider partial evacuation at least. Examples that come to mind are Abidjan, Lagos, Douala and Kinshasa, as well as the towns of the Niger Delta. Other cities, such as Dakar and Kano, are vulnerable to drought as rainfall becomes less predictable. Seawater intrusion of coastal aquifers is an additional problem to be considered. Throughout the continent there will be heightened risk of food shortages and disease.

Even in the middle case (outlined above), the trajectory for Africa under climate change is dire. For Africa, the need to make the best case a reality is desperate. Thus Africa's hope lies in pursuing a twin-track strategy. One track is the design of an adaptive strategy (infrastructure, food and water security) for the climate change to which we are committed from the excess greenhouses gases we have already emitted. The other track is a diplomatic effort to win the necessary resources from the Kyoto Protocol. If they – in concert with other low-income countries – can achieve this, they will be using the imperatives of the green agenda to fund the needs of the brown agenda.

A PROPOSAL TO ENCOURAGE BENEFICIAL CHANGE

I do not have any confidence in the validity of the 'leap-frogging' scenario. Nor do I think that developing countries should be encouraged to increase their greenhouse gas emissions so that they may become richer and hence 'developed'. This model is a dead end, and should be abandoned as soon as possible. We should all be converging on half a ton of carbon per capita per year in the shortest possible time. Even this target will also have to be reduced below half a ton as the world population continues to grow. This proposal is sometimes summarized as 'contraction and convergence'. The global quantity of emissions contracts as all people converge on a similar level of output of carbon dioxide. How might this process be encouraged?

Rights could be allocated on a per capita basis, using the familiar baseline of 1990 (Engelman, 1998). Let us set this allowance, initially, at a ton of carbon (=3.66 tons of CO_2) per year, acknowledging that this will have to be reduced, later, to half a ton or less. Establish a global carbon fund to collect revenues and a subsidiary body to develop and implement a low-carbon technology. Countries above the limit would then pay an annual fee into the fund, calculated as the product of their average excess over 1 ton and their total population. Half of this money would go into the development of new technology, while half would be passed on to countries *below* the 1 ton limit, also distributed as a product of their population and their average emission level. This would be used locally to develop infrastructure to enable citizens of poor countries to meet the stresses of climate change, both short- and long-term. Using the 1 ton limit or allowance, all African countries except South Africa would be recipients from the fund (using 1990 emission assessments from www.cnie.org/pop/CO2/rankingdata.htm). Indeed, among the world's 40 lowest emitters (sending less than 500 kg of CO_2 per capita per year), all but 13 are African.

Within each country the process would be replicated, with the high-carbon emitters (producers and consumers) paying into a national fund, some of which would be used centrally (perhaps to replace taxes on employment, savings and purchase tax on essential goods), and the rest distributed to low-carbon emitters. Some European countries are already moving in this direction, so the idea is not far-fetched. In African countries with high taxes on petrol, some form of carbon tax implicitly exists. The beauty of such a scheme is that it rewards 'low-carbon virtue' while restricting the tendency to spend the reward on high-carbon activities. It would not be that difficult to collect the tax because it could be charged at point of sale for the major sources of carbon dioxide such as petrol for vehicles and energy supply to a house or factory.

In this form, it would not capture all greenhouse gas emissions such as methane from agricultural sources. Nor would it reward people for augmenting carbon sinks. But these are refinements that could be added as required. The main advantages of such a scheme are that it would encourage a low-carbon lifestyle while discouraging a high-carbon lifestyle, and it would be relatively simple to measure, monitor and enforce, relative to the monitoring schemes that are being debated for measuring national emission reductions, carbon sequestration and so on. Of course, it should not be called a tax, so I propose that it should be called something positive, such as a carbon abatement regulation and transfer scheme (CARATS). If we take as an example a price of US$100 per ton above or below the national per capita figure, then the USA would pay in about US$112 billion annually, while China and India – the major recipients – would receive about US$18 billion and US$34 billion, respectively. Under such a scheme, Kenya would receive about US$1.3 billion. The size of the transfers could easily be moved up or down by changing the price, which is arbitrarily set in this example. In comparison with these financial flows, the global annual total for official development assistance is somewhat less than US$50 billion (Victor, 2001). Half of the receipts from this scheme would go into the global technology fund, of which the main beneficiaries would be Western companies, so it would be popular in those quarters. The limit and the price per ton would have to be adjusted to keep the fund solvent and to meet the emissions reductions actually needed to stabilize the atmospheric concentrations. A proposal like this may seem fanciful, but the likely alternative is the current impasse between the USA and the developing countries.

CONCLUSIONS

It is easy to embrace despair and conclude that there is no way to break the impasse. But a way will be found, and it will cost the rich countries *something* to finance the involvement of the poorer countries. It remains to be seen what that level of transfer will be. What is needed to give the process some momentum is an understanding that developing countries will participate in the Framework Convention on Climate Change, and that the rich countries will make their priority the reduction of *their own* emissions while providing financial assistance to poorer countries to make an attractive low-carbon technology available.

We shall probably spend a long time getting to agreement on these points. Much of that time will be wasted on specious economic arguments about starting with the most cost-effective reductions first, ignoring the fact that the longer we delay, the more difficult conditions will become for rich as well as poor. There is an economic cost attached to all the time spent on deciding where to start. The place to start is by taxing emissions from the highways, power stations and households of the West, and by directing some of the proceeds towards poverty reduction in the poorest countries of the world.

PART II

PLANNING FOR SUSTAINABLE GROWTH

Urban planning and the rationale of the market: the elimination of the intermediate urban level in Bogotá

Andrés Ortiz-Gomez

INTRODUCTION

The current transformation of city structure in developing countries has mainly been studied at the macro level by urban researchers – although market enablement policies have potentially enormous spatial impacts (see Chapter 2), little attention has been given to this issue on a more local-ized spatial scale. This chapter attempts to analyse city reconfiguration at the micro level, and to determine the impact of market forces and an increasingly free market and entrepreneurial development process on the distribution and pattern of urban services, specifically at the intermediate level.

The chapter is based on an analysis of Bogotá, the capital of Colombia. It shows how a simultaneous process of atomization and fusion has taken place in the provision of services and functions at the intermediate urban level. Some services and functions have been displaced to a more local level (atomization to the micro level), others to the metropolitan level (fusion at the macro level). The chapter shows how the increasing 'privatization' of social and planning responsibilities and the rationale of the market have caused this process of metropolization, and the atomization of urban func-tions and land uses traditionally found at the intermediate level. It further shows how these processes, by causing the 'extinction' of Bogotá's urban intermediate level (the neighbourhood), have contributed to the disinte-gration of community structures and a disaggregated pattern of urban development which is ultimately unsustainable.

The displacement and evolution of four local uses, which have con-tributed to the transformation of Bogotá's urban pattern (Figure 5.1), are examined: enclosed condominium housing; shopping centres and hyper-markets; parks and urban recreation; and elementary and high schools. The chapter argues that, paradoxically, the difficulty in adapting urban planning policies, instruments and institutional capacity for the city to the changing conditions and processes of production may have facilitated the formation of a fragmented city. This failure has, in effect, contributed to the near elimination of the intermediate level as a fundamental component of urban life (Alcaldía Mayor de Bogotá, 1999: 43).

City structure

1 Metropolitan level
2 Intermediate level
3 Project level

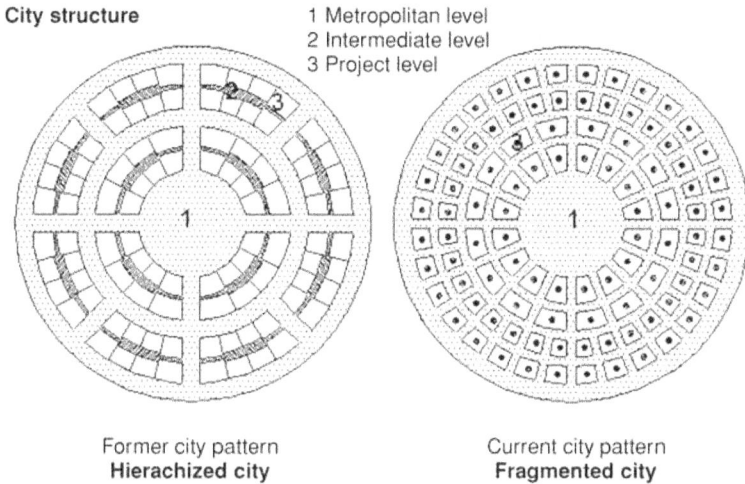

Former city pattern
Hierachized city

Current city pattern
Fragmented city

Figure 5.1   Bogotá City transformation pattern

Whether or not the demise of the urban intermediate level can be reversed, or indeed whether it should be recovered, constitutes one challenge. The more significant questions are to understand how and why cities are restructuring; how new strategies for urban planning might be developed to manage this reality; and how to develop the newly emerging structure of cities in a sustainable way. Given the forces restructuring cities and the new urban production functions, what actions are needed to recover the quality of life for communities which is lost with the loss of intermediate services and functions?

In the 1960s Webber (1968: 93) searched for 'the conception of the city that can analytically identify process-relations and form-relations'. Today, it seems to be necessary to include the market rationale as a new variable in this analysis, given that this new rationale has fundamental impacts on city structure.

Definitions

Most cities reflect a hierarchical form of service provision, from the specialist functions and uses found in city centres, through intermediate levels, to local-level centres serving daily needs. Intermediate centres are typically found in most cities, providing middle-order services and functions such as supermarkets and other large-scale retailing and service activities, a mix of business and commercial functions, larger recreational facilities, and educational establishments such as secondary schools and colleges. The intermediate level, as defined here, also constitutes the primary 'unit' of residential development. Thus, from a social perspective the intermediate level is analogous to the more traditional concept of the neighbourhood, and is the location of 'place–community'. As well as being functionally distinct, the intermediate level is also defined here from a spatial point of view – distributed in the city, usually at highly accessible poles of the city's main transport network. Finally, it is also constituted in physical terms, with site-specific buildings and land uses with identifiable developmental attributes.

INSTITUTIONAL AND POLICY CONTEXT

Institutional capacity and administrative structure in Bogotá

Critical to an explanation of the process of Bogotá's spatial transformation is an understanding of its inadequate planning machinery and weak institutional capacity. Bogotá's administration has been very centralized. Despite the fact that the city mayor, councillors and *ediles* (local councillors) are elected by the citizens, all civil servants, administrators, local mayors and managers of the decentralized institutions are selected by the city mayor. The city is divided into 20 local municipalities, but they do not have real planning powers and investment mechanisms. Their budget is minimal, and they have only regulatory and policing responsibilities. This situation has also impeded other neighbouring municipalities from joining the city's metropolitan area because they assess that integration would tend to a loss of their autonomy, rather than an opportunity to coordinate and plan the region (Londoño, 1992: 389, 396). This factor has contributed substantially to the lack of sufficient power at the metropolitan level to respond to the challenge of land-use displacement, discussed below.

The local councils were created in 1986 in order to complement the local municipalities and to enlarge the participation of the community. In theory, the law allocated them powers to manage 20 per cent of Bogotá's general budget, and allowed them to make local development plans (Garcia and Zamudio, 1997: 58). Nevertheless, local decisions and plans must always conform to a city policy. The residents elect these corporate authorities; but because of the lack of community motivation and information, and distrust in their capabilities, only 6.5 per cent of the inhabitants of Bogotá have voted for the *ediles* (members of the local council), and few know that these councils exist. Some authors think that the local councils (JALs – Junta Administration Local) instead of improving participation are simply a new link to the traditional political structures, and that their planning decisions are improvised rather than integrated within the city's strategies (Garcia and Zamudio, 1997: 27). As Leguizamón (1997: 24) says:

> decentralization has not produced all the results that were expected and proposed by their promoters, but it has achieved enough to confirm that the process is needed and has a future.

Bogotá's planning authority is the DAPD (District Administrative Department of Planning). Its main responsibilities are urban analysis, urban plan production and coordination, and the preparation of social, physical and spatial programmes. Nevertheless, in 1992 an assessment by DAPD showed that it spent 85 per cent of its resources studying and approving development and construction licences, and only 15 per cent in forward planning (Londoño, 1992: 31). City planning is a top-down process: it is not based on community information and priorities determined by the local municipalities. The Alcadía Mayor de Bogotá has not been able to control illegal development; zoning and building regulations exist, but are frequently breached without fear of effective sanctions. In Bogotá, 86 per cent of the low-income housing has been developed without construction licences. But even in many wealthy suburbs, private offices, small shops and restaurants, institutional facilities and industries have been developed in areas where their use is prohibited by plans (Garcia and Zamudio, 1997: 24).

Autonomous companies, which are increasingly becoming privatized, have managed Bogotá's infrastructure services. But they define their investment priorities independently of spatial planning priorities. This has caused a lack of institutional coordination, and inefficiency.

Planning policies and regulations

It could be said that the *Acuerdo* 7 of 1979 was the beginning of Bogotá's current urban planning era. It was a typical master plan, based on the

> dominant legal doctrine that still regards the city as no more than a bounded area comprised of demarcated plots of land in individual ownership.
>
> (Fernandes and Varley, 1998).

The *Acuerdo* 7's main objectives were (Garcia and Zamudio, 1997: 24): to retain Bogotá's surrounding rural area (*La Sabana de Bogotá*), to define the city's infrastructure boundaries, to increase urban density, and to plan urban spaces and activities by use of zoning. The planning model which was adopted in 1979 and used for 20 years had three basic limitations (Alcadía Mayor de Bogotá, 1999: 81): territorial planning was exclusively driven by regulating urban plots and local urban areas, and there was insufficient coordination and a failure to plan at the intermediate scale.

In 1990, a new urban planning framework was launched, the *Acuerdo* 6. Its policies were based on the definition of three categories of zoning: category 1, public and private uses (conservation zones, parks and open spaces, compulsory cessions, etc.); category 2, urban areas, sub-urban and rural areas; and category 3, economic activities and residential areas. The basic advance of this new *acuerdo* was that urban development opportunities were opened up by less regulatory, more flexible planning instruments. The plan provided a novel concept, setting out areas in Bogotá which could be consolidated. This concept could be applied in suburban areas subject to some conditions such as coordinated service provision, and where plots were not affected by future infrastructure projects. Also, illegal or informal urban development could be legalized and then incorporated into the urban area. Nevertheless, the key point was that these norms were based on the incorporation of new urban land exclusively on the initiative of the private sector, and the process was restricted to proposals for plots of a standard size and shape. Since 1990 the city has been planned incrementally, with no coherence between its components. The only common criteria adopted have been a road plan and regulations about uses and volumes.

> Bogotá's development model is, under these conditions, highly dependent on the time, the acting forms, and the urban parts which are determined by the market operation.

> (Alcaldía Mayor de Bogotá, 1999: 83).

Bogotá's new *Plan de Ordenamiento Territorial*, which was approved in 2000, attempts to negate the harmful urban impacts caused by *Acuerdo* 6 and 7, and has the following novel principles and strategies.

- A requirement to prepare land-use plans designed to coordinate and ensure a more cohesive and comprehensive approach to the built area, keeping the scale appropriate to the phasing and planning of the infrastructure system and other urban facilities. This concept also applies in urban conservation areas. The aim is to allow for integrated urban zones, and to make the construction of public facilities financially feasible. As we shall see, this is especially significant because *Acuerdo* 6 underpinned a process of development in urban growth which endorsed the fragmentation of the city structure and the displacement of the land uses.
- The densification of the existing developed area and the development of the vacant land within the existing urban areas in order to produce a compact city and, at the same time, the development of open spaces and proper community facilities.
- The construction of a new, comprehensively planned urban zone.

It could be said that the new *Plan de Ordenamiento Territorial* represents a fundamental improvement, redirecting Bogotá's urban structure and managing the urban intermediate level. However, if this regulation is to be effective it must be complemented with a substantial enhancement of the institutional capacity of the planning authorities.

DISPLACEMENT OF INTERMEDIATE USES

Enclosed residential developments and neighbourhood fragmentation

Two factors in combination have contributed to the displacement of residential uses. First, during the past two decades or so Bogotá has witnessed the rapid expansion of a new process of private sector residential production. This process integrates key stakeholders – investors, developers and architects – in land assembly and development for residential uses. Decreasingly constrained by urban planning policies in an environment of market enablement and more limited government intervention, private developers have expanded their role and power, responding by producing a novel form of residential development called *Conjunto cerrado.*

The opportunity to develop private condominiums and the particular form this has taken in Bogotá is the response to a second factor. The city has one of the highest levels of criminality, violence, and low detection within Latin American (Cámara de Comercio de Bogotá, 1996: 7). The everyday life of Bogotá's residents is deeply affected by the fear of crime and the changes in lifestyle it provokes. In response to this insecurity over the past 20 years in Bogotá, there has emerged a process of security privatization. In Colombia there are more than 350 private security companies, which have more than 80 000 guards (Cámara de Comercio de Bogotá, 1996: 112), and 40 per cent of this private 'army' work in Bogotá. They are responsible for the security of housing projects, shopping centres, business complexes and private and public institutions. Currently the city has three times more people working for private security firms than for the police (Gilbert, 1996: 259).

The problem of personal insecurity is clearly severe. But it is the profound impact on the form and location of residential development, combined with the emerging entrepreneurial capacity of private developers under conditions of market enablement, which is the main concern here. In Bogotá, as in Sao Paulo (Caldeira, 1996: 55), urban planning policies have been virtually powerless to resist the widespread development of a new type of housing product, the enclosed residential development (*Conjunto cerrado*). The main message in their advertising is 'do not live in the city, the city is no longer a liveable place; live in your own world inside our enclosed condominium'. Up to 1995, in the Colina Campestre sector alone, 122 *conjuntos cerrados* were developed (Pergolis, 1998: 59). Now it is possible to find a supply of *conjuntos cerrados* for high-income, middle-income and upper low-income classes across the city. In simple terms, the traditionally planned neighbourhood of open-form development with integrated land uses cannot compete with enclosed developments in an unregulated open market.

The fundamental point to emphasize is the atomization of residential areas produced by the design form and physical enclosure of the condominiums. As security costs constitute more than 60 per cent of the *conjuntos cerrados*' annual budget, the design of condominiums is based on insulating the developments from the surrounding neighbourhood by walls and steel fences, ensuring minimal access, with armed guards to control entry, and effectively privatizing community uses and communal areas by this enclosure. Private developers include within the enclosed condominiums as many additional services as possible; these services appeal to residents' ambitions and an imagined enclosed social world.

Urban planning regulations have had limited impact in controlling this process. Beyond the need to accord with very basic planning require-ments under *Acuerdo* 6 – access standards, linkage to the city's road net-work, fulfilling density and plot ratio standards – these condominiums have been developed in an unconstrained way. Opportunities to create a balanced land-use pattern and integrated mix of uses, linked to the wider pattern and provision of a neighbourhood, have been ignored. The enclosed developments are thus autonomous islands. By ignoring the local spatial context and connectivity with each other and the local neigh-bourhood, their development strongly contributes to the fragmentation of the city's intermediate level. This process not only leads to a reconfigura-tion of the neighbourhood, it has also created the atomization of the city.

Under the current urban regulations, enclosed developments are scarcely regulated. They can be developed in any residential sector in the city within plots smaller than 40 000 m². There is no provision for public roads or open spaces, there is only one access and they are essentially autonomous.

Finally, the size of project phases has been reduced as an effective way of minimizing financial risk. The reduction in size of phases is also a useful way of guarding against the impact of rapid changes in customer taste or economic capacity. The aim now is to build projects with the shortest possible duration of design, construction and selling time. Con-sequently, Bogotá is being planned and developed in smaller fragments, which fuels the speculative cycle and further accelerates the atomization of the residential elements.

Shopping metropolization

In 1975 *Unicentro*, a pioneering form of shopping centre in Colombia, was developed in the northern high-income suburbs of the city. In the 1980s other shopping centres for the city's elite were also constructed. Further large-scale centres of similar design have subsequently been built for middle-income communities, and for low-income areas of Bogotá as well. This commenced the process of the 'deconstruction' of local and intermediate centre shopping facilities, which accelerated in the late 1980s when Bogotá's current commercial era began – the first hypermarket was opened. The local store Exito launched this new con-cept, based on shops of greater than 10 000 m² of retail area and focus-ing their market strategy on accessibility, price, quantity and quality of goods offered, services, parking facilities and security. In the 1990s, glob-alization and an open market provided the entry point for transnational retail stores such as Carrefour, Makro and Home Centre. This consoli-dated the now established pattern of retailing by locating stores on the main roads and on the periphery of the city. This phenomenon has evolved more dramatically in other Latin American cities such as Mexico City and Buenos Aires.

As the city planning document describes the impact:

The conjuncture between arterial road junctions and the massive transport flows in Bogotá has produced the appearance of unplanned nodes. At these points there has been a remarkable concentration of the city's commercial activities.

(Alcadía Mayor de Bogotá, 1999: 51).

This coincidence has been the target point for the private hypermarket chains to locate new stores, as this location guarantees a metropolitan coverage. The average catchment area covered by each store is about 1100 hectares and a population of just over 230 000 inhabitants. In other words, each superstore serves more than 20 existing neighbourhoods (Almacenes, 1998/9, unpublished study). It is estimated that nearly 60 per cent of customers take more than 15 minutes travel time from their home to the shopping centre, illustrating how far the customers live from the stores. Their location is at points of maximum access and demand catchment, such that local shops and small markets within neighbourhoods cannot easily compete. Against the competitive power of the superstores, planning regulations have negligible impact. This process should be planned.

The outcome, after some 25 years of retail relocation in the city driven by the rationale of the market, has been the decay of intermediate centres and the consequential metropolization of this function. Additionally, the increasing size of hypermarkets means that land is one of the most significant variable costs. This fact is an important explanation of their peripheralization and consequent metropolization. A spiral has started in which the hypermarket clusters that are being formed in new city sub-centres in Bogotá generate additional land value increments and the consequent displacement of existing urban uses.

The city's urban regulations for commercial uses have been based on the principle that 'the bigger the shopping project, the wider the road front'. This requirement removes big commercial projects from local neighbourhoods and concentrates them on the city's main avenues. Moreover, Bogotá's planning authorities leave the final decisions about the stores' specific locations to private developers and commercial investors. The legislation was more focused on where shopping uses should not be, instead of where they should be located, thus encouraging new unplanned centres of activity.

Recreation and parks – fragmentation and metropolization

At the beginning of the previous century in Bogotá, recreational land use was based on the concept of the city as 'shared space', which generated the provision of open space and plazas as meeting places for citizens and for social interaction. During the 1950s and 1960s the concept was further developed, as the city itself expanded, based on planning policies to provide integrated neighbourhoods. These plans included requirements for open space and parks with sports facilities for each new community.

However, in the 1980s and 1990s, as in the case of residential development discussed above, the city regulations for new urban land subdivision were almost exclusively based on the interests of private sector owners and developers. Open space provision is largely residual after residential and commercial land uses have been maximized in terms of plots size and shape. The only obligation private developers have concerning recreation facilities is to provide the standard ratio of open space, but the regulations have not allowed the planning authorities to determine the character of the open space in terms of layout, facilities and landscaping. Moreover, the developers have been more interested in fulfilling the city's open space and recreational land-use regulations inside their projects – the condominiums – in order to make the development more competitive and attractive in the market.

Bank loans represent more than 60 per cent of the financial resources invested in new housing developments in Bogotá. Thus a small reduction in financial cost can dramatically improve the project feasibility. The reduction in project duration has been a frequently used strategy by developers in Bogotá to achieve cost reduction. This has been achieved by dividing a project into many autonomous smaller phases. As a result, parks and open space required in accordance with the planning regulations have also been proportionately reduced in size, and produced in a very piecemeal way, because they serve only one project phase instead of the whole new project or neighbourhood.

These processes have caused both a reduction in open space provision and the atomization of this space – in which the city ends up being a sum of fractions that have been individually planned, with little coherence between them. The decline of local recreation facilities reflects not so much a lack of demand, but the unprofitable value of urban public goods such as parks and green areas. This reality is clearly illustrated in Figure 5.2, which demonstrates the evolution of Bogotá's urban space location.

The absence of sports and recreational public facilities has been a traditional characteristic of the city. Conversely, the substantial lack of green spaces at the intermediate scale has been substituted with private recreation facilities such as country clubs and private or cooperative recreation centres (*Cajas de Compensacion Familiar*) (Alcadía Mayor de Bogotá, 1999: 62), which have been developed in large lots at the city's periphery. Under market enablement, the inevitable decline in public goods provision is matched by a prodigious growth in demand for private clubs and recreational facilities.

A final twist in this process is that city shopping malls have been increasingly transformed into recreation centres for people who have been 'deprived' of public recreational facilities in the past. The commercial entrepreneurs have seen this as a great business opportunity. The impact of these twin processes has been the fragmentation and metropolization of recreation and park facilities.

(a)

(b)

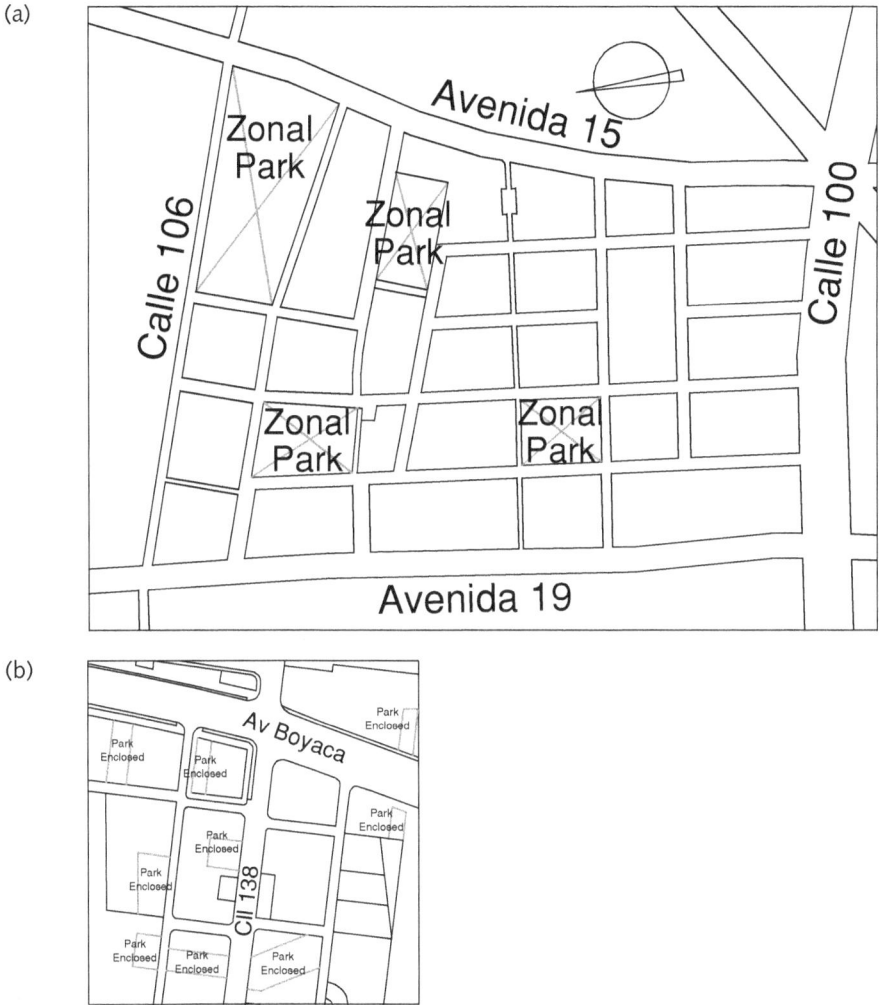

Figure 5.2   Parks and open spaces: urban pattern comparison. (a) El Chico neighbourhood, developed in the 1960s; (b) La Colina neighbourhood, developed in the 1990s. Both plans are on the same scale

Metropolization of school locations

In Bogotá, in 1997 over 1 331 000 children were studying in primary and high school. Primary schools served about 90 per cent of the eligible population, while high schools served about 83 per cent of the people. Taking data from 1994, the failure rate of students was 60 per cent higher in public (state) schools than in private institutions, and only 40 per cent of students from the state sector achieved the expected academic level (SED, 1998: 7, 11, 13). Because public education has been of such low quality and there have been insufficient places in state schools, by 1995 over half the children of school age attended private schools. As Table 5.1 shows, private schools comprise nearly 80 per cent of the total number, and about 70 per cent of classes.

Not surprisingly, as the 1993 CASEN (*senso del departamento adminis-trativo de catastro*) census shows, there is a close correlation between income and private education (Table 5.2).

Although private education has undergone this major transition, there has been no attempt to prepare an urban policy framework to plan the location strategy, the distribution of private sector education and its inte-gration with state provision and the overall process of urbanization. There is no concept of school catchment areas, and there are no obligations for private housing developers to build complementary educational facilities. Private schools can be located anywhere within the city limits where insti-tutional use is allowed. The planning regulations have been ineffectual. As a result, some areas of the city have a concentration of schools whereas in other areas there is a notable deficit in school provision.

Because the northern part of the city was the most affluent, it was here that new shopping and offices project were located during the 1980s and

Table 5.1 Schools distribution between sectors* (1999)

Number of:	Public (state) schools	Private schools	Total
Schools	700	2664	3364
Classes	1289	2980	4269

*Given that public schools have more children per level than private institutions, and that the majority of public schools have two timetables a day (morning and afternoon groups), the imbalance is greater whether the distribution between sectors is analysed taking into account the schools quantity.

Source: SED (1998).

Table 5.2 Percentage of families paying for education (1993)

Family earning (in multiples of minimum salary)*	Public (state) schools (per cent)	Private schools (per cent)
<1	91.2	8.8
1–2	62.5	37.5
2–5	45.5	54.5
5–10	35.0	65.0
10–20	16.6	83.4
All families	50.3**	49.3

*One minimum salary in 1999 = US$125.

*From 1993 to 1995 the number of students studying in private schools had increased by 8 per cent.

Source: SED (1998: 10).

1990s, creating new multi-use areas. This process exerted great pressure on the land market because high demand was constrained by the very limited supply of land. Given that educational institutions occupied many of the larger plots, private developers began acquiring these as the best alternative for new projects. Educational sites reached enormous values caused by land speculation in this area of Bogotá.

As a result of this process, many private schools sold their former sites and moved outside the city to the northern periphery. Private providers know that the public have little real choice, and for that reason they can take the demand for granted in these locations. Competition is clearly imperfect, but the consequence is the collapse of socially and spatially more sustainable urban forms. A recent study (Montenegro, 1999) suggests that more than 100 schools had been built in this area of Bogotá, where large sites could be acquired and much improved facilities built for just a fraction of the returns on the sales of former sites. The same phenomenon is happening in other Colombian cities such as Medellín, Cali and Barranquilla. Although Bogotá's planning regulations prohibit development in these areas, developers are secure in the knowledge that there is virtually no risk of penalization or prosecution because of the planning authority's incapacity. As Fernandes observes: 'Many illegal forms of land occupation and construction can be observed among the more privileged groups in society' (Fernandes and Varley, 1998: 15).

Private primary, elementary and high schools in Bogotá have tended to concentrate on the same sites. In this way they can reduce their operating costs with the maximum utilization of their facilities and equipment. These cost-driven processes have eliminated existing and prevented the development of new, more local community- and neighbourhood-based educational provision closer to residential areas. Additionally, their most important market segments are found in communities that represent higher social economic strata, are bilingual, or include religious groups.

Figure 5.3 illustrates the impact the disaggregation of school location has had on travel-to-school patterns in Bogotá. Based on a sample of school bus journeys to only five schools, the enormous catchment areas over which the pupils travel is readily evident. Again we can see how this fourth land use has shifted to a metropolitan level and lost connectivity with the intermediate level of urban service and functions.

IMPACTS ON THE CITY

Urban and spatial effects

These examples illustrate the profound impacts that market enablement and the lack of effective planning powers have had on the spatial structure of Bogotá. The intensity of developers' interests is completely transforming the city's urban pattern and form, as urban planning policies are following

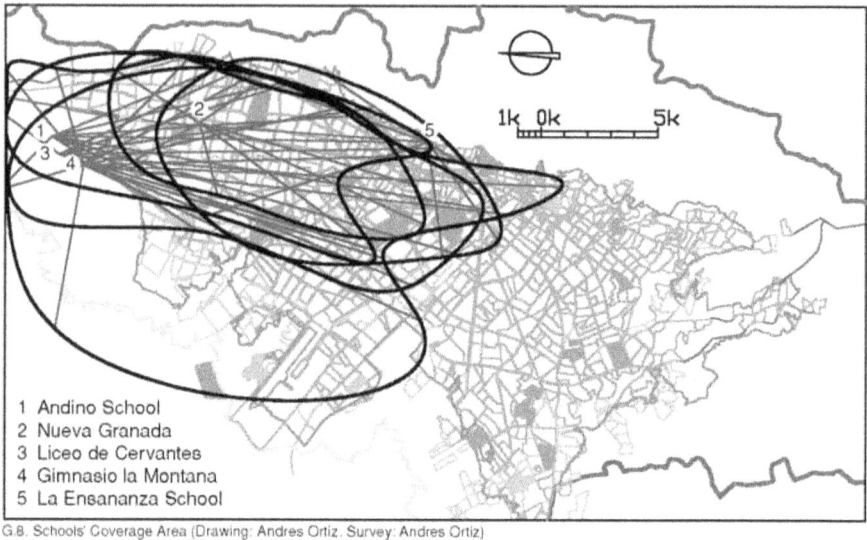

1 Andino School
2 Nueva Granada
3 Liceo de Cervantes
4 Gimnasio la Montana
5 La Ensananza School

G.8. Schools' Coverage Area (Drawing: Andres Ortiz. Survey: Andres Ortiz)

Figure 5.3   School catchment areas, Bogotá City

private actions and interventions. This section reviews some of the impacts of this process.

A fundamental failure of Bogotá's urban policy has been to see legislation as an objective in itself, not as an instrument to implement an urban plan (Ministerio de Desarrollo Económico, 1995: 227). The city has lost its hierarchical urban system; now there are dispersed activities at nodal points in the urban network. There is effectively no strategic-level urban planning at the macro scale. The notion of land uses and functions integrated at different spatial levels; the concept of centres, especially at the intermediate level; the spatial disposition of the city – none of these characteristics appears valid. Bogotá is now characterized by atomization and pragmatic intervention and development decisions (Pergolis, 1998: 17). In summary, 'The particular form of land occupation that has developed depends upon the local pattern of landownership, the price of peripheral land, the attitude of the political authorities and the pace of urban growth' (Gilbert, 1998: 88).

In Bogotá, social and community control over the street and public spaces is now very weak. Paradoxically, instead of improving perceptions of security, enclosed developments are increasing the fear of insecurity outside them. This insulation of housing projects is causing the atomization of neighbourhoods which are no longer served by open and recreational space, or shopping facilities, in an integrated way. Finally, it is important to note that the peripheralization of local uses has enormously expanded the city's uncontrolled spread of residential areas.

Social and community effects

It could be argued that urban residential fragmentation results not from a market-led development process, which has reconfigured urban structure in Bogotá, but from the interplay of more profound social and political forces (Pergolis, 1998: 1). Where there is fragile commitment to 'democracy, solidarity, the community organization, and collaboration with the authorities . . . there is the extinction of the neighbourhood (Cámara de Comercio de Bogotá, 1996: 45). In the case of Bogotá, the rationale for individualizing space (because of security fears), and a development process that also atomizes residential space, seem to have gone hand-in-hand. It is certainly the case that the harmful destruction of the intermediate level derives from the now current belief that 'the feeling of city character must start in the locality' (Leguizamón, 1997: 24).

The outcome of this process of enclosed developments is that 'the fear of crime is helping to create distance and separation among social groups and, thus, to enforce segregation' (Caldeira, 1996: 63). This situation is especially dramatic in Bogotá because it further accentuates a city whose socio-economic structure is already 'one of the most spatially differentiated cities by income group' (Mohan, 1994: 267). The combined effects of spatial and social fragmentation, which derive from the new development/architectural solution, based on private security, further contribute to 'the erosion of the legitimacy of the state and its ability to maintain its monopoly over the use of force' (Burgess, 1998: 8). Urban development processes undermine the role of state and public interests, which further promote the atomization of the city in a seemingly endless process.

When schools, recreation and shopping areas (the fundamental bases of the city social structure) are also disconnected from neighbourhoods, the citizens lose the essential resources and opportunities to create communities. As we have seen in the case of Bogotá, the concentration of private schools, hypermarkets and recreational centres at the periphery is a phenomenon which has caused detrimental impacts on the quality of life and the mobility patterns of children and adults (Alcadía Mayor de Bogotá, 1999: 58).

Environmental effects

At the urban level, one of the most profound effects caused by metropolization and fragmentation of local uses is the physical separation of activities, thus increasing the need for movement. This is particularly true in Bogotá, where in 1990 the average daily journey to work was 90 minutes (Gilbert, 1996: 67), while according to current research the average daily journey to private schools in the northern periphery, for example, is 130 minutes.

The fact that in the northern periphery of the city there are more than 100 schools means that nearly 2000 school buses and 16 000 private cars must travel twice a day to this area (author's calculation). Motor vehicle emissions are the principal source of atmospheric pollution in Bogotá, representing 60 per cent of the total air pollution (Alcadía Mayor de Bogotá, 1999: 22). In the city centre the noise level reaches more than 90 decibels, and in some of the city's commercial areas it reaches 80 decibels.

Enclosed condominiums and the atomization of parks and open space lead to severe deterioration in the quality of the urban landscape. The change of use of former schools to shopping and employment centres in the city has caused a significant reduction in the provision of green areas and sports fields in residential neighbourhoods.

ELIMINATION OF THE INTERMEDIATE URBAN LEVEL AND THE RATIONALE OF THE MARKET

The following sections analyse how neoliberal economic principles and the free market rationale have brought about the elimination of the intermediate urban level in Bogotá. The objectives of private developers are assessed against some basic economic and market concepts and definitions, in order to determine the extent to which the rationale of the market is a priority for urban entrepreneurial decision-making in urban development.

The central tension in the urban development marketplace is between the development entrepreneur's wish for profitability and risk minimization, and the mediating role of government to ensure that the wider needs of the community are taken into account. While the entrepreneurs should act within the legal framework of planning and other regulations, it is also argued that they should have responsibility to the community and should act in an ethical and socially responsible way. As we have seen in Bogotá, the challenge under conditions of neoliberal market enablement policies is that the regulatory framework of the state seems powerless to deploy appropriate instruments and modes of intervention to correct the destructive effects of the urban market on the quality of the city and its sustainability.

The complex relationships between individual, collective, private and public spaces are fundamental to the morphology of the city and its social development. Yet, where the balance between market and state interests in managing these relationships is disturbed, as seems to be the case in Bogotá, it would appear that the basic economic tenets of market enablement inhibit the capacity of the government to intervene in the operation of the urban land market. This is necessary in order to define spatially and socially more appropriate and efficient forms of urban development.

Market economy (supply, demand, competition and monopoly)

Where urban services and resources such as land are in short supply, and the planning machinery fails to regulate the supply process effectively, development tends to be located not where it is most needed, but where land is cheapest or profitability can be maximized. It is within the context of this basic principle that the lack of balanced supply and demand for land, and the increasingly speculative characteristics of Bogotá's land market, are the fundamental causes of the peripheralization of many urban land uses in the city.

The processes of capital accumulation and the tendency to create monopoly power in the urban development process in Bogotá, as in many other cities of the developing world, have been accentuated by the inflow of large quantities of international capital. This further strengthens the power and freedom of development interests to manage the pattern of urban growth and city structure, at the same time ignoring urban planning and social priorities.

From the commercial development point of view, the most important strength of big cities is their large population and resources. Private projects in a competitive market must make the most of this potential – hence the frequent tendency to develop projects that maximize access to the metropolitan level in order to capture a bigger market.

Marketing (market mix, segmentation, position and consumer behaviour)

Urban projects have many components – these can be varied in order to increase customer appeal and therefore sales of the product. From the perspective of the city and community, two critical elements are the location of projects and the urban context in which they are developed. But from the private development perspective in Bogotá, it is precisely these important spatial and community effects which are ignored in private development. In this context, the target of the market is towards specific private sector 'community' characteristics such as profession, income and social class. Neighbourhoods or 'spatial communities' are rarely the main determinant in their decision-making process.

Costs analysis (direct, indirect, fixed and variable costs)

Applied in the context of urban development, this concept assumes that the best plan will be the one that delivers the greatest quantity of economic benefits in relation to economic costs. The relation between costs (in these examples primarily, though not exclusively, land costs) and project location is therefore strongly affecting Bogotá's urban development patterns and driving the unplanned process of growth. As a result, the distribution of urban services within the city is inappropriate to community needs and sustainable urban form.

While developers focus on the cost analysis, which affects the commercial viability of projects, they ignore the public costs caused by their decisions. In the case of Bogotá these public costs are evident in increasing pollution, declining security (although as a welfare good, not strictly measured in monetary terms), increasing congestion, and so on. The rise in these costs indicates a city that is becoming decreasingly sustainable in economic terms, and also less sustainable environmentally and socially.

Risk evaluation (financial, legal, and market risks)

As a general principle, it can be said that business risks are smaller when the potential market is bigger. Therefore urban services, which are developed by the private sector, have a tendency to operate on a metropolitan level instead of an intermediate or local level. We can see this basic principle being played out in Bogotá.

As has already been said, the financial costs and changes in the market preferences are especially risky in the production of 'urban commodities' because of the long timescale required in order to build them. Consequently, urban developers in Bogotá are showing a preference for smaller project phases. The effect of this shift on the development process is a key point that planning authorities must take into account in order to manage the development of Bogotá effectively within broadly free market imperatives.

A final point to note with regard to risks is that when local authorities and planning institutions are weak, informal developers and, in the case of Bogotá, formal sector developers will ignore legal risks.

PLANNING RESPONSES: MANAGING THE NEW REALITY AND ANTICIPATING THE FUTURE

In order to tackle the current problems and to redirect the evolution of the city, it is necessary to reconceive appropriate and flexible strategies and instruments. What is needed is 'strategic or adaptive or situational planning which retains a broad perspective of a limited number of variables and issues considered to be of strategic importance' (Fernandes and Varley, 1998: 267). What might be the main dimensions of such an approach? Although specific to the case of Bogotá, it is contended that these approaches have wider resonance and applicability to many fast-growing cities of the developing world.

Strategic or purposeful planning

Bogotá's authorities need strengthening in order to accomplish the planning proposals and the *Plan de Ordenamiento Territorial* strategies, and to ensure that influential individuals will not be able to subvert them. Greater support is needed to ensure that urban planning instruments and regulations are adhered to, and that illegal developments by privileged landowners are not tolerated.

Second, a major challenge is to exert 'democratic leadership' in the participatory process in order to ensure that urban strategic goals are not subverted or by-passed. Improved governance and civil society are the cornerstones of this objective. Bogotá's urban regulations and administrative structure have the potential to work well. But decentralization and more locally based forms of governance are needed to achieve a better understanding of participatory decision-making and its implications in urban planning.

The existence of neighbourhoods in Bogotá does not necessarily mean that these communities are organized for effective participation. As we have seen, the twin processes of atomization and metropolization of the city have undermined the traditional place–community relationship. To promote participation, what is needed in Bogotá, summarizing Hall (1992), is more than mere consultation; . . . involvement in the people in making plans for themselves. In Bogotá, the government must win credibility by showing that the people's opinions are really taken into account in the city's plans.

'Planning would also incorporate the social goals embodied in encouraging the mixed use of space' (Burgess et al., 1997: 121). Mixed land use, in which the physical separation of activities is limited, is desirable. A planning strategy such as this makes sense to private developers seeking financially feasible development. For example, a highly profitable shopping area within a housing development could compensate for the cost of free land provision for education and recreation. In this way, 'planning gain' through cross-subsidy would produce a more sustainable urban form and a spatially more coherent configuration of the city.

As Zetter notes in Chapter 2, there is a need for coherent urban land policies linked to planning strategies in order to promote sustainable urban development. These should enable the delivery of an affordable and orderly supply of land within a strategic planning framework. Private-use rights should be retained, consistent with public needs and interests. Above all, in the case of Bogotá's chaotic land market, these policies must offer long-term investment stability to private developers without the negative impact of speculation.

If the current trend is 'towards a decline in the state's role as direct producer of goods and services and an increase in incentives to private sector investment in strategic or priority areas for development' (Fernandes and Varley, 1998: 258), then the predominance of private development interests in Bogotá could be a positive asset. Nevertheless, in order to achieve the urban objectives and counteract land market pressures, this opportunity must be managed and planned within the framework of public–private partnership.

In order to achieve a more satisfactory redistribution of land uses in convenient locations in Bogotá, closer involvement between the public sector, private developers, private institutions (e.g. schools), companies (e.g. hypermarkets) and the community is fundamental, along with the acceptance of mutual interest. 'New relationships between public authorities and the private sector can be established in a number of ways, and there are various strategies for involving the private sector in the provision of public services' (Fernandes and Varley, 1998: 263).

Adaptive and flexible planning

Local Plans (*Planes parciales*), which are the core of Bogotá's new urban regulations and planning mechanisms, must be the arena where the city's planning strategies can be adapted to the neighbourhood reality.

> The problems arising from rapid city growth are best dealt with by observing and understanding these patterns and designing flexible and self-correcting institutional frameworks that are capable of responding to the variegated needs of the city components.
>
> (Mohan, 1994: 272).

For instance, the fact that insufficient commercial areas and residential neighbourhoods in the city have been planned has caused the illegal adaptation of former houses to shops and the metropolization of hypermarkets, with the harmful effects noted above.

Resurrecting major city-wide control of the urban planning process does not necessarily mean that this would work against free market forces and private sector interests. The point here is that 'it is necessary to understand the operation of the system as a whole in order to control it effectively; unless this is done, actions taken to control one part of the system may have completely unexpected effects elsewhere' (Hall, 1992: 229). At the same time, if the urban planning regulations are to be respected they must be adapted for Bogotá's needs, and suitable for the private developers and community capabilities. Only within such a framework and with a strengthened local authority will an informal, market-driven, sometimes illegal and ultimately unsustainable urbanization process be managed.

Bogotá's urban development strategy must be formulated in an adaptive way so as to reorganize the production of public and private institutional facilities – schools, open space and recreational facilities. These are significant fixes in the morphology of a city and its development dynamics. Therefore it is fundamental that they are incorporated in a flexible way into the city's planning strategies for new development and regeneration. Private developers must be obliged to reserve suitable land for community infrastructure and open spaces, not in isolated parcels but in coherent packages. In practical terms, if the city plan is to be economically efficient, socially responsive and environmentally sustainable, its objectives can be achieved only through urban partnerships that are more responsive to the market rationale. 'However, partnerships should not be seen merely as a means of extending market forces, but rather as a means of reaping social and environmental benefits from them' (Payne, 2000: 8–9).

Finally, in view of the fact that most *Bogotanos* increasingly interact in an expanding urban realm beyond their immediate locality, the city planning authorities must find ways to adapt strategies that take into account the spatial and non-spatial communities. Much of what Webber elaborated nearly 30 years ago is relevant to Bogotá today. The planning agencies must 'find the use locations that offer the best opportunity for interaction with participants in all the realms in which they participate'. This can be done by 'seeking to accommodate place-conditions to the non-place interactions of the inhabitants' (Webber, 1968: 137, 146). Accepting that the current situation must evolve and be improved, rather than embarking on wholesale city reconstruction, it could be said that the most suitable plan for Bogotá should articulate both models.

Strategic or pragmatic planning

Restructuring of the pattern of urban development and preparation of the city for future development pressures are two fundamental objectives for Bogotá. Pivotal projects and programmes in accordance with the requirements of communities or particular city areas are now needed. This should be complemented by the following approach:

> *the role of governments should be to inspire, enable and facilitate formal private sector initiative through an appropriate policy framework, rather than to involve themselves in project implementation.*

> (Payne, 2000: 5).

Currently Bogotá's municipality is undertaking urban renovation projects in order to 'recover' central areas and, at the same time, control the outward expansion of the city. This is a crucial opportunity to relocate private schools, shopping areas and recreational facilities, and to counteract gross deficiencies in the provision of community facilities: it is estimated that 50 per cent of Bogotá's developed area requires improvement programmes of this kind (Alcaldía Mayor de Bogotá, 1999).

The new city's *Plan de Ordenamiento Territorial* includes the possibility of using 'transferable development rights' (Alcaldía Mayor de Bogotá, 1999: 121). With this legal instrument private landowners, who would be obliged to supply land at zero cost in areas where a school or a recreational area is required, could be compensated by disassociating the development rights from the serviced land and 'awarded transferable development rights certificates for use in other approved areas' (Payne, 2000: 14). Such an approach would also be more equitable for those community services and private schools that are still located in very expensive areas, but would be prevented from capitalizing their assets as happens now. Instead, they could be compensated for the inability to sell their development rights.

Paradoxically, Bogotá's fast growth is also an opportunity to balance the distribution of schools and recreational facilities. Between 2000 and 2020, the city must supply new land for housing and complementary services for 158 000 people per year (3 160 000 new inhabitants); that means over 10 500 hectares of land in 20 years. In other words, the 107 schools, the hypermarkets, clubs and recreational cooperatives already located in the northern part of the city could serve the surrounding projects that will be developed in the next seven years.[1] A strategic plan is necessary in order to ensure that private developers involved in peripheral housing projects which are served by social and other facilities already in place, are required to supply the land and construct a new communal infrastructure in the developed areas where there is clearly a deficiency in provision. This could be defined as a 'planned strategy of cross-compensation'.

CONCLUSIONS

The increasing privatization of social and planning responsibilities and the rationale of the market are a fundamental cause of the metropolization and atomization of local uses in Bogotá. As argued above, the neoliberal and market-driven paradigm is not only causing transformations in the macro-level structure of the city, it is also affecting the micro level within the city and leading to its reconfiguration. These phenomena have not been effectively counteracted in the city by urban planning policies and authorities. The consequence is the destruction of the urban intermediate level which, in turn, is an important contributor to the process of Bogotá's community disintegration, the disaggregation of its urban structure, and an environmentally unsustainable city.

This urban transformation process is not exclusive to Bogotá. Some common tendencies are shared with other cities: enclosed residential developments and the insecurity of mega-cities, as in Sao Paulo and Caracas (Caldeira, 1996: 55); hypermarkets and the metropolization of retailing, as in Mexico and Buenos Aires; the new concepts of urban recreation and non-spatial communities. Equally, issues such as the peripheralization of school provision and the fragmentation of open spaces and parks indicate characteristics that are more specific to Bogotá. The four uses examined in this chapter are only part of this process of urban transformation; other activities such as industrial and office development are also being affected.

The policy failure – both spatial and non-spatial – to tackle these profound changes is attributable to the limited institutional capacity and the inflexible, top-down planning system of the Bogotá authorities. Failure to understand the macro- and micro-level dynamics driving the reconfiguration of the city has prevented the authorities from dealing simultaneously and in a coordinated way with planning, design, environmental and other strategies. If the urban planning system is to manage effectively the contemporary patterns and process of change in Bogotá, then it is imperative to engage the market rationale as a fundamental component in the evolution of the city. This should not be considered more important than social goals and environmental sustainability, but must be coordinated together with them.

Finding the modalities of a planning system and the policies and instruments to tackle the neoliberal urban development paradigm is a major challenge. The conclusion drawn here is that the rationale of the market is not per se opposed to urban community interests, the hierarchical pattern of urban structure and environmental priorities. Simply, it does not respond to these characteristics when they do not form part of the financial equation. Thus, as discussed above, the private sector is not interested in a level of the urban hierarchy which is no longer sufficiently large to provide an attractive potential market for the majority of urban enterprises. Currently, developers are unwilling to risk investment at the intermediate scale. In short, from the private sector point of view, the intermediate, zonal level is not good business.

Accordingly, it is not feasible for planning policies to recover the former concept of Bogotá's integrated neighbourhoods and the urban intermediate level. The reality of Bogotá's urban fragmentation must be accepted. Rather, a new spatial structure for the current non-spatial communities and their 'space realm' must be planned and adapted. The crucial objectives are: to prevent further fragmentation of the city and its irreconcilable inequalities; to recover the quality of urban life and economic livelihoods; to curtail environmental degradation; and to counteract urban diseconomies. These objectives could be realized within a new and flexible urban structure designed to respond to the current rationale of city development. At the same time, it is important for the strategy to recognize that people still closely identify with the neighbourhood. A new role must be created for the intermediate level which accommodates it within a reconfigured structure of the city.

CHAPTER SIX

Public sector capacity-building and urban policy change in the Kingdom of Lesotho: implications for international development assistance

Cormac Davey

There are three main reasons for the new interest of international development agencies in urban poverty alleviation in developing countries. First, cities and towns are the 'engines of national economic growth' and a focal point through which poverty can be addressed. Second, trends towards the localization of decision-making have placed greater responsibilities on local and municipal governments. Third, for the first time in human history more people, many of them among the poorest, are living in cities and towns.

A number of international development agencies, including the World Bank, the UK Department for International Development (DFID), the Canadian International Development Agency and the Asian Development Bank have recently published urban strategies with a strong focus on poverty reduction (DFID, 2001). The European Union is also developing sustainable urban development guidelines. These strategies and guidelines all prioritize the need for effective urban governance, which requires well-managed national and local public sector institutions. Consequently the international community will have an increased responsibility to demonstrate that their development assistance can improve the capacity of public sector institutions to manage pro-poor urban development.

This chapter, drawing from the author's recent experience as a technical adviser to the Government of the Kingdom of Lesotho,[1] seeks to identify the key factors contributing towards improving the effectiveness of development assistance, which is primarily aimed at public sector institutional strengthening and urban policy change. While measuring development assistance in the urban sector is difficult, the experience provides a number of important lessons. First, political will, public sector accountability and engagement with a wider constituency of stakeholders are critical issues if development assistance is to facilitate more sustainable change. Second, piloting a multi-stakeholder approach to urban land development provides a highly fertile method for encouraging dialogue on urban policy change.

The chapter concludes with a brief discussion, based on the lessons learned, of the implications for future DFID support for urban development in Lesotho, and presents findings that can inform improvements in the role of development assistance in developing countries.

EVOLUTION OF DEVELOPMENT ASSISTANCE FOR URBAN DEVELOPMENT

The Kingdom of Lesotho is a small, land-locked and mountainous country surrounded by the Republic of South Africa. Its population is approximately 2.05 million, with a growth rate of 2.3 per cent (Economist Intelligence Unit, 1997). To date there has been little need for development assistance in support of urban development, as Lesotho is a predominantly rural country. However, as in most of southern Africa, it is now experiencing a rapid increase in its urban population. Approximately 25 per cent of the population currently live in urban areas, but this is growing annually at a rate of 6 per cent (Economist Intelligence Unit, 1997). The 1995 World Bank Poverty Study[2] estimated the extent of urban poverty at 27 per cent of the national urban population. Maseru, the capital, currently has an estimated population of 150 000 (UNDP Lesotho, 1997). This realization calls for new strategies in development assistance for urban development and poverty reduction. A brief chronology of development assistance to urban development in Lesotho over the past 20 years provides a useful basis for discussion.

The support of DFID to urban development in Lesotho has been minimal. However, its experience serves to highlight the evolution of thinking on how development assistance can address urban development issues. Development assistance has been channelled in three phases through the Directorate of Lands, Housing and Urban Development (DLHUD) – a national-level sector department under the Ministry of Local Government, with broad responsibilities for land development, housing and planning. Phase I (1980–90) involved the provision of expatriate staff to fill line-management positions. Additional support was given to the development of urban sanitation improvement programmes and an urban land development scheme. During phase II (1990–96), DFID supported progress towards institutional strengthening and capacity-building, which involved technical training, the withdrawal of full-time expatriate staff, and the incorporation of project-related agencies into the institutional structure of DLHUD. Both phases were classic ring-fenced projects that took place in parallel with other donor inputs focused on surveys and mapping and physical planning support. Changes to urban policy were minimal during this time, but the case for change had been strongly argued.

During the final monitoring mission of phase II, DFID sent a small team to Lesotho to assess the potential for a further phase of support to DLHUD. It found that while phase II had been moderately effective, it had not resulted in a sustainable outcome as DLHUD was still deemed to be dependent on long-term external support. Critical institutional problems identified within DLHUD included the following.

- Weak management, manifest in difficult communications between senior management staff. This was compounded by a lack of a functional business plan to integrate activities.
- Lack of attention to human resources, which had resulted in poor staff retention, low morale, demotivation, and largely unfocused and inappropriately skilled staff. The institution was thus unable to tackle new issues resulting from rapid urbanization and increasing urban poverty.
- Failure to resolve its weak institutional status, weak influence relative to other public sector agencies, and unclear role within the local government system, the emerging private sector and civil society.
- Neglect of the promotion of a service culture, resulting in an unaccountable public service that was unable to manage an appropriate service for its clients.
- Poor revenue generation from services, making it reliant on the transfer of scarce central government funds.

The DFID mission team recognized that any further development assistance to DLHUD would need to address these institutional issues within the broader macropolitical developments affecting Lesotho. This included the need for Lesotho to reposition itself for the post-apartheid era, its growing economic dependence on the South African economy, and ongoing internal political instability. In addition, a number of current Government of Lesotho (GoL) policies for the establishment of local government, public sector reforms (including a review of public sector pay and grading), and a general drive to improve public sector performance and efficiency, were identified as key opportunities.

DEVELOPING AN INSTITUTIONAL CAPACITY-BUILDING PROGRAMME

The DFID mission team undertook the design of phase III based on the findings of the evaluation. A project memorandum was produced along with a logical framework (a project management tool used by DFID). The goal of the project was identified as improving the supply of available land for industrial, commercial and residential development. The purpose of phase III was to enable DLHUD to undertake its function without reliance on continued external support. The outputs of the project focused on strengthening organizational and management capacity, commercialization and decentralization of core functions, policy development along the lines of a more market-oriented approach, skills training, and the development of a business plan to guide and prioritize activities. There was also some provision for developing community-driven urban planning processes in the context of the Habitat Agenda. The activity level of the logical framework and the observable verifiable indicators, as well as their means of verification, were not documented. Development assistance was to be channelled to DLHUD through the placement of a Physical Planning Technical Cooperation Officer (TCO) and a Link Organization. The TCO role was to be a narrowly defined technical role within the Physical Planning Department. The Link Organization's role was to provide DLHUD – through the use of 90 weeks' consultancy time and a training budget over two years – with the necessary resources and technical assistance to take forward a programme of public sector reform in the land, planning and housing sectors. A Link Manager would be appointed to oversee the implementation of the project. Subsequent to DFID and GoL approval, the project commenced in October 1997 with the arrival in post of the TCO. The Link Organization and Manager were not put in place until March 1998.

The identification and design process for phase III was flawed. First, the design of the project did not sufficiently involve DLHUD staff or its clients, failing to facilitate partnership or participation with the public or private sector or with civil society groups. This weakened the robustness of the project framework which, as a result, did not effectively assess the risks to project success. Second, the mission team was not sufficiently equipped to design an institutional capacity-building project. It is significant that a governance and institutions adviser was not part of this team, which weakened the internal logic of the project framework and technical assistance inputs, which were unfocused and lacked priority. Finally, the decision of DFID and the GoL to commence the project at this time, despite the failure of DLHUD to take forward outputs under phase II; the absence of a completed project framework; and the late appointment of the Link Organization and Manager, were questionable. This leads one to suspect that neither DFID nor the GoL placed much emphasis on the project or its role within their broader development programme in Lesotho. The fact that the TCO was not supported by DLHUD in a narrow physical planning role demonstrates a lack of attention to detail and local ownership. In addition, DLHUD perceived that the project management approach was being imposed, giving them little influence over the use of project funds, particularly the training budget. This caused frustration and adversely affected the development of local commitment during project implementation.

PROJECT METHODOLOGY

The methodology for project and change management was developed during the project inception phase. Significantly at this stage, the project framework was finalized. The methodology for building local ownership and sustainable outputs revolved around setting up work streams in which senior management had responsibility for project outputs and implementing project activities. Each work stream broadly correlated with project out-puts documented in the project framework. The ethos of the project was to adopt a classic change-management approach, utilizing consultative and participatory processes around a strategic plan for the future. A concern to build in political support external to DLHUD led to the establishment of a Project Advisory Team, which included the Permanent Secretary of the Ministry of Local Government and the Chief Economic Planner at the Ministry of Local Government. The team had responsibilities for approving the project and future amendments, as well as reviewing progress and monitoring reports.

The TCO was repositioned and brought into the mainstream of project implementation as Project Adviser, but still retained specialist inputs regarding broad planning issues. Essentially this involved working more broadly across all the work streams and liaising with other key DLHUD staff and local counterparts, as well as the Link Manager and Link Organization consultants. Finally, a study visit to the UK was organized for the Commissioner of Lands – the most senior manager within DLHUD, appointed by the Minister of Local Government. The purpose of the trip was primarily to influence the Commissioner of Lands to support a change process through exposure to institutional thinking on land and development policies.

While the approach went some way to addressing the flaws in the design process, it fell short of what was required. Senior DLHUD managers responsible for land, housing, physical planning and urban development divisions were not keen to take on responsibility for work streams, fearing increased accountability demands and, in some cases, due to their fundamental opposition to the project's objectives. An opportunity to review the logic of the project and prioritize inputs was not taken. In particular, the role of DLHUD as a public sector agency was not questioned. The study visit failed in the long term to spark a different management approach. It is likely that a more carefully organized trip to a neighbouring country, rather than the to the UK, involving other senior DLHUD staff, would have served a better purpose – a key team-building opportunity was missed. Finally, the TCO had to walk a difficult tightrope, representing DLHUD on the one hand while undertaking day-to-day management of the Link Manager on the other. The Commissioner of Lands increasingly sought to use the TCO to do work that was the responsibility of DLHUD managers, while the Link Manager came to rely too much on the TCO in communications with DLHUD. Consequently, when the TCO left Lesotho, communications between DLHUD and the Link Manager were not sufficiently developed.

OUTCOMES OF THE DEVELOPMENT ASSISTANCE

Phase III of development assistance to DLHUD has been largely unsuccessful. The project purpose, as agreed in the project framework, was not achieved. The focus of outputs towards institutional strengthening and management change was eventually abandoned, having had little impact, in favour of limited 'apolitical' technical and training inputs. Key factors were the unrealistic logic and focus of the project given the short time frame, a deteriorating management approach within DLHUD, and ongoing political instability during the period of the project.[3] While the project did, over time, become more focused on key priorities based around urban development, the Link Manager was unable to influence or address the risks within the context of the project.[4] The Commissioner of Lands was increasingly intent, under pressure from his superiors, to drive his vision. Unfortunately, this was not effectively communicated to the senior managers in DLHUD, who became increasingly distant, retreating into their technical roles away from their management responsibilities. Junior staff within DLHUD were inevitably caught in the crossfire. As a result, the Link Manger took a lead role in driving change processes, without supporting counterparts. Consequently, many activities did not lead to successful or sustainable outcomes. Despite these constraints, the Link Manager and various consultants did play a key role in facilitating a number of successful processes which have encouraged policy dialogue, raised awareness and understanding, and introduced DLHUD to multi-stakeholder partnership approaches to urban land development. Even where progress was made, however, implementation was complicated by perceived difficulties in the public service of working with other stakeholders, such as local chiefs, landowners and local government. The lack of recognition of the role of urban development in poverty reduction and urbanization was perhaps a more serious limiting factor. A more detailed look at the outcomes of the work streams and their impact on urban policy change will help illuminate these issues further.

Deconcentration versus decentralization

Two regional and a number of district offices have been established, and a skeleton staff deployed. However, they are not fully functional or able to provide an effective public service. Development assistance was not able to influence this process. Link Organization consultants facilitated a number of workshops and consultations. A number of report-based outputs were produced, which made time-bound recommendations on the institutional options and phased process to be adopted for effective decentralization to take place within the context of establishing local government. The Commissioner of Lands dismissed this work, primarily because its recommendations did not conform to the approach being adopted, which was predicated on putting people into offices, rather than on effective service provision. In addition, the recommendations required broader change – the transfer of resources and decision-making powers to regional officers and local government bodies. Furthermore, there was no appetite to undertake changes to planning legislation to establish multidisciplinary and interdepartmental urban and regional planning. This clearly threatened Maseru-based authority. Given the complexities of vested interests within both the GoL and DLHUD, it was perhaps an overly ambitious and unrealistic undertaking to expect change.

Implementing a business culture

A business plan was produced which, after three years, provides a potential framework against which future progress can be measured. In this case, development assistance was able to play an important role in facilitating the completion of the plan. A multi-stakeholder process was engaged to assist DLHUD in assessing its role and priorities as a public sector agency and its relationship with a broader constituency of stakeholders. The process succeeded because it addressed the concerns of both the Commissioner of Lands and DLHUD senior managers. The former needed a mechanism to hold senior management to account; the latter wanted a realistic document that provided a medium-term framework within which they could plan their work. Despite this progress, there still remains division within DLHUD over whether the role of DLHUD should be as a facilitating and enabling, or welfare-focused, public sector agency. The involvement of a wider stakeholder constituency has, however, provided new insight, increasing pressure on DLHUD to make visible changes to the lives of ordinary Basotho. Unfortunately, weak accountability, lack of responsibility of senior management for meeting objectives, and a poor management culture will undermine implementation.

Failing human resources

The development of human resources was not improved. Development assistance was not able to play any significant part in facilitating more effective management of human resources, which included the production of a staff training plan. While DLHUD appointed a Human Resource Officer, this was not a serious attempt to address issues of low morale and demotivation within the organization, associated with lack of promotion and reward. This appears to be a low priority within the GoL, despite the fact that most staff view it as important. The lack of transparency is a real problem, causing concerns over nepotism by a powerful elite. A training plan and monitoring process were produced, but were not acceptable to the Commissioner of Lands. This was mainly due to disagreements between DLHUD and the Link Manager on the purpose of the training budget and human resource management. This was a lost opportunity, in which the junior and aspiring staff suffered, further undermining morale. Essentially, agreement could not be reached on the disbursement or use of funds to DLHUD. The Link Manager preferred to use the training fund for on-the-job and in-house training, and to keep control in order to widen training opportunities and offer incentives to staff. DLHUD continued to perceive the need for traditional overseas postgraduate training. The Commissioner of Lands also wanted control of the fund to ensure a filtering of candidates for privileged access to overseas training opportunities. Consequently there was little incentive for DLHUD to produce a plan. As a result, limited and ad hoc use was made of the funds.

Action planning: practical approaches to land management

Increasing frustration with the slow progress and management problems encouraged a more pragmatic approach through which improvements could be made to management and DLHUD performance. The Link Manager facilitated the development of a follow-up multi-stakeholder process to explore urban land development issues, with a view to informing urban policy change. While the outcome of the process was disappointing, given the focus on management change and poverty reduction, it did succeed in raising awareness and training staff in design and project management. Improved relationships and awareness of other stakeholders' views and positions were also positive outcomes, despite the difficult nature of the task. It was established that a broad range of stakeholders could explore and debate together issues around the pragmatic and mutual goals of planned urban development. Crucially, there was willingness to question the appropriateness of planning standards, regulations and legislation.

The process highlighted some of the key institutional constraints at the heart of urban policy change. While technical and management proposals for the piloting of a peri-urban land development approach in Maseru were produced, they were largely abandoned in favour of a more traditional approach to land development. First, while progress was initially very positive, senior staff within DLHUD became divided over the approach. Some embraced the fact that piloting involved risk, while fear and scepticism prevented others from supporting it. Importantly, the Commissioner of Lands, while initially supportive – establishing a project team and allocating resources – increasingly became impatient with the slow progress and put pressure on the process to deliver designs and implementation at the expense of stakeholder involvement, which undermined the approach. As a result, tensions between government, local chiefs and landowners, who found it difficult to trust government, have increased. In the absence of strong enforcement this is likely to result in acceleration of informal land subdivision, increasing the cost to project implementation. Second, DLHUD's relationship with Maseru City Council and other service providers has been adversely affected. Maseru City Council, feeling its authority was being usurped by DLHUD, viewed the project with increasing suspicion and some resentment. Ultimately, DHLUD's views remained more powerful. While development is proceeding, albeit slowly, a crucial opportunity for testing new approaches leading to sustainable changes to urban policy has been lost and the fear is that stakeholder positions could be further entrenched.

LESSONS LEARNED: IMPLICATIONS FOR DEVELOPMENT ASSISTANCE

- *Stronger development assistance framework between the donor and recipient government and DFID.* A clear framework of agreement is necessary, which clarifies development priorities related to the wider macropolitical and economic context between the recipient government and the donor, in order to cultivate political commitment and accountability. In the absence of a clear framework, greater efforts need to be made to include the central ministry responsible from the outset in discussions around identifying project support. In addition, care must be taken to ensure development assistance is not overly ambitious, given the complexity of the political and institutional policy environment.
- *Development assistance is demand led and driven by the recipient institution.* The recipient institution must drive the identification and design of development assistance. Clarity is required from the outset to ensure that the right balance and focus of development assistance is agreed. This is particularly important in agreeing the scope and nature of participatory approaches, stakeholder involvement, and the project framework.
- *Greater commitment to undertaking stakeholder analysis throughout the project cycle.* The involvement of a broader constituency of stakeholders and the analysis of their roles and views is necessary to strengthen the project framework. This will help illuminate valuable insight into the institutional or micro-project context, such as the structure for human resource management, which is a key gateway through which sustainable change is channelled. Relevant risks for successful implementation are also more likely to be correctly identified. Both donor and recipient institutions need to be clear as to who their key supporters are, as well as identifying opponents and key stakeholders. These factors and risks should be clearly addressed as part of the project design.
- *Project activities, including monitoring, must be properly and clearly articulated and agreed during project design.* Project outputs must be sufficiently measurable and achievable; the lack of these conditions will undermine a sense of purpose and achievement. This will require that a management information system is in place and there is understanding of how progress can be measured – processes can be improved to undertake this during the project, but a framework for start-up procedures must be established. A commitment and procedure for monitoring must be agreed between the donor and recipient institutions during the project design phase. This should be developed with a view to enhancing existing procedures, where these exist, and should be linked into government-wide systems. Once agreed, every effort should be made to support and maintain this process.

This will be crucial in order that local mechanisms for decision-making and accountability are developed.

- *The recipient institution must play a full role in the appointment of donor consultants and technical staff.* The recipient institution must play a full partner role in approving the appointment of donor and local personnel or counterparts, who will be responsible for implementation and achieving results. This must be a fair and transparent process based on a full appraisal of donor representatives and consultants.

- *Project inception must address the key management change issues from the outset.* The often problematic management tensions must be dealt with from the outset. For example, acquiescence on the part of the donor to continuing poor management practice will undermine all project activities. Although difficult, and requiring a sensitive approach, this is crucial. If this cannot be addressed sufficiently, development assistance should be conditional or, in extreme circumstances, withdrawn. The project inception period should also be used to allow local project and expatriate staff to establish working relationships and parameters – an equal relationship should be fostered. Study visits should be undertaken as part of developing team-building around commitment, ownership and understanding.

- *Practical pilot projects should be considered explicitly within the project design.* The potential benefits of a practical pilot project have been clearly demonstrated as a vehicle for developing operational experience and learning around the important issues of defining the role of public sector institutions. In the case of DLHUD, it also demonstrated how, in the absence of progress elsewhere, it can provide a means to drive change. However, by considering the role of a pilot project during the design phase, adequate resources can be allocated and the poaching of resources from other project activities avoided.

- *Emphasis must be given to employing the right mix of technical and human skills.* The role of technical assistance is critical to the implementation of a well designed project. It is therefore important that those staff engaged to facilitate change must have the appropriate human skills, attitudes and technical abilities. There is clearly a balance to be struck with regard to donor and management consultants using the project to provide training for their staff, particularly when difficult circumstance are encountered.

- *Project evaluation must highlight good practice and lessons learnt and be disseminated within the donor institution and recipient government.* It is important that project evaluation is undertaken and divorced from the identification of new project assistance, as was the experience with phase III of the Lesotho project . This will allow time for effective lesson-learning, dissemination and reflection on the best way forward. The recipient institution should be encouraged to undertake its own evaluation of experience.

CONCLUSIONS

The issue of urban development is crucial to Lesotho's future and economic development if the needs of present and future citizens are to be meet. Access to land, shelter and services and the effective planning of the urban areas are critical, particularly if the well-being and livelihoods of the urban poor are to be improved. The DLHUD is critical to these objectives. Drawing from the lessons learned, it is evident that before moving forward both DFID and DLHUD need to evaluate and reflect on this experience within the context of the broader macropolitical environment and international context.

For DFID, this will require a willingness to engage more effectively with urban development issues within the framework of decentralization and the establishment of local government in Lesotho. In addition, the poverty focus of DFID will require a more committed approach to project identification and design if it is not to be implicated in maintaining the status quo. The case of the pilot land development project is an interesting example. The abandonment by DLHUD of much of the market-oriented, stakeholder and partnerships approaches to land development will adversely affect the livelihoods of existing land-users, and will reduce the scope for drawing public benefit from land development for the advantage of the poor. Clearly, DFID cannot support such non-poor approaches.

Donors, more generally, need to look for innovative and robust approaches to delivering development assistance which address the need for political commitment and local ownership at both national and local levels. New donor-initiated anti-poverty planning frameworks, such as the World Bank's Comprehensive Development Framework and the International Monetary Fund's (IMF) Poverty Reduction Strategies for Highly Indebted Poor Countries offer the potential for an improved approach.[5] Lesotho has recently commenced with the development of a poverty reduction strategy with the World Bank, IMF and other Donors, including DFID. The DLHUD and other local stakeholders will need to engage in this process to ensure that a broader national consensus is developed in Lesotho that takes into account the needs of the urban poor and the role of urban development in regional and national development. Finally, within this broader framework consideration should be given to focusing support on a broader range of stakeholders, such as local government and, in particular, civil society groups. Direct funding for local development through civil society groups working in partnership with municipal and local authorities and other partners, including central government, should be encouraged.

CHAPTER SEVEN

Property taxation, public finance and sustainable development: the case of Belém, Brazil

José Júlio Lima

Property taxation, public finance and the relationships between them have constituted only partial elements of the sustainable development debate, although the issue of urban management has included these matters in the context of development promotion (UNCED, 1992: 54, 56). But the capacity of local governments to generate revenue by property taxation on the one hand, and their requirements for infrastructure investment on the other, dictate local development patterns and thus the quality of urban environments in which people live. It follows that any examination of local government processes and development decision-making should include public finance issues in order to evaluate the extent to which they constrain or support the achievement of sustainable urban development in a wider sense.

To investigate the issue, this chapter considers the relationships between social components of sustainable development and local administration instruments. More specifically, the chapter aims to identify consequences of property taxation assessment and public infrastructure investment, at the local government level, for city development and the distribution of services. It identifies factors that arise from the transformation of rural areas to urban and, in particular, how urban form is influenced by public finance and property taxation. The chapter draws on the case of Belém, Brazil to demonstrate these issues.

The chapter briefly discusses the role of the city in the sustainable development debate. Comparisons between the impact of the sustainability debate in developing and developed countries suggest that urban management and planning need to be reviewed to include public finance and property taxation in order to help promote sustainability. The case of Belém is then explored to illustrate how the built form and property assessment, as part of a local government finance system, contribute (or not) to the achievement of sustainability from the point of view of the provision of a better quality of life.

THE CITY, BUILT FORM AND THE SUSTAINABLE DEVELOPMENT DEBATE

In general, as some other chapters in this book have illustrated, the concept of sustainability has not engaged in detail with issues of urban built form, especially in the developing world. This contrasts with the literature on cities and sustainable development in developed countries. Here the objective of 'sustainable built form' (Elkin et al., 1991) is taken into account, and considerable emphasis is now given to the importance of more recently emerging concepts such as the compact city. Concepts such as these have helped forge the link between built form and urban sustainability in terms of density and mixed uses, in order to conform with some principles of sustainable development (e.g. Jenks et al., 1996). This is not to argue that emphasis on intensification and densification of cities of the developed world is either desirable or appropriate for cities in developing countries with a very different urban context – indeed, the case of Belém questions this 'conceptual transfer'. Rather, the point here is that urban built form, although differing between developed and developing cities, is a neglected but nonetheless important component in Brazil, as in other developing countries. More specifically, the debate on urban built form and its relationship to property taxation and revenue-raising procedures is also relevant, but equally limited in the context of cities in the developing world.

Thus these debates in developing countries are conceptualized in terms such as 'sustainable urbanization' (Hardoy et al., 1992a). This is more than a difference in terminology from 'sustainable built form'; 'urbanization' refers to a process under way and regards the built form as the product of this process, rather than as an integral input into sustainable development strategies. Factors such as appropriate and adequate provision of housing and transport for different income levels of the population are significant in city planning strategies, in theory if not in practice – their relationship to sustainability is espoused in terms of not 'compromising the ability of future generations to achieve their needs and aspirations' (WCED, 1987: 8). However, the main concern about sustainability in such cities tends to be dominated by the processes and impacts of population growth rates, and less by the relationship between built form and the achievement of sustainable development through the location of population, density and compactness policies, and the provision of services within the urban environment (Elkin et al., 1991). As sustainable development in this context only briefly addresses built form, there is consequently an even poorer understanding of how the structure of these cities is determined by public finance needs, and how these needs link to the objective of sustainable development.

Underlying these contrasting perspectives is the relative capacity to manage the development of the built form of cities. In developed countries, urban development policies rely on well-developed institutional structures capable of managing the implementation of city building and the regulation of the built form. With greater financial resources derived from public revenues such as property taxation, and institutional structures that facilitate investment, 'sustainability in the city' is associated directly with encouragement of development of the existing fabric within the limits of economic feasibility and the maintenance of existing urban values of social vitality and cohesion.

In developing countries, urban development also aims to increase economic growth and the productivity of the city. However, the imperative of economic growth tends to subjugate wider environmental objectives and policies such as sustainable built form. Moreover, the desirability of pursuing multiple city development objectives – for example, economic growth, efficiency, sustainability – calls for expansion in the capacity of public authorities to act as managers of city structure rather than providers of urban services, as in the past (Hardoy et al., 1992a: 131). But in much of the developing world the existing inappropriate legal framework and weak capacity, based on bureaucratic and centralized decision-making, needs reform in order to manage a process of city building, over the longer term, which will be undertaken mainly by the private sector or public/private partnerships, especially for the provision of public services and infrastructure. In this context, urban revenue and land and property taxation policies and instruments become critically significant variables. On the one hand they determine the extent to which city administrations will be able to fund development in partnership with the private sector and reach a more equitable distribution of services. On the other hand, they offer new tools to regulate the development of the built form. In this way, therefore, the issue of property taxation links to wider objectives of achieving sustainable built forms in fast-growing urban areas.

BELÉM

Belém lies on the fringe of the Amazon region, and is located at the intersection of the Pará (a tributary of the Amazon River) and Guamá Rivers. The population of Belém has grown from 633 000 in the 1970s to approximately 1 200 000 in 1991 (COGEP, 1992). The growth rate in the 1960s was 4.5 per cent per annum; in the 1970s, 4.7 per cent per annum; and in the 1980s, 2.7 per cent per annum. The peripheral growth rate of 11.3 per cent in the 1970s (Ribeiro and Lago, 1995: 374) was the highest among Brazil's Metropolitan Regions, and produced profound changes to the urban physical structure of the Great Belém Region.

This transformation of the rural areas into an urban region typically illustrates the three distinct patterns of 'internal differentiation of Latin American cities' (Bahr and Mertins, 1992: 66).

- 'An older pattern in the concentric rings in the city centre', observable in the city centre of Belém where the Portuguese established a fort in the seventeenth century, followed by elite occupation.

- 'A pattern characterized by settlement expansion along axes', which in Belém was initiated by the substitution in the 1960s of two rail tracks by main roads, which became part of the city's internal road network.
- 'A cellular, discontinuous settlement structure at or ahead of the current periphery'; this process is extremely rapid and is characterized by informal illegal settlements, government-sponsored building projects and, to a lesser extent, upper-class residential areas.

Up to the 1950s the development of the city core was driven by the economic force of the export boom in rubber. In this lengthy period, the urban layout was characterized by formal grids in which urban neighbourhoods were added as extensions of the first colonial occupation. The rural area between the city core and a second district was gradually occupied, because access to the area was facilitated by the road network which advanced in that direction.

Then piecemeal development began to alter the logic of the formal grid. Following occupation by institutions, such as the navy and army, on the areas immediately surrounding the most urbanized core, housing estates were located on the margins of the former rail axes which, with the construction of major roads improving access between these areas and the city, became more significant axes for urban expansion. Rural land was increasingly urbanized through the building of social housing schemes funded by central government and, more recently, of fenced middle-class condominiums surrounded by illegal land invasions. This process of urban peripheral development expanded very rapidly, especially in the past decade. It presents a 'deformed grid', produced by the aggregation of housing estates and land invasions, lacking a comprehensive or cohesive urban form and characterized by gross shortages in infrastructure, notably in areas occupied by the urban poor. The level of physical segregation is accentuated by the condominiums, which are replacing the pattern dictated by the housing policies of the 1970s and 1980s as middle-class people choose a condominium rather than a centrally located flat.

In summary, the repercussions of these modifications to the city structure caused by development on the urban periphery – typical of many cities in the developing world – are threefold and interlinked. First, the processes of urban transformation have produced a very fragmented spatial structure/built form as newly urbanized areas are needed to provide adequate housing and other land uses for the rapidly growing population of the city. Second, this disaggregated urban structure and the disparities in building types highlight marked social segregation. Third, a gross lack of affordable and sustainable infrastructure accompanies these patterns and processes. It is the last outcome that provides a bridge to the central concern of this chapter.

Here two critical questions are relevant. The first concerns the financial capacity of local government to implement infrastructure supply policies (primarily for the basic needs of water and sanitation), and to incorporate infrastructure maintenance into administrative procedures. The second issue is a related question concerning the built form. To what extent are the existing management, planning and development control mechanisms of local government able to cope with rural/urban transformations in terms of sustainable development? For example, what is the potential for compact service provision rather than expensive extensions of water and sanitation networks? A discussion of the relationship between urban public finance and urban form attempts to address the first question and suggest answers to the second.

LOCAL PUBLIC FINANCE IN BELÉM

Urban public finance, a most important tool for implementing urban development policies in Brazil, has two components : revenue-raising and expenditure. The first is important because locally raised income is decisive for the capacity of local government to provide and maintain services; the latter because expenditure, as it appears in the municipal budget, reflects how priorities, in terms of the location of services and consequently of the social groups targeted, are determined. Overall, the appraisal of urban public finance in Belém shows how property taxation, as a component of urban revenue generation, and patterns of expenditure have decisive roles in decision-making, affecting the promotion of sustainable development.

Revenue-raising

In contrast to their lack in other Latin American cities, Brazilian local government finances have been strengthened by the 1988 Constitution. The main measures that have been adopted are an increase in the number of taxes which the municipality can now directly raise, and 'limited earmarking of transfers from revenues' (Cammack et al., 1993), that is, money can be moved from one category of expenditure to another. Table 7.1 shows a summary of Brazilian local revenue sources used throughout the country after 1988.

The importance of the *Imposto Predial e Territorial Urbano* (urban land and property tax; IPTU) in a local authority's financial structure can be seen in terms of the significant amount it raises. In Belém it represents an average of 35 per cent of all municipality revenue (SEFIN/PMB, 1998a). In Rio de Janeiro in 1984, 11.5 per cent of local expenditure was financed from property taxation; in São Paulo it was 13.8 per cent (Bahl and Linn, 1992: 62). Revenues derived from property taxation provide local government with investment for the provision of urban services and infrastructure in newly or already occupied areas. Property taxation and subsequent revenue raised constitute parts of a mechanism that, for the purposes of this discussion, is called the taxation cycle. It is a chain initiated by property-specific valorization for taxation assessment; which continues with rev-

Table 7.1   Brazilian local revenue sources

Source	Description
Urban land and property taxation (*Imposto Predial e Territorial Urbano*, IPTU)	Urban land-use type and property tax by area and type of activity
Service land uses taxation (*Imposto sobre Serviços*, ISS)	Tax levied on over 100 different categories of business
Vehicles and fuel tax (*Imposto sobre Veiculos e combustiveis*, IVVC)	Retail sales tax on gasoline and fuels
Real estate transactions tax (*Imposto sobre a Transmissão de Bens Imóveis*, ICTBI)	Property sales tax
Other duties	Fees for building licences, advertising, and user charges (for solid waste management, public lighting)

Source: Nickson (1995): 125.

enues actually received and includes the overall revenue income from local government actions. The chain follows, depending on the level of urbanization in the area, new revenue is raised and infrastructure costs recovered to make possible further investment.

A second tax is assessed according to the urban distribution of businesses (*Imposto sobre Serviços*, service land-uses taxation; ISS). Over 100 categories of business are identified and registered. The registration includes the legal status of the company and the names of individuals, in the case of professionals. Although the location of a business within the city has consequences for land-use patterns, the business tax list has no information about where the business is located. The other taxes identified in Table 7.1 are administered directly by local government following procedures entirely determined by federal legislation.

Observing the role of these taxation sources in the municipal budget of Belém in 1991 (Table 7.2), locally raised revenue was 24 per cent of all income; the rest came from central and state transfers (Prefeitura Municipal de Belém, 1993). Of locally raised revenue, the highest proportion came from tax levied on businesses (31 per cent), followed by property taxation (14 per cent). Accordingly, the distribution of buildings and the number of businesses have large implications for the revenue-raising capacity of local government.

In Brazil's property taxation system, all households pay taxes assessed according to the valorization of the land, depending on the location of the property and primarily related to existing infrastructure; and a valuation of the buildings, depending on market value, the characteristics of the buildings and the land, including their uses (Meirelles, 1998). Property taxation is characterized by a base in which property is assessed according to its estimated annual rental value, which depends on the market price. While

Table 7.2   Belém – municipal revenue, 1991

Source	Revenue (US$)	Percentage
Locally raised revenue	**22 967 583**	**24**
ISS	7 192 216	31
IPTU	2 966 129	14
Other taxes	3 258 154	14
IVVC	2 126 904	9
ITBI	955 295	4
Properties (owned rented premises)	6 468 885	28
Transfers	**76 497 599**	**75**
Transfer from central government (FPM)	16 379 290	
Transfer from state (ICMS)	49 786 147	
Other transfers	8 861 880	
Other sources	**1 470 282**	**1**
Total	**92 696 297**	**100**

Source: Prefeitura Municipal de Belém (1993).

there is a relationship between the two values, actual market values are always higher. This tax, in principle, is levied on all properties located within municipal boundaries.

More specifically, in relation to the rate structure, the incidence of taxes due from property (IPTU) varies, but is reliant on four main interrelated factors: valuation of the property (a plot or a building and its plot) related to its use; location; development stage; and form of occupation (whether the property is owned or rented). Only the more significant elements of property taxation related to the context of this chapter are now considered.

With regard to the rateable value of the land, local government registers show which streets are provided with which services (road paving, water supply, drainage, sewerage, garbage collection, electricity, public transport, etc.); the provision of services is one component in computing the value of the property for taxation purposes (valorization). The developable area of the plot (using parameters such as maximum plot coverage of building, floor area ratio and length of frontage) and the physical quality of the site are also taken into account as other components in assessing the tax. On maps of the streets, these factors are indicated by an index – the value of linear frontage – placed alongside the frontage of the blocks along that street. The combination of variables appears in the generic values plans (*planta genérica de valores*) which form part of the cadastre for the city.

As regards the rateable value of buildings, this takes into account the size of buildings, the quality of construction (luxury, high, medium, popular, low and primary), and the state of building maintenance and condition (good, satisfactory and bad) (SEFIN/PMB, 1991a,b, 1998a,b). The combination of these variables results in the basic table of building per square metre (*tabela básica de metro quadrado de construção*), another piece of the municipal cadastre. Another component of the property tax relates to the nature of the tenure (rented or owned) and type of occupancy (residential, business, etc.). The incidence of building taxation is divided between individual households or businesses in proportion to their occupancy of the building's floor area.

The overall rateable value is thus determined by the sum of land and property valuation calculated annually according to market price revaluation procedures. The rates payable are multiplied by the appropriate *aliquot* – fraction of the property value to be rated. The fractions employed in the final calculation are for:

- owned or rented residential properties
- non-residential properties
- non-built properties.

The cadastre includes maps – the generic values plan and the basic table of building per square metre – and other information constituting the basis of property taxation. The cadastre is a critical instrument because it provides comprehensive information about the physical basis of local property taxes, the valorization of streets according to the provision of services, as well as unique information about every property – registration, physical and ownership characteristics, and market valuation.

Each year the local authorities collect revenue from property occupants using these maps. Each city has a different system, and every city has a different procedure for calculation, although following the same national revenue principles. Annually, the local administration must conduct a survey to assess how the market is behaving, and update gradients of land prices for the whole city. Technically, tax gradients take into account all the variables discussed above, such as the buildable areas established by floor area ratio per zone, plot sizes, and differences in the provision of infrastructure. Assessing market values and tax gradients is, however, something that is artificially judged. Moreover, variations in the valorization of streets show that a time lag is allowed before imposition of the tax after a service has been provided, to enable occupants to adjust to an increased tax.

Property taxes are then calculated in 'municipal fiscal units', and each unit corresponds to a certain amount of currency. The ratio (or value) of a unit related to the actual monetary value and valorization procedures are established by a municipal law approved by city councillors every year. All the information and calculation procedures are available for public scrutiny in the finance secretary's office. Although the process is regulated by specific laws, the annual updating and the tax gradients are usually politically manipulated. It is important to note that while final decisions are approved by local councillors, this is usually without discussion by the elected council.

A number of conclusions can be drawn from this process in relation to managing the built form of the city and the distributional consequences.

The distribution of values in the cadastral maps illustrates the pattern of service delivery as it has developed in the process of urbanization of

Brazilian cities. But the setting, coverage and assessment procedures of property taxation also reflect the morphological and social patterns in the city. The physical structure of the city, especially the location of houses and businesses, plays an important role in assessment of the IPTU. The setting of the tax base and the mechanisms of calculation are related to the built form; revenue levels reveal the relationships between the social distribution of population in the urban area and the characteristics of locations such as infrastructure provision, natural features, and grid configuration in residential areas. The location of a site within the overall city structure gives each plot a value; each street has its own value assessed according to the existence of infrastructure along it.

Establishing street alignments is fundamental to both property taxation and building permission. In areas without secure tenure, entry into the formal housing sector through payment of property tax is the starting point for obtaining building permission. In granting permission for the proposed building or plot, street alignment definition is physically determined in accordance with engineering designs for streets and water channels. Theoretically this should work, but problems arise because there is no exchange of information or updating of projects carried out by different agencies, for example, those who provide light and water.

The incidence of taxes could be classified as fiscally neutral because the distribution of rates accords with the property value, not the economic and/or social status of the occupant, although the two may be related. The social effect of the taxes, however, is that this 'neutral' system tends to lack equity in its incidence (Bahl and Linn, 1992), as we shall see. Moreover, as Bahl and Linn contend for much of the developing world, including Brazil, 'Actual assessed value (rateable value) is generally below market value because of infrequent reassessment and poor assessment practices' (Bahl and Linn, 1992: 91). A consequence of both the negative distributional effects and the failure to generate revenue on a current market value base is that, in recent years (from 1997 onwards), since the left wing Workers Party came to power, updating the cadastre of the city has been a priority. A survey covering all properties in the municipality has revealed an increase of more than a third of existing properties that have not previously been assessed. The survey has indicated the need to integrate all revenue procedures. *Aliquots* have also been reviewed, which brought much controversy. A large number of owners, from both high- and low-income groups, have objected to the new taxation values assessed after the new survey. The official response was that it was not the *aliquot* used that increased; rather that infrastructure has been upgraded in the areas and consequently taxation had increased. What appears to be happening is a tentative move by the new local government administration to use new powers to compensate poor areas by improving the infrastructure, made possible by increased revenue raised after the cadastre has been reviewed for already developed, higher-income group areas.

More specifically in the case of Belém, there are a number of problems in the use of the property taxation system in peripheral settlements.

The valorization of different locations needs to be reviewed because infrastructure provision appears not to be the determining factor, especially on the periphery. The valorization seems to be randomly assessed. As taxes differ according to the location of properties and businesses, the fragmented and single use-oriented residential periphery of Belém has been assessed and given low values, while the centre has values hundreds of times greater than those of the periphery.

Rateable values of social housing estates are assessed similarly to those in consolidated areas of the city – although, as poorer areas, the service needs are greater than the tax base can provide. Social housing estates should be planned to take into account their future impact on local taxation. Their infrastructure needs should be financed according to the capacity of local government to assess rates on the city as a whole in the first instance, and to promote more equity in the distribution of public expenditure patterns. Integration of social housing estates with the rest of the city should be promoted by changes in the allocation of finance.

Inherited contradictions in the tax base of peripheral areas do not justify the lack of service provision. This happens because housing settlements are historically those with less local government investment, therefore with limited revenue-raising capacity. The result is a cycle of poor infrastructure provision in areas where inhabitants have weak political representation and few opportunities to improve their living conditions.

Expenditure

The other aspect of urban finances to be considered is the pattern of expenditure. In Brazil, expenditure patterns depend on priorities established in the municipal budget. This results, in most cases, in policies that accord with political clientelism (Batley, 1993). Only in recent years has participatory decision-making on expenditure been partially implemented in some cities (Bava, 1995). If steps are to be taken to promote sustainability as a social as well as an environmental policy objective, decision-making will need to be less influenced by the urban elites, and more concerned with the needs of poorer areas.

Budget and pattern of expenditure affect the built form of cities. In Belém in the 1980s, the emphasis on transport (Table 7.3) meant expenditure on the road network of the centre. Only one out of four improved roads was on the periphery, and only two social housing estates on the periphery had improvements made to roads in them. Expenditure to consolidate the fragmented built form into the urban structure was not even perceived as necessary or desirable. Yet problems of accessibility to the city centre created by the growth and design of the peripheral settlements go beyond a purely physical concern – they affect the relationship between the overall integration of the city and, as this chapter contends, the creation of a more socially sustainable pattern of development through the implementation of services by local government.

Table 7.3 Expenditure by Belém local authority, 1980–89

Function	Average (per cent)
Transport	23.72
Administration/planning	16.97
Education and culture	12.57
Sanitation	12.45
Urbanism	8.75
Welfare	8.01
Health	5.49
Services	1.40
Legislative	8.23
Other*	2.41

*Expenditure on electricity, telecommunications and advertisements.

Source: Souza (1992), quoting from Belém Municipal Balance, Finances Secretary, 1980–89.

CONCLUSION: THE IMPACTS OF A 'SELF-PERPETUATING' TAXATION CYCLE ON SUSTAINABILITY

Impacts of public finance structures, as the Brazilian case explored here suggests, can be considered in terms of a policy implementation gap. Shortcomings in the implementation of policies create locational disadvantages that accentuate the inequalities in urban form, both in the centre and on the periphery of the city. To overcome this, property taxation and investments need to be coordinated with other local government measures. Urban planning processes should include budget and fiscal measures, in terms of the impact of development proposals on public servicing costs and revenue-raising potential. This does not commonly happen in Brazil, and still less is there consideration of equity and distributional consequences.

Public finance structures, illustrated in this chapter, reveal what can be termed a taxation cycle, which has adverse impacts on local urban policy effectiveness because of a lack of coordination between development control and the allocation of funding for infrastructure. This, in part, is caused by property valorization procedures, based mainly on the presence or absence of infrastructure. Where infrastructure provision is low, valorization is low, and therefore expenditure on infrastructure is low. To improve social sustainability, intervention to end this self-limiting system is needed. While in the centre the poor and 'unequally' distributed infrastructure provision seems to be ameliorated by advantages provided in the configuration of the area as a whole, on the periphery no benefits appear to accrue from urban form to ease the problems of poor infrastructure provision. Indeed, political influence of higher-income groups, pressing for expenditure to improve their locations, increases the disparity of provision.

Overall, in the city, as suggested by the cadastre of Belém, the combination of urban form and infrastructure patterns determine locational differences inherent in urban structures. As shown in the assessment of valorization procedures for taxation purposes, such differences have differential roles in the revenue-investment cycle and thus have implications for sustainability of the urban communities in Brazilian cities. The recognition of these relationships indicates the rationale to overcome this self-perpetuating cycle.

Alterations to the taxation system require a review of the relationship between the amount of revenue raised and infrastructure provision, in particular, in areas with scarce infrastructure and low revenue-raising capacity. Rather than acceding to the political pressures that manipulate property values, the tax base and developer-led demands for infrastructure, use should be made of existing fiscal laws and urban regulations to provide infrastructure in areas where it is needed to sustain, socially and spatially, the locations in the city occupied by vulnerable groups. Accordingly, in peripheral areas the presence of upgraded infrastructure, which will of itself raise the tax base in hitherto neglected areas, dwellers would make a graded contribution to the higher tax. This would be accompanied by a redistribution process balancing total expenditure between well-established areas and those on the periphery. This balancing should be determined by a combination of social and spatial indicators to compensate disadvantaged social groups.

The implementation of housing and urban policies in the developing world in recent years demonstrates a poorly established understanding of the relationship between the built form of cities and development location (especially housing), on the one hand, and the fiscal opportunities and consequences for city development and planning strategies, on the other. Zoning laws have historically facilitated real estate expansion and inhibited urban upgrading, because of the lack of flexibility and neglect of poor areas in need of social housing services. In Brazil, the outcomes were made worse by the centralized nature of municipal administrations, which have been susceptible to the influence of powerful groups and individuals. This has prevented local administrations from developing longer-term social objectives, articulated for the benefit of communities located on the periphery.

In order for spatial growth in urban areas to be more carefully planned and regulated, there is an evident need for urban management to include public fiscal instruments as a vital component of sustainable development. This would help satisfy the desperate need for poor urban dwellers to have access to basic urban infrastructure prior to housing development, and for the maintenance of services after housing estates are built. At the same time, this would also better assist the achievement of the aims of equity and social justice. The rationale for this approach, as this chapter argues, is the manner in which public finance affects sustainability. This is the basis for contemplating new ways to address the typical urban scenario of most developing countries, their social stratification and social instability, with their adverse implications for future generations.

CHAPTER EIGHT

Urban livelihoods, shocks and stresses

David Sanderson

Urbanization is bringing about one of the greatest demographic and social transformations in history. One set of statistics sums up the situation well. In 1900, 233 million people (14 per cent of the world's population) lived in cities. In 2000 it was three billion (47 per cent). By 2020 it will be 4.4 billion: 60 per cent of the world's population. Most of this growth is occurring in towns and cities in Africa, Asia and Latin America, among many of the poorest members of society. In urban settlements, livelihoods strategies are complex. Contexts are changing and uncertain, with rapid urban growth, increasing crime, an ill-equipped public sector, and intense competition for limited resources. Household members employ varied living strategies, often living on credit, surviving and competing in markets, undertaking seasonal work, and working in an informal economy. As Hugh Stretton states:

The life of a modern city is very complicated. The citizens have intricate patterns of common and conflicting interests and tastes and beliefs, and individually and collectively they have very unequal capacities to get what they want for themselves or from one another. From that tangle of powers and purposes comes a social life so complicated and partly unpredictable that any understanding of it has to be incomplete.

(Stretton, 1978).

Within this complication, a livelihoods-based approach offers a route map for describing how people obtain assets, what they do with them, what gets in their way in obtaining them, and who controls the resources on which assets are based. Importantly, it includes the concept that assets buffer households against shocks (such as natural disasters or emergencies), as well as longer-term stresses (such as ill health or unemployment). Assets are not only physical, e.g. land, they are also social, e.g. good relations with neighbours; human, e.g. good entrepreneurial skills; financial, e.g. savings; and, importantly, political, e.g. having a say in democratic processes.

Several development organizations are currently in the process of developing livelihood-based understandings of poverty. Most understandings emerge from Chambers and Conway's description of livelihoods:

A livelihood comprises the capabilities, assets (both natural and social) and activities required for a means of living; a livelihood is sustainable which can cope with and recover from stresses and shocks, maintain or enhance its capabilities and assets, both now and in the future, while not undermining the natural resource base.

(Chambers and Conway, 1992).

Figure 8.1 illustrates CARE's household livelihood security (HLS) approach. HLS is described as 'sustainable and adequate access to income and other resources to meet basic needs, and to build up assets to withstand shocks and stresses' (Sanderson, 1999a). This can be represented diagrammatically as follows:

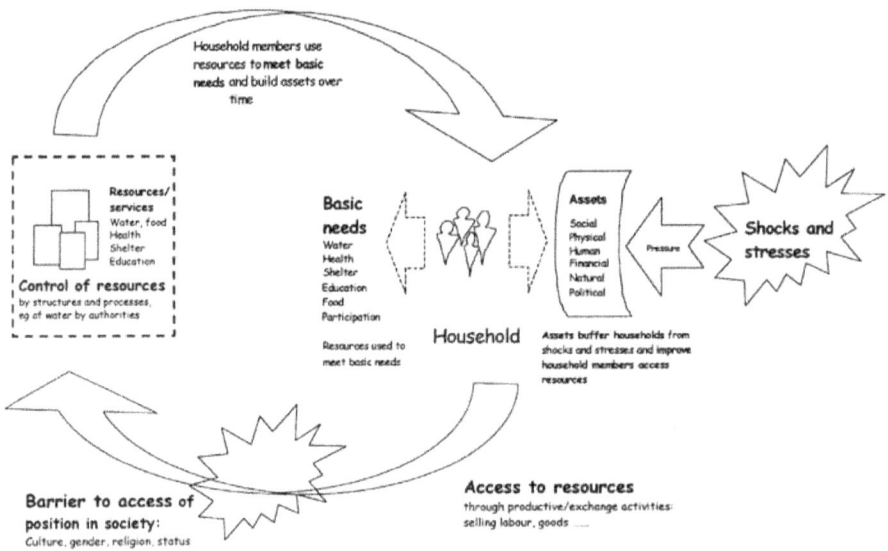

Figure 8.1 CARE's household livelihood security approach

The sequence followed by the diagram in Figure 8.1, beginning at the household and following the arrows, is:

1. Household members have basic needs: food, water, shelter, education, etc.
2. To meet needs, household members access resources or services, e.g. water, food, shelter, healthcare, electricity. Most access is gained through payment. Payment is secured by undertaking productive activities, e.g. selling labour to gain income to pay for resources needed.
3. There are barriers to accessing resources/services which, for the poor, usually prevent or reduce the quality and quantity of resources accessible. Two barriers (of which there may be many) are:

- position in society, e.g. culture, gender, religion, status, being poor
- control of resources by *structures*, e.g. government, private sector employers, and *processes*, e.g. laws, regulations (which may discriminate against the poor).

4. Depending on the degree of success in overcoming barriers, resources/services secured by household members are used to:
   - meet immediate basic needs
   - build up assets (social, physical, financial and human) over time.

5. Assets are used to:
   - buffer households against stresses and shocks, e.g. sickness, fires, sudden unemployment
   - increase the ability to improve access, e.g. improved education (human assets) may lead to better jobs.

The HLS approach, as with other livelihood-based understandings, is used as a programming tool for developing and implementing poverty reduction development interventions. To these ends it offers uses in the following contexts.

- Linking micro- to macro-issues. The livelihood-based approach does not advocate community-level or municipal interventions; rather it describes the links between all levels that affect poor urban dwellers, from how households secure a means of living to the policies that control them.
- Highlighting the layering and complexity of controls by institutions and their regulations that affect the poor's access to resources. While controls on the poor may be legal, e.g. by municipalities, they may also result from illegal activity, e.g. drug gangs that control neighbourhoods.
- Indicating access to resources as a key concept, including the ability of poor urban dwellers to access healthcare, food, employment, shelter or political power.
- Stating the importance of income as a means of accessing many of those resources, e.g. food, clothing, building materials, education.
- Emphasizing the importance of household-level assets, including non-physical assets, e.g. political, social, human, as well as physical assets.

ASPECTS OF LIVELIHOOD-BASED UNDERSTANDINGS

The control of resources by structures and processes

According to Carney (1998), control of resources is by the two components of *structures* (private and public organizations), i.e. who controls; and *processes* (policies, laws, regulations, 'rules of the game'), i.e. the mechanisms for control. The structures controlling resources can be complex: they include formal institutions, such as municipalities, city authorities and privatized utilities, and, increasingly, informal/unregulated structures such as water vendors. Some of their activity is illegal, although access may depend on cash payment and/or position in society, for example, squatters on unregulated land may find securing municipal services difficult.

Cities are notable for the often complex and sometimes contradictory layering of both structures and processes – within any given city there may be several municipalities, a city authority, and specific housing and infrastructure agencies. Coordination among these different groups may often be weak or non-existent.

At the heart of most resource access issues is landownership. Land touches on access to work (squatters will endure terrible conditions to be close to sources of income), and is a key asset to secure, as for most, ownership brings greatly enhanced security. A further complication relates to degree of ownership: a neighbourhood may say it owns its houses because it has electricity and has been resident for 40 years, while the municipality master plan has the neighbourhood area designated as a park. Above all, land issues are politically charged, and are one of the critical issues facing urban management.

Access to resources through selling labour

Unlike rural areas, where the primary activity may be farming to consume produce (Maxwell, 1999), most productive time in cities is devoted to acquiring money to purchase resources. Key to this for many urban poor is through the selling of labour (Hamdi et al., 1998). The dominance of the cash market has strength in the diversity of ways available for securing resources through purchases, but can be weak in being reliant on the market for resources whose availability and cost may vary or be disproportionately expensive. Also, work and city living for many urban poor residents is seasonal. Large numbers of people migrate to and from cities according to the seasons and rural–urban-based sources of work. During the monsoon season in Bangladesh, the numbers of bicycle rickshaw pullers grows dramatically.

Priorities in assets

A key aspect of many livelihoods approaches regards the role of assets in strengthening households. Descriptions of assets vary, but the following are common to several interpretations.

Financial assets

Most resource access in urban areas results from cash exchanges. For the urban poor, as with other city-dwellers, the building of financial assets is almost always the primary activity for greater livelihood security. Financial assets are often fragile; many urban poor live by arranging complex systems of loans and debt servicing, borrowing small amounts and calling in debts from others to pay bills as they arise. A large proportion of the urban poor are forced to work in the informal sector, earning low incomes for long hours of work. Competition for work is intense, usually making incomes very low. For such workers, insurance, healthcare or sick pay do not exist. Working in poor conditions serves to increase long-term vulnerability to disease and ill health. This is increasingly the case regarding child labour, where many lifelong health problems can begin.

The informal economy allows for a diversity of ways for earning income to acquire resources. However, those resources can come at a high price, where the poorest often pay more than their better-off neighbours for basic services. Research in Lusaka, Zambia found water purchased by low-income groups to be nearly ten times more expensive than a subsequently installed water supply system. Food can also come at a high cost, despite the existence in some countries of 'urban agriculture': food expenditures can make up as much as 60 per cent to 80 per cent of total expenditure amongst low-income households. Yet recent studies by Ruel et al. (1999) in Ghana point to increasing malnutrition among the urban poor.

Physical assets

Tenure is a key physical asset to acquire. Squatters and slum-dwellers will endure dangerous conditions to be close to sources of income, while in the rental sector many families may share crowded, poor quality, illegally divided tenements. In central Delhi, for instance, a large squatter settlement has lived within the designated flood plane of the Yamuna River for over 25 years. The settlement is forced to evacuate at least once a year to the busy roadside while their shelters are flooded for upwards of one month. Yet the settlement is thriving, with small businesses, a school and a vibrant property market. The regular flooding is seen as the price to pay for living in the centre of the city for low cost (Sharma and Gupta, 1998). Having a degree of ownership of land, therefore, is often the beginning point for households to consolidate shelters.

Human assets

Cities provide a variety of opportunities for earning incomes. Many poor urban dwellers prioritize education for their children in their livelihood decisions regarding, for instance, moving to cities, or sending significant amounts of household income for tuition fees. The benefit of different household members entering into a range of activities based on skills, knowledge and ability increases the chances of sustaining a household. However, some strategies serve to increase vulnerability, threatening household sustainability: young children working in factories may miss out on an adequate education, and on childhood, and may suffer damaged health.

Social assets

Low-income urban settlements are often characterized as having limited social assets – lack of extended family structure, established networks of contacts or strong relationships of trust. However, for many newly urbanizing groups, which rely on mutual help and support, social assets can be strong. Many livelihoods project interventions concern the building of social assets. Focusing on the threat of disaster can be a key resource in developing sustainable risk reduction measures. In work carried out in Lima, Peru among low-income market traders by the NGO ECOCIUDAD (Sanderson, 1999b), mutual distrust between the voluntary fire services and market traders was cited as a major problem. Fire services were never called by traders when fire broke out, and the fire services were frustrated at not being alerted. Through the organization of meetings and joint training events, misunderstandings between both parties were addressed. The firemen and women became accepted by traders as professionals performing a useful job in protecting their livelihoods. In time, as the level of mutual trust improved, the local fire service organized mock evacuations with traders, and advised on fire reduction measures which the traders enacted. The fire station was also repainted with donations from the traders and became a forum for neighbourhood meetings.

Political assets

> If urban poverty is recognized to include voicelessness and powerlessness within the political system – for instance, the lack of possibilities for low-income groups to make demands within the political system and to get a fair response – this also adds a new dimension to poverty reduction.
>
> (Satterthwaite, 2001).

Organized voting and strong political alliances are common phenomena in low-income settlements. Often, squatter settlements receive improvements in exchange for supporting a particular candidate for a political appointment. Well-organized neighbourhoods with political support are better able to lobby for improvements, tenure, etc.

Position in society (barriers to access) and rapid change

Cities are marked by rapid change: growth in housing stock, shifting populations, economic changes in neighbourhoods (improving or declining), growth and regularization of settlements, etc. Low-income inhabitants of rapidly growing cities are defined by their class, culture and religion, as well as by age or gender. Newly arriving whole communities or households from the same region may settle in one area. Communities known to come from unpopular areas, from a minority religion, or from a despised social class may find their access to employment/income more difficult than others. It is in this scenario of the 'permanence of change' that urban dwellers are often called upon to adapt, change and diversify survival strategies. Within the city, some groups are especially vulnerable due to their position.

- Children – the urban phenomenon of 'street children'. It is estimated that approximately 100 000 street children reside in Delhi alone (Heissler, 1998). Increasingly, children may be forced into working in factories in poor working conditions, which may in the long term substantially reduce quality of life.
- Women – are generally more severely affected than men by poor and overcrowded housing and by inadequate healthcare, as they take most responsibility for looking after children, caring for sick family members and managing the household.
- Youth, especially in Africa – due largely to natural increase, large numbers of urban society are teenagers and those in their early twenties, with little or no opportunity for formal employment and limited access to good education.

BARRIERS TO ACHIEVING A SUSTAINABLE LIVELIHOOD

A livelihood is sustainable when it 'can cope with and recover from the stress and shocks, maintain its capability and assets, and provide sustainable livelihood opportunities for the next generation' (Chambers and Conway, 1992). To these ends, HLS is a goal to which interventions contribute. It serves to identify the range of factors affecting poverty, ranging from the micro individual/household level (management of assets and resources) to macro-level governmental structures and processes that affect household access to resources. Poverty is said to be absolute when individuals or groups are unable to meet their basic needs adequately (Gross et al., 1995). From a livelihoods perspective, contributory factors to this include the following, in varying degrees.

- Access – an inability to carry out adequate productive activities, e.g. through illness, or because the opportunities for adequate productive activities do not exist, e.g. through a surplus of labour.
- Barriers to access – due to position in society, e.g. being a woman prevents getting work that pays an adequate wage, or belonging to a low caste in India prevents getting a better job.
- Control of resources by others preventing access – e.g. private landlords increase rents which uses up some of the income that would have been used to pay for food; electricity authority regulations prevent a community from gaining an electrical connection.
- Inadequate resources – e.g. water supply is available for only two hours a day due to water shortages and a poor water delivery system, or roads within a low-income settlement are not maintained.

▥ Structures and processes that increase community vulnerability – e.g. government regulations prevent an adequate water supply to a squatter community dwelling on illegal land.
▥ Resource availability is limited or low – due to poor governmental management, weak policies, war and/or debt. This results in many different manifestations, from lack of a fire service to no healthcare facilities.
▥ Poor use of resources at household level – e.g. incremental building of poor quality shelters that eventually collapse or catch fire easily, or contaminating drinking water through poor hygiene.
▥ Shocks – extreme events that a household does not have the resources to withstand. These range in scale and nature, and may be a natural hazard, e.g. a fire or earthquake, or a political emergency.
▥ Stresses – eroding assets and increasing household vulnerability, e.g. long-term sickness within a family and the consequent pressures on other family members, overcrowding in a small dwelling, alcoholism, or hyperinflation diminishing purchasing power and destroying savings.
▥ Inadequate assets – e.g. a breadwinner with poor health and nutritional status is more likely to be ill for longer; or lack of savings to send children to school reduces the subsequent generation's chances to gain better access to resources through finding a better-paid job.

SHOCKS AND STRESSES

It is almost always those with limited assets to withstand shocks who are the most vulnerable. Shocks include natural disasters, such as earthquake, fire, cyclone; man-made, such as industrial accident; or result from war or political emergencies. They may also be economic, related to markets (Maxwell, 1996), for example, hyperinflation that erodes savings. On average, 85 000 people die each year as a result of natural disasters, and nearly five million are made homeless. At the end of 1999, 40 countries and territories were the victim of 'official' humanitarian emergencies in the world. Among health emergencies, the AIDS pandemic stands out: Zambia's workforce is likely to be 17 per cent smaller by 2015 as a result of AIDS.

Such events come in different sizes and over longer periods. For millions of poor urban dwellers, managing shocks and stresses is an everyday occurrence, less noticed by outsiders, but just as insidious. This may include the fires that wipe out squatter neighbourhoods, the cumulative health problems resulting from poorly ventilated shelter, or the long-term effects of pollution on children.

At household level, assets buffer households against shock events. A shock occurs, by definition, when a household is overwhelmed by a large, negative event. Assets are 'swept away'. This may be the destruction of a shelter by a mudslide, the ruination of a community by ethnic violence, or the loss of family income through loss of income-earners. Household-level livelihood strategies therefore concern the building of assets over time to reduce vulnerability. In this respect, risk reduction at community level becomes a development activity.

Building social assets can increase the chances of greater self-reliance among households and neighbourhoods. A recent example is provided from the Venezuela floods in Catuche, a neighbourhood of the country's capital city, Caracas. According to Manuel Larreal from the organization Ecumenical Action-ACT, 'the organization of the neighbourhood and the solidarity of the people saved hundreds of lives' (Jeffrey, 2000). He states that on the night of 15 December 1999, 'as the flooding progressed, community members mobilized to assist one another'. Neighbours who knew each other and had worked together for years swiftly communicated the news of the rising water. Older residents were helped from their homes by younger neighbours. When a few were reluctant to leave because they did not believe the threat or because they were afraid their few possessions could be stolen, neighbours broke down doors and carried people forcibly to safety.

> *In one incident where we were trying unsuccessfully to kick down the heavy door of a woman who refused to leave her house, a young gang member came along, pulled out a pistol and fired into the lock, allowing the door to be opened. The gang member then pointed his gun at the woman and ordered her out of her house. Seconds after she left the dwelling, the house fell into the raging current.*
>
> *(Jeffrey, 2000)*

In Catuche, 'perhaps as few as 15 people died, a very small figure compared to other similar neighbourhoods where hundreds lost their lives' (Jeffrey, 2000). These life-saving actions resulted only after several years of community activities addressing development issues concerning shelter and sanitation. From a livelihoods perspective, the social assets built up over time resulted in preparedness actions that saved many lives.

The example from Catuche describes a simple but effective neighbourhood-level intervention that resulted in saved lives. At a city management and policy level, actions leading to reduced risk also need to be taken. In the language of livelihoods, the structures and processes that control access of the poor to income and resources need to be aware of the risks that poor urban dwellers face, and take steps to reduce them. To these ends, most good urban programming works at both neighbourhood and policy formulation levels. But much urban legislation still results, if sometimes unintentionally, in increased vulnerability of the poor: the prevention of permanent services to illegal settlements can increase ill health, while the withholding of tenure inhibits consolidation of buildings, resulting in poorly built shelters that easily collapse, catch fire or harbour disease.

A deeper problem, however, lies in the continuing separation of disaster management from urban and development planning. Governments frequently have entirely different ministries responsible for emergency management and urban development, one with little knowledge of the other's activities. For example, India's Ministry of Urban Affairs' Draft National Slum Policy 1999 makes no reference to the vulnerability of slum-dwellers to natural disaster. Yet the same ministry estimates that 1 per cent of India's total housing stock is destroyed by natural disaster each year (Ministry of Urban Affairs and Employment, 1999).

LEARNING FROM LIVELIHOODS APPROACHES

This separation is also evident within development organizations, including donors, intergovernmental organizations and NGOs. There will always be a need for external assistance when emergencies occur, and agencies have a crucial role to play in providing an appropriate response. However, this separation is perpetuated and encouraged within many organizations: staff are either emergency people or development people.

Livelihood-based approaches provide one opportunity for viewing emergencies and development issues within one unifying approach: one that fundamentally sees shocks and stresses as part of everyday life. This approach can provide valuable opportunities for development practitioners to develop new tools and approaches for both emergency and development situations. To these ends, the following case study seeks to illustrate a livelihood-based understanding relating to a participatory urban livelihoods assessment carried out in Kosovo in 2000 by an interdisciplinary team led by CARE.

Urban livelihoods assessment, Kosovo

The 1999–2000 conflict in Kosovo marked the climax of 12 years of organized discrimination and state-supported violence against Kosovo's Albanian community in the Former Republic of Yugoslavia. Before 1989, Kosovo enjoyed a level of autonomy from Serbia as part of the Republic. This changed over the following 10 years through the systematic sidelining of Albanian Kosovars in political institutions, the formal economy and employment. During the violence that reached its peak in early 1999, at least 850 000 ethnic Albanians were forced to flee to neighbouring countries. Over the course of the conflict as many as 10 000 people in Kosovo were killed. Following the NATO bombings and the withdrawal of Serbian forces, most Kosovar Albanians returned. As Albanian Kosovars returned in mid–1999, up to 33 000 ethnic Serbs fled, most leaving for Serbia.

The objective of the assessment was to provide a profile of poverty in Kosovo to assist participating agencies in directing future programming. Data gathering was undertaken in 18 settlements throughout Kosovo, comprising 15 villages and three urban neighbourhoods. Assessments were undertaken by teams of four, two men and two women, drawn from participating agencies. Serb teams visited Serb settlements; Albanian teams visited Albanian settlements.

The assessment approach utilized HLS as the key tool for organizing the information gathered, while participatory rapid appraisal (PRA) was used to gather the information. Table 8.1 illustrates the HLS components and the PRA tool used to gather information relating to each component. The left-hand column shows the various components of HLS: context, assets, access, vulnerability, etc. The second column comprises the specific questions to be analysed; the third and fourth columns comprise the PRA tools for gathering information relating to the HLS components; and the final column lists the stakeholder themes identified and their relationship to the framework and tools.

The HLS approach provided the conceptual framework for linking and describing the issues that affect and perpetuate poverty in both urban and rural settlements. These ranged from uncertainties of governance to the use of household-level assets; and from neighbourhood-wide issues of infrastructure to individual concerns over safety. To these ends, the framework yielded questions relating to:

- how household members access resources, e.g. through work, loans or welfare
- barriers that prevent access, e.g. ethnicity, gender, unemployment, location, unemployment, destruction and scarcity of resources
- the ability of households to build and use household assets (physical, financial, natural, social)
- structures that control resources: existing governance structures and long-term uncertainty.

Information was gathered over a period of four weeks. At the end of this time the team reconvened for a five-day findings review workshop. Through a series of sessions, findings were compared and contrasted and conclusions drawn. This provided the basis for further analysis and the production of a final report by the consultant.

The use of a livelihoods framework proved useful in the following ways.

- Equal application to villages and neighbourhoods. The same livelihoods understanding was applied to both. Differences emerged in the emphases and complexities given to particular issues, e.g. in urban neighbourhoods many relief and development organizations were known about, compared to fewer in villages; in urban neighbourhoods unemployment was the big issue, but it received less emphasis in the villages.
- As a basis for holistic analysis. The framework includes aspects affecting governance as well as employment. This also helped mitigate prescribed information being sought: no particular aspect was

Table 8.1   Information to be collected and tools used in relation to stakeholder themes

Livelihoods	component	What we need to know	Principal tool for collection	Secondary tools
Context	Institutions	Presence and importance of community-level institutions; interaction of population with external institutions; control of resources by institutions at community or neighbourhood level; attitude to new institutions; participation; nature of government and institutions; access to governance	Venn diagram	Household interviews; focus group discussions; key informants
	Natural resources	Food-economy zone; presence of common property resources; availability and access to producer resources; access to land	Area mapping	Secondary data; key informants
	Infrastructure	Availability of education, health, social services; water and sanitation infrastructure; roads and transport infrastructure	Area mapping	Venn diagram; interviews; secondary data
	Cultural environment	Ethnicity; religion and gender	Secondary data	Livelihood profile; interviews; focus group discussions
	Political environment	Broader political context in Kosovo; political parties at community level; access to voting; feelings of insecurity/uncertainty at household and community level	Secondary data	Venn diagram; interviews; key informants
	Resettlement patterns	Number and dates of migration and resettlement; perceptions of security and risk; presence of landmines; physical isolation; participation; attitude to new institutions	Key informant interview	Mapping; interviews

Table 8.1 Information to be collected and tools used in relation to stakeholder themes *contd.*

Livelihoods	component	What we need to know	Principal tool for collection	Secondary tools
	Processes (rules, regulations etc.)	Impact of rules, regulations and policies on households and communities; potential impact of taxation; access to passports; impact of judicial processes; perception of new institutions; institutions at community level; participation	Venn diagram	Secondary data; interviews; key informants
Household assets	Social	Exchanges of goods and services; assistance to or from extended family networks; membership in community groups; nature of interactions with other households; social capital; remittances; physical isolation; gender; distribution of poverty within communities; participation	Household interview	Livelihood profile
	Physical	Housing; agricultural implements; vehicles; machinery; shops; household-level water and sanitation facilities; household economy; shelter; depth and distribution of poverty; water and sanitation; food security and agriculture	Household interview	Livelihood profile
	Human	Education level; ability to work; dependency ratio; education; health; gender; household economy; time allocation; participation; food security and agriculture	Household interview	Livelihood profile

			Household interview	Livelihood profile
	Natural	Land; access to common property resources; distribution of poverty within communities; land-holding; household economy; food security and agriculture	Household interview	
Livelihood strategies	Production, processing, exchange and income-generating activities	Pre-war activities; type of activities undertaken by each household member; level of contribution to household economy; coping strategies; access to employment; income-generating activities; access to credit; contribution of remittances to household livelihood; distribution of poverty within households; remittances; pension; gender; food security and agriculture; economic activities; household economy; access to finance; time allocation	Household interviews	Economy activity analysis; livelihood profile; key informant interviews
Vulnerability to shocks and stresses		Pre-war condition of household; coping strategy of household during war; ability to recover from war; time of return; process of resettlement; current status of household; barriers to recovery; other stresses (e.g. illness); shelter/housing; distribution of poverty within communities; institutions at the community level; remittances; social capital; economic activities; household economy; pension; gender; access to finances	Household interviews	Economic activity analysis; livelihood profile; key informant interviews

promoted above another as an issue on which to gather information, in order to reduce any biases or 'pet issues' of the team.

- Flexibility: generic headings such as vulnerability, access and controls allowed the framework to work in the specific Kosovo context. For example, the presence of UN forces and the new legislature could be described in terms of structures and processes controlling resources; united but marginalized Serb groups could be described in terms of possessing strong social and human assets, while remaining highly vulnerable.
- For including intangible as well as tangible assets. As well physical items, information on human and social capital was also gathered. This was considered important to give a truer picture of the status of Kosovo.
- As the basis of a common understanding and rationale for a complex situation. This was particularly important given the scale of the research, the range of complexities present in Kosovo, and the large research team involved, as well as the large client group (ten agencies in Kosovo).

CONCLUDING REMARKS

If the increasing vulnerability to disasters of the poor is not addressed by policy, management or implementation, then, simply put, urban living for them cannot be sustainable. At policy level, gaps between disasters and urban planning need to be closed. Proactive measures to reduce the threat of disaster need to be an integral aspect of urban planning.

Livelihoods approaches to urban poverty problems provide one way of seeing vulnerability to shocks and stresses as an integral part of the development picture. Development practitioners from government organizations and NGOs have the opportunity to weave considerations of risk and vulnerability into their development programmes. Moreover, they have a duty. Not to do so is bad stewardship of time and resources in initiatives that might fail when large-scale shocks occur. Development practitioners need to consider that the threat of disaster is part of everyday life, while emergency practitioners need to understand the development context of their interventions.

While livelihoods programming is at a comparatively early stage in its development, the livelihoods framework has much to offer for understanding the dynamics of urban poverty and the role that disasters play. Such approaches place the vulnerable at the centre and, in so doing, aim to make city-dwelling more sustainable, in particular for the poor.

International agency shelter policy in the 1990s: experience from Mozambique and Costa Rica

Paul Jenkins and Harry Smith

The United Nations and the World Bank issued important policy statements for the shelter sector at the end of the 1980s and beginning of the 1990s, and followed these up with programme activities during the decade, which themselves had implicit policy directions. This chapter looks at the experience of application of these policy statements in UN- and/or World Bank-funded projects in two regions of the developing world – Mozambique in sub-Saharan Africa and Costa Rica in Central America.

Although there are significant differences between these countries, analysis of the empirical experience shows certain similarities, particularly with respect to the institutional form of action and relationships between the three main sectors: the state, the private sector and civil society. Despite explicit statements supporting strengthened roles for civil society in shelter provision by the UN, in practice the focus for both agencies has been on improved relationships between the public and private sectors, especially referring to urban management. In both countries, however, macro-economic forces have actually reduced state roles and capacity, while not necessarily attracting sufficient effective private sector action.

The chapter exposes the need to incorporate civil society in shelter policy and practice, by opening spaces for negotiation with 'horizontal' actors in civil society, as well as permitting more traditional 'vertical' forms of political negotiation. The basis for the argument is inevitably summarized, and the authors acknowledge the danger of subjectivity in such seemingly broad assessments (for more sources see Jenkins, 1998, 2001b; Smith, 1999; Smith and Valverde, 2001). The divergence of practice from theory in the sector, and a lack of theoretical bases by which to analyse new approaches, which has limited their development, are also noted (Jenkins and Smith, 2001b).

BACKGROUND AND REVIEW OF THE MAIN INTERNATIONAL AID AGENCIES' POLICIES IN THE 1990S

A brief history of international aid agency involvement in the shelter sector

International aid agency involvement in the shelter sector varied in approach throughout the second half of the twentieth century, responding to prevailing development paradigms, economic conditions and geopolitics. In the 1950s, when modernization was the prevailing paradigm, participation of international agencies in shelter activities was constrained to limited technical assistance and loans for house construction.[1] Under the Kenyesian paradigm, however, in the 1960s international aid was considered important as a means to redress developing nations' lack of state capacity to invest in housing to promote wider economic development. Financial support for savings and loans associations, as well as for industrialized housing production, was provided by agencies such as USAID which, in addition, supported self-help housing, particularly in Latin America.[2]

Kenyesian-based strategies such as 'basic needs' and 'redistribution with growth' came to dominate the lending strategies of international development agencies in the 1970s and 1980s in Latin America, Africa and Asia, and led to the direct promotion of 'self-help' housing policies as opposed to conventional housing delivery. The World Bank became a major player in lending for urban development and housing, systematically attempting to influence policy formulation through lending policy. Key principles promoted by the World Bank were affordability, cost recovery and replicability, which were accepted by all the major international agencies by the mid-1970s (Burgess, 1992). Four phases in the development of what can be loosely termed 'self-help' housing policy have been identified (Burgess, 1992; Pugh, 1994, 1997) – sites and services (early to mid–1970s); upgrading (late 1970s); extension to employment and community organization, as well as to housing finance institutions (early 1980s); and a focus on programmes as opposed to projects (late 1980s).

During the 1980s there was a shift in development paradigm towards neoliberalism, in particular in the World Bank approach, which began to consider the role of housing finance systems in the macro-economy, focusing on reforming the housing system as a whole and on increased housing supply. This period laid the foundations for the development of the World Bank's 'enabling markets' approach in the late 1980s and early 1990s. A different view of 'enablement' was that developed by the UN, which drew on the 'supports paradigm' (Habraken, 1972; Turner, 1982; Hamdi and Goethert, 1989). These two approaches to enablement, one centred on markets and the other on communities, are described below.

The UN policy position in the 1990s

The *Global Report on Human Settlements 1986* (UNCHS, 1987) put forward a new housing strategy replacing what it called the 'new orthodoxy'[3], the objective of which was defined as:

> *making conditions for self-help and mutual aid as favourable as possible, through sets of enabling action in support of locally determined, self-organized, and self-managed settlement programmes.*

(UNCHS, 1987: 195)

The main elements of the strategy were *settlement-wide action*, in order to deal with problems posed by very large numbers of poor people, and *enabling actions at the local level*, so as to provide for effective autonomy for community-based groups. Responsibilities were divided between government, which would manage the growth of settlements, and community-based self-help groups, which would carry out improvements at the local level.

The UN Centre for Human Settlements (UNCHS) approach to enabling strategies, however, underwent important changes which have been analysed by Pugh (1997), on whose account we draw here. After the first approach to enabling strategies as localized and based on the grassroots in human settlements, in *A New Agenda for Human Settlements* (UNCHS, 1989) enablement was regarded more as facilitatory, with connection to the generalities of the state–market–NGO–household relationship. The idea of enablement had started moving towards society as a whole, not involving only the poor, although in practice it would include community-based applications in housing, employment, infrastructure and the environment. *The Global Strategy for Shelter to the Year 2000* (UNCHS, 1990) provided a further step towards economically oriented enabling strategies, enablement being defined as:

> a concept to mobilize resources and apply entrepreneurial skills for increased housing and infrastructure production, by establishing legislative, institutional and financial frameworks that will enable formal and informal business sectors, non-government organizations and community groups to make optimal contributions to development.

> *(UNCHS, 1990: 7)*

Thus the UNCHS's initial community-based approach to enabling strategies gradually changed towards what would eventually be expressed as the World Bank's enabling strategy based on housing markets. In addition, this approach increasingly focused on issues of governance, as expressed in the Habitat Agenda adopted at the Habitat II Conference in Istanbul in 1996, where the UNCHS agenda centred on transparency, accountability, justice, effectiveness and efficiency of governance in towns, cities and metropolitan areas, as well as on participation (UN, 1996).[4]

A further strand of UN policy that developed during the 1990s was the promotion of urban sustainability through the Sustainable Cities Programme, run jointly by UNCHS and the United Nations Environment Programme (UNEP). The aim of this programme is to build capacities in environmental planning and management at the local level, and it has developed pilot experiences of 'consultative and participatory processes in environmental planning and management in a number of cities' (Wegelin, 1994: 135). In addition, 'community development' has been addressed through UNCHS's Community Development Programme (CDP),[5] which has also reflected the incorporation of an enabling approach. These programmes, together with Best Practices and others, highlight the shift in UNCHS's involvement in shelter provision from promoting shelter solutions on the ground in a project-based approach to supporting the exchange of information, capacity-building and partnerships on a programme basis.

The World Bank's policy position

The World Bank developed its own approach to 'enablement' (World Bank, 1991, 1993). These policy papers expressed the need 'to put development assistance in the urban sector in the context of broader objectives of economic development and macro-economic performance' (World Bank, 1991: 4), and reflected a shift towards the promotion of city-wide policy reform, institutional development and high-priority investments. Central to this approach was the consideration of housing primarily as a market sector with a significant effect and dependence on the economy as a whole, its performance being determined by market forces. The poor were portrayed as victims of the failure of housing markets, and therefore their problems could be alleviated if these markets were enabled to work. Consequently, governments were advised to abandon their role as producers of housing in favour of an enabling role in managing the housing sector as a whole (World Bank, 1993: 2).

In the mid–1990s the World Bank continued to lend finance for urban infrastructure and housing projects, but increasingly tied these to reorganization of market-oriented delivery systems. However, in addition to the economic conditionalities for 'market enablement', the World Bank also began to add political conditionalities of good governance. The stress in general is on the reorganization of government's role in market regulation and urban development as essential to ensure more effective urban economies as the 'engine for development' with 'associated increasing incomes'. The argument is that governments have for too long been dealing with the symptoms of urban housing problems, not the basic causes. The role of governments in this context should be to create appropriate governmental institutions to manage the housing sector market overall with minimum interference, yet defend public interests. An important factor influencing this approach is the change of emphasis in the underlying development philosophy to concentrate on structural adjustment, which basically is geared to remove the various forms of economic insulation between developing countries and the world markets (Pugh, 1995b). By the mid–1980s most World Bank lending had already become tied to structural adjustment, and the effect of structural adjustment programmes in reducing disposable incomes for lower-income groups has been in direct conflict with the self-help housing philosophies of the previous decade and a half.

World Bank finance since the late 1990s focuses on housing finance systems and municipal development. Urban policy reform is promoted, strongly linked to macro-economic development and restructuring. Special focus points are housing finance and urban management institutions; legislation on land (development of property rights) and facilitatory town planning; infrastructure improvements; partnerships for service provision; better organization and competition in building industry; anti-poverty subsidization; and environmental protection/management. The overall package, according to Pugh, is 'very demanding, requiring well developed public administration, effective coordination among participants, and complex systems of cooperation' (Pugh, 1995b: 70).

The Urban Management Programme

The Urban Management Programme (UMP) was developed in 1986 by the World Bank, UNCHS (Habitat) and the UN Development Programme (UNDP),[6] and implemented in three phases during the period studied here (1986–92; 1992–96 and 1997–99). It was designed 'to strengthen the contribution that cities in developing countries make towards human development, including economic growth, social development, and the reduction of poverty' (Wegelin, 1994: 127), and it also linked housing to the wider urban economy, promoting the use of housing as a vehicle for economic growth.

The first phase concentrated on the development of policy framework and discussion papers on municipal finance, infrastructure management, urban land management and the urban environment. The second was centred on raising awareness levels and promoting the quality of urban research and the orientation to more practicable policy alternatives (Jones and Ward, 1994: 37–38). The UMP was not funded to undertake projects, but to contribute to setting up regional networks of institutions involved in urban management[7] – to facilitate and catalyse the initiation of consultative processes, to monitor their implementation, and to facilitate replication (Wegelin, 1994). In this sense the UMP was to dovetail with the Sustainable Cities Programme, among others. The aim at the end of Phase 2 was to have delivered an operational South–South technical assistance network dealing with critical urban management issues. It was envisaged that the third phase would complete the process of 'institutionally anchoring the regional assistance networks' (Wegelin, 1994: 135) and securing long-term structural funding (from programme clients rather than from donors).

The UMP was therefore seen as part of an effort to increase local capacity to address needs in the urban sector, rather than to implement specific programmes. It shares the same ethos of supporting the exchange of information, capacity-building and partnerships on a programme basis evident in other UNCHS programmes of the 1990s.

THE EXPERIENCE IN MOZAMBIQUE

An overview of activity

The two main international agencies active in the shelter sector in Mozambique since independence in 1975 have been the UN (UNDP and

UNCHS) and, later on, the World Bank.[8] The UN has been involved for a substantial part of the post-independence period in Mozambique through a series of projects including Self-help Housing (1975–79); Assistance to Human Settlement Planning (1980–85); Training for the National Institute of Physical Planning (1987–91); Contribution to a National Housing Policy (1987–91); and the National Housing and Urban Development Programme (1991–94).

The World Bank has been involved for a shorter period, as Mozambique was not a member of the International Monetary Fund, with which it did not sign agreements until 1984, thus holding up other multilateral agreements. The World Bank's engagement has therefore always been within the overall umbrella of structural adjustment, although basic elements of adjustment have not been applied directly to the shelter sector projects. Specific shelter sector projects have been the Urban Rehabilitation Project (1987–94) and the Local Government Reform Programme (1992–99).

UN and World Bank involvement in the urban shelter sector in Mozambique over the past 25 years broadly reflects the themes shown in Table 9.1. These themes closely reflect the interests of the international agencies at the time – sites and services and self-help housing (1970s), national shelter strategies and programmes (mid–1980s to mid–1990s), and urban management (1990s). The exception is the first World Bank project which, arguably, represented the 'learning by doing' project approach from the 1970s, despite being implemented in the late 1980s when the World Bank had moved to the housing systems approach. Not only was this project out of step with current World Bank lending policy for the shelter sector in the developing world, but there was never any attempt to apply the cost-recovery/affordability theme which the project stage approach had so strongly stressed. In fact this project might be seen to a great extent as a 'sweetener' project by the World Bank, keen to start urban sector operations in the country. The evaluation of the project, however, brought in the critiques of the earlier approach, and the second project (the Local Government Reform Programme) conformed more closely with the current World Bank themes in the shelter sector (urban management). Again, however, in this case the project was never linked into the wider Urban Management Programme sponsored by the Bank, UNDP and UNCHS, as the project was exclusively implemented by the World Bank.[9]

An analysis of activities

All of the projects to date have been based in central government institutions, even if implementation has been at local government level. Generally, while responding to Mozambican government requests for assistance, the nature of the request has differed considerably from the nature of what has been accepted for funding by the international agency. The final pro-

Table 9.1   Mozambique projects and agencies 1975–99

Project type	1975–79	1980–83	1984–87	1988–91	1992–95	1996–99
Sites-and-services/ self-help housing projects	UN			WB	WB	
Squatter settlement upgrading projects	UN					WB
Basic infrastructure provision (on site)	UN			WB	WB	WB
Physical planning		UN		UN		WB
Training programmes	UN	UN		UN		
National policy/global shelter strategy				UN		
National shelter programme approach					UN	
Infrastructure rehabilitation				WB	WB	
Housing rehabilitation				WB	WB	
Core housing construction				WB	WB	
Small-scale credit				WB	WB	
Environmental management						WB
Land management						WB
Urban management						WB

UN, United Nations; WB, World Bank.

jects have all primarily reflected the international agencies' interests. In many cases the level of involvement of Mozambican personnel in the project formulation has been limited – due partly to technical capacity, but also to political weakness. Most projects have reported considerable difficulties in functioning as their local counterpart institutions have been so weak technically and administratively, although this is also a reflection of the relatively low profile of urban shelter activities at the political level.

In most cases special project implementation units were created within the central government institution responsible, sometimes with local government offshoots. In all cases the severe shortage of skilled Mozambican personnel has led to the projects being highly dependent on foreign technical assistance, while absorbing a high proportion of the available Mozambican technical personnel. A significant amount of the foreign technical assistance, in the later projects in particular, was through short-term consultants, in some cases employing Mozambicans who were leaving government employment (due to falling real wages), but in others foreign consultants, many of whom did not speak Portuguese.

All projects have had training elements, but in most cases these have been minor aspects of the project and have suffered from the lack of basically trained personnel to benefit from the project-based training. Only in two cases did the projects actually develop basic training programmes, for topographers and for basic and medium-level physical planners. The World Bank projects, in particular, have not contributed significantly to training, while absorbing high numbers of the scarce trained personnel. Another aspect, partly resulting from the lack of state capacity, has been the concentration of UN and World Bank projects in the sector in the main urban areas. Most of the activities actually implemented in the above projects have been in the capital, Maputo, with some in the second largest urban area, Beira; only in the last project have there been a limited number of pilot projects in other urban centres, Pemba, Nampula and Quelimane (Jenkins, 2000).

In general, the projects have also suffered from lack of adequate coordination between the major donors, as well as with other national and local initiatives. The attempt by the UN to adopt a coordinated 'programme approach' in the early 1990s was not accepted by the other donor agencies involved in the sector – particularly the World Bank – and the Mozambican government was not interested or able to demand higher levels of coordination. Consequently, evaluation of the projects has been project-specific and not sector-wide. Evaluations have stressed the over-ambitious nature of the project documents – themselves generally reflecting complex requirements relating to donor agency policies as well as the extent of the needs to be addressed in Mozambique.

One of the basic problems is that, to be approved, international agency project approaches have to satisfy criteria set by the headquarter organizations. Rarely are these easily applied in the Mozambican institutional reality, and hence the projects are seen post factum as 'complex'. This is exacerbated by the tendency of both government and donors to widen the scope of projects, as it is virtually impossible to achieve key project objectives without achieving certain 'secondary' preconditions. However, the lack of technical and administrative capacity – the precondition for effective implementation – is so widespread that no project is able or willing to tackle it. The result is the need to create a special unit with better skilled Mozambican staff as well as foreign assistance to be able to implement at least some of the project objectives.

The other basic problem concerns the context in which the projects have been located within the Mozambican economic and political reality. Being one of the poorest countries by both UN and World Bank standards (World Bank, 2000a), the levels of poverty in Mozambican urban areas have been so high that there has been a need to redefine standards of poverty. Poverty is as much an urban as a rural phenomenon – overall, rural poverty levels have been assessed at 70 per cent in absolute poverty, with the urban population at 60 per cent, even with a redefined level of absolute poverty.[10] As elsewhere in sub-Saharan Africa, urbanization is increasing fast, with 40 per cent of the population classified as urban, expected to rise to 57 per cent in 2025 – a rise of some 12 million urban dwellers as opposed to 3 million rural dwellers.[11] Maputo is generally considered to have lower overall poverty levels than other urban areas, yet studies indicate that, in 2000, some 50 per cent of the approximately 180 000 households are in absolute poverty (60 per cent of these are destitute). This situation is deteriorating due to macro-economic changes with widespread formal sector job loss, but as yet is not compensated by alternative new employment prospects for the underskilled (Jenkins, 2000). This has affected all projects' ability to deliver, but more so for those that have been based on cost recovery and affordability. In practice, no major project in the shelter sector supported by an international agency in Mozambique since independence has recovered costs – whether nominal or actual.

Concerning the political context, the anti-urban bias of the post-independence Frelimo period with its strong command structure left little room for state investment in urban shelter (Jenkins, forthcoming). The reality that state-built housing programmes were not going to be the typically socialist solution came to be politically accepted by 1984, at the time of the IVth Party Congress of the ruling party, Frelimo, which also faced up to the limitations of state capacity in other sectors of the economy. The resulting change of policy direction, however, was never consolidated either politically or in practice, despite efforts at local government level to support local projects. The international agencies ignored these political changes as they professed to be non-political. However, at the national level they were inevitably allied to international political pressure to withdraw from the socialist orientation and alliance with the Soviet bloc, which led eventually to changes in the constitution of 1990.[12] Again, while professing not to become involved in politics, the World Bank has, de facto, pushed for local government decentralization as an element of the democratization process, and exclusively associated later assistance with this. However, central government agencies have again been the channel for this assistance, which has tended to be implemented by international consultancy firms.

THE EXPERIENCE IN COSTA RICA

An overview of international agency activity in Costa Rica

The UN has been involved in the shelter sector in Costa Rica from the late 1980s and throughout the 1990s, through a series of projects linked to the Global Shelter Strategy and to the UNCHS's Community Development Programme, including the National Shelter Strategy for Costa Rica (1988–91); the Project for the Strengthening of Community Self-Management in the Development and Operation of Human Settlements (PROFAC; 1991–98); and the Resource Facility for Sustainable Development of Human Settlements in Central America (CERCA; 1997–99).

The National Shelter Strategy for Costa Rica was prepared to strengthen a housing programme already initiated in 1986 as a result of negotiations between the Costa Rican government and strong national civil society 'housing fronts'. The objectives of this UNCHS/Government of Finland project, which began in 1988, were consistent with 'enabling strategies' as set out implicitly in the UNCHS *Guidelines for the Preparation of Shelter Programmes* (Wakely et al., 1992). PROFAC was part of UNCHS's Community Development Programme, and its key objectives were to involve local communities with the aim of ensuring optimal use of public investment, as well as changing attitudes and procedures in central and local government, so as to be more conducive to community participation. CERCA's objective was to promote decentralized, participatory management of human settlements in Central America, and its strategic approach was to strengthen operational partnerships involving central governments, local governments and community organizations throughout the region. It therefore intended to address partnerships, enablement, capacity-building and institutional development, as set out in the Habitat Agenda.

In contrast with the involvement of UNCHS in shelter, the World Bank has not engaged directly with this sector in Costa Rica, but has made inputs to other sectors such as transport, education, health, and water supply and sewerage. The main external sources of funding for shelter in Costa Rica during the late 1980s and early 1990s were: USAID, mainly through loans for sites and services programmes and seed funding for the National Housing Fund (FONAVI); the Central American Bank for Economic Integration (BCIE), through credit for the National Housing Bank; the Canadian government, through funding for a rural housing foundation; the Inter-American Development Bank (IDB), lending for sites and services programmes; and the Swedish government, which has provided funding on several occasions for the housing NGO FUPROVI. USAID eventually pulled out of Costa Rica in 1996, and during the 1990s the IDB shifted its focus in Costa Rica from sites and services to urban planning and land titling.

The experience in Costa Rica is therefore directly relevant for any evaluation of UN shelter policies in the 1990s. It also allows some degree of evaluation of the World Bank's policy approach to shelter because, although the World Bank has not been directly involved in shelter in Costa Rica, the Costa Rican government's policies do reflect the 'enabling' approach promoted by the World Bank.

An analysis of international agency activities in Costa Rica

As in the case of Mozambique, projects have been based in central government, reflecting the highly centralized character of government in Costa Rica. This centralization is evident in the implementation of agency-funded projects, which are overwhelmingly urban and located in the Central Valley, in the Greater Metropolitan Area around the capital city of

San José. The balance between response to government requests for assistance and international agency-driven initiatives has been mixed, although final projects have always reflected the international agencies' agendas. The level of involvement of Costa Rican personnel in project formulation and implementation has been high, in terms of both government staff and local consultants. This reflects not only the availability of trained staff, but also the high profile of shelter activities at the political level.

However, somewhat paradoxically, the level of Costa Rican staff involvement has reflected the relatively small size of the Ministry of Housing and Human Settlements, where between one-fifth and a quarter of total staff were involved in UN projects in the late 1990s. This in itself might not be a weakness, except for the fact that the two UN projects that were in operation ended before the end of the decade, having been designed to run a limited period of time. These projects do leave a legacy of personnel trained in community and institutional facilitation and capacity-building (community development and social workers), but have not had an impact on the training of technical personnel. Government technical personnel – concentrated mainly in the National Institute of Housing and Urban Planning, a parastatal agency – has not been addressed directly by these programmes.

In general, the projects have achieved some degree of coordination between programmes within each international agency, and between international agency project implementation units and local institutions, if not between major donors. Thus, international agency project implementation units (in particular the UN) have worked within national programmes such as the National Plan Against Poverty, 1994–98. This coordination has not been devoid of problems, and often has not optimized its effectiveness due to institutional constraints: lack of delegation of power within participating government organizations; administrative weakness (especially of local government); institutional rivalries. It is likely that these constraints, together with the top-down origin of the UN initiatives and the – to some extent unavoidable – lack of full engagement with political contexts, might help explain the extremely limited impact of the UN projects on the ground.[13] For example, despite the UNCHS rhetoric about 'enabling communities', the projects implemented in Costa Rica have done little to address the weakness of second-tier community organizations which resulted from the co-option of the national housing fronts by central government in the late 1980s (Smith, 1999; Smith and Valverde, 2001).

In addition, other than the National Shelter Strategy, there has been little interaction between UN projects and the financial components of the national shelter policy, which has developed along the lines of the World Bank's version of 'enablement'. It can be argued that the main reforms introduced in the housing sector as a result of the 1986 negotiations developed four of the seven enabling instruments advocated by the World Bank (1993): the development of property rights; the development of mortgage finance; the rationalization of subsidies; and the development of an institutional framework for managing the housing sector. The success of this approach has relied heavily on the subsidy element, and the continuity or increase of the house-production rate in Costa Rica depends on the sustainability of this subsidy. However, cost recovery, one of the World Bank's requisites, is not generally accomplished, and was one of the concerns in the evaluation of IDB sites-and-services projects implemented in the late 1980s and early 1990s (Rojas, 1995).

It could be argued that UNCHS has used Costa Rica as a safe testing ground for the implementation of institutional aspects of enabling strategies, in a favourable environment in terms of political stability, long national experience in 'community development' and political prominence of shelter issues. As such, the UN projects have responded more to internal UNCHS project phasing constraints and interests, and have not engaged with the more politically and economically sensitive and onerous issues of land and finance for housing. The latter have been addressed by national policies, international development banks and national aid agencies, in a way that is consistent with World Bank shelter policy and that is therefore acceptable to major donors. Indeed, the Housing Finance System established in Costa Rica has favoured a market-based approach in the sense that it has encouraged the participation of private sector actors in the management of housing finance and in house-building, albeit on the basis of heavy government subsidization through one-off capital grants to low-income households.

AN ANALYSIS OF THE EXPERIENCE

The basis for analysis – state, market and civil society

This chapter has adopted an institutionalist approach[14] to analysing the experience of international agency shelter policy in the two case study countries, focusing on the roles of the state, the market and civil society in housing. This tripartite model underlies much of the literature on the housing debate (Turner 1988a,b; UNDP, 1993: 1).

Analysis of the relative weighting for role of each sector in UN/World Bank policy documents

The United Nation's first major statement of enabling strategies specifically defined roles for two sectors – the state and civil society – seeking to optimize the division of responsibilities between these 'by allowing each party to do what it is best equipped to do' (UNCHS, 1987: 198).[15] Governments were assigned the most important role and were expected to act primarily at the level of legislation and regulation (or de-regulation), as well as providing some credit and managing growth at settlement level. The role of communities was seen as operating at a local level, through 'Well-trained and self-regulating community organisations [that] could assume responsibility for certain aspects ... thereby relieving pressures on project agencies' UNCHS (1987: 203). This required the strengthening of community organizations, which was another recommendation in UNCHS (1987). NGOs were also given a role, although a relatively minor one, being seen as specialized subcontractors; as community group mediators to access different kinds of support; and as third parties in collaborative projects. Finally, the private sector was virtually ignored in this UN statement, meriting only a brief mention in relation to its participation in providing low-cost materials (UNCHS, 1987: 197).

In the World Bank's (1993) statement of enabling strategies there was an implicit market-based view of society as composed of individuals and individual households, participating as consumers and producers. Roles for the different sectors were defined around these concepts. Thus, governments were explicitly recommended to abandon their role as producers of housing and adopt a new 'enabling' role, which involved the implementation of macroeconomic policies that would allow housing markets to operate efficiently.[16] House production was therefore to be left primarily to the market, and the recommendations given in World Bank (1993) were addressed to governments and aimed at facilitating the operation of housing markets. Little was said of the actual operation of housing markets and the specific roles of private sector agents involved. Civil society was hardly addressed at all and its role in housing delivery was not clarified. World Bank (1993: 6) recognized there is a role for the informal sector and even suggested that its activities are the most likely to benefit from enabling strategies, though it did not expand on what this role is, in the World Bank's view, other than an 'important submarket' (World Bank, 1993: 58). The only specific role given to community-based organizations (and NGOs) was as participants in institutions that oversee and manage the performance of the housing sector as a whole.

Analysis of the relative weighting of actual activity in the two case studies

In Mozambique, while the international agencies have concentrated almost exclusively on state support, overall there has been unwillingness to face up to the realities of state capacity in the sector – whether political, economic, administrative or technical. Although there was latterly some attempt to involve other actors within the private sector and civil society, especially in housing, recent research has shown that the formal housing market is interested only in acting on behalf of the proportionally small national and international elite, and there has been little interest (to date) within the national or local government in developing programmes that involve the informal market and/or elements of civil society (Jenkins, 1999). In general, for historical reasons as well as due to the continuing social and economic crises, organized civil society is weak, whether in terms of vertical links – society–state – or horizontal links – associational forms within society (Jenkins, 2001b). Non-associational forms of linkage, however, are the essential ingredient in both household survival and the socio-economic engagement of the majority (Jenkins, 1998). However, efforts to develop capacity within civil society in the sector (through, for example, local community involvement in planning and land management) have not been supported by the international agencies in any substantial way – to a great extent, as the state has not wanted these institutions to compete with it. The resulting situation is that the non-regulated informal sector dominates housing, land delivery and development, with growing illegal land speculation related to the embryonic formal housing market (Jenkins, 2001a).

In Costa Rica, UN project activities have, in general terms, been heavily weighted towards the state, in particular in the National Shelter Strategy for Costa Rica and in CERCA.[17] The main counterpoint to this is the experience of PROFAC, which dealt much more directly with community organizations although, as was indicated above, it did not engage significantly with second-tier community organizations that might have provided a more effective basis for the intended community capacity-building, as well as being better placed to exercise improved negotiation skills in its dealings with government and with the private sector. The latter is glaringly absent from the UN projects, closely reflecting the weighting in UN policy documents noted above. In contrast, in its first eight years (1987–94) the operation of the housing finance system – which, in effect, incorporates much of the World Bank 'enabling markets' approach – saw an overall increase in the role of the private sector, especially housing mutuals, in the management of housing finance. The participation of state institutions in the disbursement of housing subsidies and loans decreased, and community organizations can access such funding only through these private sector and state 'authorized agents'. The growth in housing backlog has been halted, but communities' and households' capacity to provide themselves with housing through means other than state subsidy has not improved.

CONCLUSIONS

The cases of Mozambique and Costa Rica illustrate the implementation of 'enabling' housing policies and programmes, as formulated by international agencies, aiming in both cases for a reduced role for the state and an increased participation of the market, with limited degrees of promotion of civil society involvement. The domination in practice of the World Bank 'enabling markets' approach over the UN's 'enabling communities' approach has not been effective in facing up to the real situation in Mozambique, and is leading to increasing reliance on state subsidies in Costa Rica.

Three major conclusions can be drawn from the cases analysed here. First, general policies formulated by international agencies cannot be successfully applied in different national contexts without responding to the social, economic, cultural, institutional and political context in which they are meant to operate. In Mozambique, the lack of assessment of affordability in the light of extreme poverty, and the lack of analysis of market capacity in the shelter sector, are examples of this. In Costa Rica, a higher awareness of the implications of the four-yearly electoral process, for example, might have mitigated the negative impact of the 1998 general elections on community self-management processes established by PROFAC.

Second, shelter policy needs to reassert a more balanced approach to all three major actors in housing – state, market and civil society – rather than hinging on the nexus between only two of these actors. This balance can be achieved only through opening spaces of negotiation involving all actors with a role in housing, and the case studies show that it is of particular importance to open up spaces for civil society, which is currently not being given opportunities for full engagement. This will involve political change and activism in cases where civil society is weak – something generally eschewed by international agencies which, however, have pursued their own political agendas and been active in promoting market activity (Jenkins, 2001c).

Finally, the state has an important role to play in the developing world, and state capacity needs to be strengthened, not weakened. This is true for supporting both market activity and civil society engagement. But it is the quality of the state involvement that matters, rather than the quantity (Jenkins and Smith, 2001b). In Mozambique the state was unsuccessful in supporting the provision of housing, even during its socialist period. Its role has decreased after structural adjustment with a continuing lack of success in addressing housing provision under a market-oriented economy. In Costa Rica a relatively strong state has increasingly been channelling resources through private sector organizations and has reduced housing backlog, but it has failed to address the underlying reasons for the continuing decrease in housing affordability and has thus created a greater dependence on public subsidy. This situation in Costa Rica needs to be addressed through a higher state capacity to influence housing markets, not simply through an unsustainable level of subsidy.

These initial conclusions are based on the comparative analysis of international assistance to shelter policy-making and implementation in two very different countries. Further comparative analysis of housing policy in other countries is needed to increase critical understanding, as well as to formulate alternatives more attuned to local needs and context. Overall, there is a need for renewed analysis that draws on theoretical models – albeit not necessarily the 'meta-theories' of the past – which go beyond the more pragmatic assessment and realignment of international policies. The lack of theoretical development in the sector from the end of the so-called self-help debate in the early 1990s, with its eventual polarization of theory and practice, needs to be overcome. The challenge is to develop theoretical and analytical approaches articulated with both emerging theories of globalization and economic development under market entitlement conditions, as well as empirical experience.

Authoritarianism and sustainability in Cairo: what failed urban development projects tell us about Egyptian politics[1]

W. Judson Dorman

Healthy and secure environments for the urban poor in developing countries cannot be imposed top-down. The success of development interventions to establish them depends, at least in part, on the mobilization of their residents as active contributors or tax-payers. Such mobilization is necessary not only for the success of the initial implementation, but also for long-term sustainability – so that maintenance and replication do not depend on continual infusions of donor resources. More broadly, the concept of sustainable development requires that the intervention's beneficiaries take responsibility for the gains made and their preservation.

While this definition of sustainability may seem narrow, demands for social mobilization are implicit in various development discourses, including the notion of project cost-recovery, the aided self-help paradigm, and the current literature on participation. Although the precise method differs, all are concerned with extracting the resources latent in beneficiary communities and using them in support of particular interventions. They are also – most obviously in the case of participation – linked to issues of governance reform, as a means of making governments more accountable and responsive to those who live under them. In turn, such reform is likely to contribute to the sustainability of project-level improvements to the urban environment.

This chapter explores the counter-argument – that in many developing countries an authoritarian political environment precludes community mobilization or governance reform on any meaningful scale. While practitioners and academics are hardly oblivious to such constraints, they often regard them as something that either has to be endured, or can be dealt with through improved project methodology. This fails to acknowledge the extent to which the non-mobilizational character of authoritarian regimes can undermine the achievement of sustainable development objectives, despite the use of varied approaches and the expenditure of considerable resources.

To substantiate this claim, I examine the Egyptian state's governance of the Cairo informal housing sector, defined as communities established outside the framework of state administration and planning.[2] I use as case studies a series of internationally backed – and generally unsuccessful – urban development programmes undertaken since the late 1970s. They suggest that while donors have repeatedly attempted replicable, sustainable and sometimes even participatory projects, these efforts have been repeatedly frustrated by Egyptian government agencies. Of course, programme failures cannot be blamed entirely on the state, and this chapter is not subtitled 'why projects fail'. Nonetheless, it is clear that its officials and institutions have consistently acted to preserve a top-down political economy in which an unaccountable state allocates infrastructure without a corresponding degree of taxation or other form of social extraction. Avoiding direct governance and the consequent mobilization of informal communities, they have eschewed Cairo's sustainable development. While the development programmes considered here have provided resources for this distribution, they also challenged the allocative political economy by requiring state agencies to take a more extractive approach to urban management.

DURABLE AUTHORITARIANISM

Although there is debate as to the causes, the Middle East has become well known as a region resistant to the global trend – in evidence since the late 1980s – towards political liberalization. One means of understanding the regional resilience of authoritarianism is through the 'rentier' or 'distributive state' paradigm (Vandewalle, 1998). This was originally formulated with reference to those states whose economies are largely based on oil exports. Oil production is generally external to the producer's domestic economy, with the resulting revenue usually accruing directly to the state.

States deriving their revenues in this manner are generally able to dispense with taxing and fostering domestic capital accumulation. In the absence of such fiscal imperatives, state–society relations tend to be characterized by the top-down distribution of goods and services which becomes the primary mode of governance. Some have further concluded – although it does not inevitably follow – that the absence of revenue imperatives further relieves the state from the necessity of seeking the consent of the governed; in other words, 'no taxation' is seen as resulting in 'no representation' (Anderson, 1997). In such circumstances, bottom-up political activity hardly ceases. Rather, it becomes a process whereby individuals and groups seek preferential access to the oil rent – ultimately serving to reinforce the political status quo (Luciani, 1987).

EGYPT: A SEMI-RENTIER STATE

While not a major petroleum exporter, since the late 1950s Egypt has had access to analytically similar exogenous income flows. Those directly available to the state include oil revenue, foreign aid, international credits, Suez canal tolls and, to an extent, tourism revenues. Remittances from Egyptians employed abroad, by contrast, flow to society but have also provided substantial sources of foreign exchange since the 1970s. The extent and precise composition of the exogenous revenue stream has varied considerably over time. Between the mid–1970s and 1980s – the period immediately following the economic opening to the West – they amounted to approximately US$59 billion and may have accounted for up to half of Egypt's annual GDP during the 1980s (Handoussa, 1991a; Waterbury, 1993). Despite subsequent fluctuations in the extent of the flows, Egypt continues to depend on external income (Weiss and Wurzel, 1998).

Egypt's military-dominated regime – established by Nasser after the Free Officers' seizure of power in 1952, and continued under the Sadat and Mubarak governments – resembles the distributive-state model in a number of crucial respects. For example, successive Egyptian governments have been very reluctant to undertake social extraction. Direct taxation of the population has been only a minor source of revenue, and Egyptian governments have financed investment using externally generated resources (Waterbury, 1985; ERF, 2000). While state distribution has never kept pace with demand, by the late 1980s consumer subsidies – only one of the channels through which the state allocates resources – consumed over half the annual budget (Harik, 1997). However insufficient they may be, such transfers are seen as traded for political acquiescence – constituting a putative 'social contract' (Singerman, 1996). Finally, domestic political activity – at all levels of society – is often concerned with gaining preferential access to state resources and the channels of devolved patronage within which its distribution takes place (Waterbury, 1976).

Egypt's post–1952 regime can thus be characterized as 'distributive authoritarian'. Consistent with Linz's (1970) classic definition of authoritarianism, its reproduction has been predicated on social demobilization rather than on the active support of the governed. While the role of coercion and strategies of containment cannot be discounted, external income has been crucial in two respects. First, successive governments organized along distributive authoritarian lines have achieved social demobilization both through co-option and by making access to state largesse – rather than formal representation – the primary goal of political competition. Second, although budget shortfalls and western pressures to reduce macroeconomic demand led the Mubarak government to cut back state distribution in the 1990s, the absence of revenue and accumulation imperatives means that Egyptian governments have, nonetheless, been relatively non-interventionist in society (Harik, 1997; Weiss and Wurzel, 1998). Fluctuations in distribution notwithstanding, they have generally refrained from direct social extraction in ways that might trigger unrest and provoke demands for representation (Waterbury, 1985).

The risk-avoidance tendencies intrinsic to the distributive authoritarian type of regime mean that the domestic policies of successive governments have tended to follow the proverbial path of least resistance, avoiding public choices between competing interest groups around which dissent might be mobilized. This is governance by doing as little as possible. Another aspect of the regime type is the state's neglect of certain sectors within Egyptian society. Even before 1952, the Egyptian state only ever ruled the country's 'main axes' directly – relying on intermediaries to control the urban and rural peripheries (Roussillion, 1998). Such practices of indirect rule continue, further reinforced by the post–1952 regime's predominantly distributive mode of governance. In situations where governments are unable or unwilling to allocate resources, the state is likely to be conspicuous in its absence.

THE GROWTH OF INFORMAL CAIRO

One measure of the authoritarian character of state governance is that Cairo is not governed by a single metropolitan authority (Sullivan, 1983). Rather, it is divided administratively between three autonomous units known as governorates. The Cairo governorate, which includes the city's historic centre, occupies the east bank of the Nile, with the exception of the Shubra al-Kheima industrial area in the north which is in the Qalyubiyya governorate (see Figure 10.1). The entire west bank is in the Giza governorate. Nominal bureaucratic coordination among them does not disguise the divide-and-rule strategy and the lack of effective governance mechanisms latent in the absence of a city-wide administration (PADCO Inc. et al., 1982; Sullivan, 1983; G. El Kadi, personal communication, 1992). Moreover, the dispersed administration is nationally rather than locally appointed. Governors, frequently military or police veterans, are directly named by the president – and are primarily concerned with maintaining control over the city, which is regarded as a potential security problem (Ino et al., 1989; Sullivan, 1983; Mayfield, 1996).

Another measure of such state–society relations can be found in the genesis and growth of the Cairo informal housing sector. The most recent estimates indicate that it currently houses over 7 million Egyptians, amounting to more than 60 per cent of the city's inhabitants (Sims, 2000). Empirically, informal urbanization in Cairo is best understood as the product of substantial migration from the 1940s until the 1970s, coupled with subsequent high rates of natural increase at least through the 1980s (Sims, 2000). The resulting housing demand has never been matched with an adequate supply of public housing for middle- to lower-income groups. The state's preferred means of provision – highly subsidized apartment blocks – amounted to little more than 5 per cent of annual housing production and has largely benefited the middle to upper classes. Later government efforts to encourage formal private-sector production in the 1970s similarly failed to reach low-income consumers (Harik, 1997).

Yet the government rhetoric of the 1970s, that Cairo faced housing shortages of up to 3.6 million units, was patently false (G. El Kadi, personal

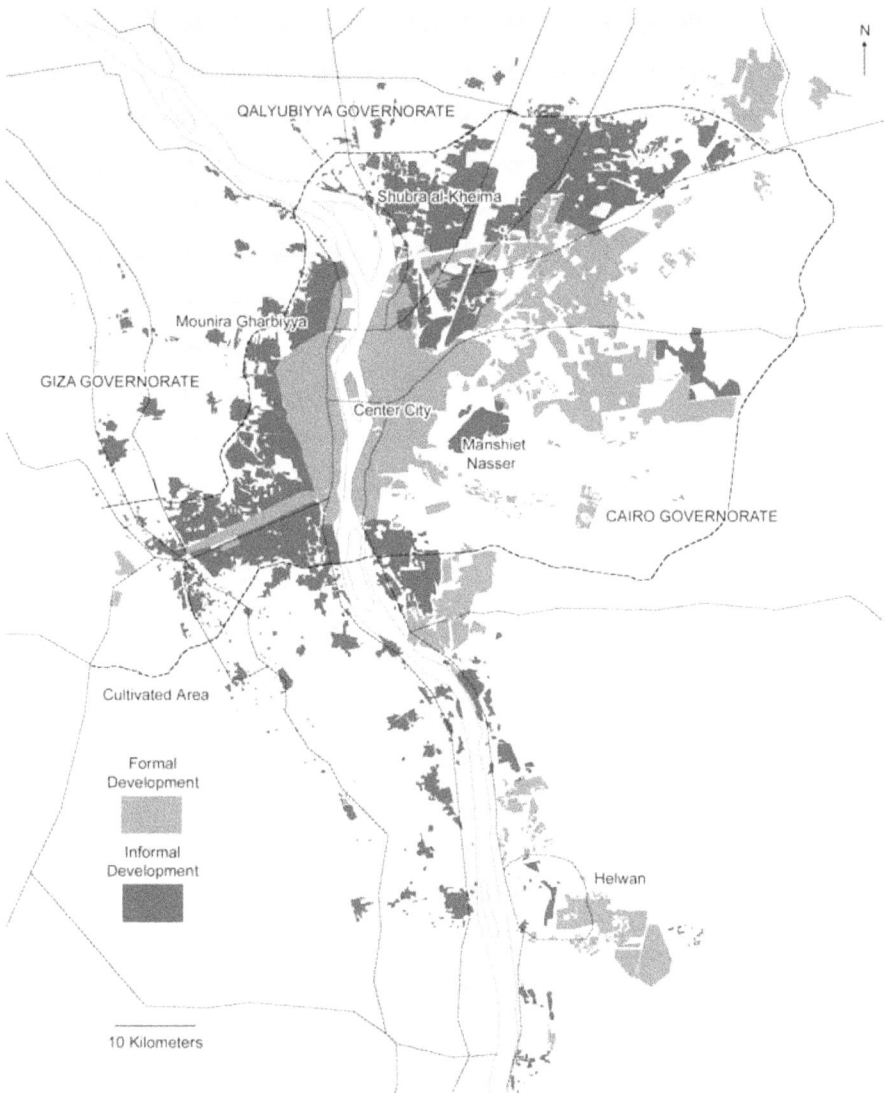

Figure 10.1   Cairo Metropolitan Area

communication, 1992). Sector production – histo rically absorbing up to 50 per cent of private investment (Handoussa, 1991b) – had more than kept pace with family creation rates through the 1980s; the 1986 census revealed that there were 1.8 million empty flats in the city (Harik, 1997). Much of the demand, however, has been satisfied by the informal sector. While remittances from Egyptians employed abroad provided the capital through the mid–1980s, a stagnant agrarian economy encouraged the illegal subdivision of agricultural land on the city periphery for residential development (Abt Associates et al., 1982). Such growth consumed between 330 and 590 hectares per annum from 1966 to 1982, and 150 hectares to 1989, producing sprawling zones of densely populated informal settlements and leaving very little cultivated land within Cairo's nominal boundaries (G. El Kadi, personal communication, 1992). As they are established illegally, such settlements lack formal planning and are usually denied connections to public infrastructure – at least in the early phases of their growth.

Although such settlements account for over 80 per cent of the informal urbanization in Cairo, there are other kinds of informal communities (Sims, 2000). These occupy land nominally owned by the state and/or land of uncertain tenure; some are situated on desert land bordering the built-up area, while others are within long-established neighbourhoods (Oldham et al., 1987; Sims, 1998). Generally more impoverished than communities of the urban-fringe type, they have also been the location of most Western aid interventions. Their diversity notwithstanding, informal communities of all types share an ambiguous relationship with the Egyptian state.

STATE RESPONSES

Strictly speaking, 'informal' urbanization is illegal. Urban-periphery settlements violate numerous laws for preserving scarce agricultural land, as well as urban planning and building standards regulations[3]; the other types usually encroach on public land. Some scholars have argued that the very existence of certain informal communities is an implicit political challenge to the Egyptian state (Ismail, 1996). Public pronouncements to the contrary, state officials have generally avoided confrontation, preferring to ignore such settlements (Environmental Quality International, quoted by Taher, 1997a).

Towards the end of the 1980s, the informal housing sector appeared to enter the official agenda as Mubarak's government discovered militant Islamist groups established in a number of such communities, most notoriously in the north Giza neighbourhood of Mounira Gharbiyya (Ibrahim, 1996). Despite plans announced in 1993 to upgrade or demolish such areas systematically, relatively little has been done.[4] Indeed, declared campaigns against informal areas actually occur every few years and follow a cycle of nominal indifference, replaced by official indignation and giving over to promises of upgrading and legalization (Zaghloul, 1994).

In Cairo, at least, the informality of the informal housing sector stems from this combination of nominal illegality with de facto, if inconsistent, government toleration. The state's tacit acceptance of such communities is confirmed by its periodic distribution of utilities and other services. Apart from the western-funded programmes discussed below, however, such allocations are rarely planned and systematic. Rather, they are ad hoc, often because of bottom-up pressures and through clientelist channels (Tekçe et al., 1994; Sherif et al., 1996).

WESTERN ASSISTANCE

The Egyptian state's failure either to upgrade or demolish Cairo's informal neighbourhoods systematically is conventionally explained as an absence of capacity. Put simply, the state lacks the resources to rehouse the millions of Cairenes who would be affected. While this explanation is indisputably true, it neglects the efforts made by a succession of Western donors – embracing a variety of approaches – to foster an administratively competent state, which would be better able to manage the provision of housing and urban services. The failure of these donor initiatives to influence government urban-development policies suggests that the constraints on the state are at least partially self-inflicted, and perhaps related to the political survival strategies of the post–1952 political order.

Aided self-help

US Agency for International Development (USAID) and World Bank missions in the 1970s concluded that Egypt's ostensible housing shortage was a consequence of the state's highly subsidized provision of apartment blocks – mainly to upper-income consumers – and the failure to mobilize private savings. Both organizations attempted to reform sector policies by demonstration projects intended to show that the state could more effectively house lower-income groups through reduced subsidies, increased cost-recovery and lowered construction standards. Recovery and reinvestment of project costs in a revolving fund would enable the housing-provision process to become at least partially self-financed. While it may seem problematic to attempt to recover costs from low-income project beneficiaries, donors have not always opposed housing and utility subsidies per se. Instead, they have urged that they be transparent and explicitly targeted at the poor (Joint Housing Team, 1976; World Bank, 1986a).

Moreover, donors have seen their efforts as broadly compatible with informal urbanization in Egypt, a market-driven process entailing ample cost-recovery and mobilization of private savings. Their demonstration projects also drew upon the aided self-help paradigm, the conventional wisdom of the 1970s. This maintained that informal homesteaders had an inherent dynamism. If not treated as criminals, but rather supported through development assistance and land titling (sometimes referred to as regularization), they would be capable of solving their own housing problems (Joint Housing and Community Upgrading Team, 1977; World Bank, 1986a; Tekçe et al., 1994). The following sections examine two projects in the aided self-help category.

Egypt Urban Development Project

This US$14 million World Bank programme nominally ran from 1978–85 and included a component for the upgrading of existing Cairene informal settlements. It was mainly implemented in Manshiet Nasser, a settlement located on state land on the eastern edge of Cairo's historic core. Cost-recovery was to be achieved by the sale of land titles to the upgrading beneficiaries. Servicing was to be coupled with strengthening of the state's sector agencies so as to institutionalize the Bank's approach to shelter provision (World Bank, 1986a).

The Egyptian government had initially requested that the Bank fund its conventional housing projects, rather than supporting an upgrading scheme. Once the project had been apparently agreed on, its start was delayed almost a year because of Egyptian administrative upheavals. In 1978–79, as part of an ostensible decentralization of local government, the housing ministry was restructured and responsibility for upgrading informal areas was transferred to the governorates. The sector agencies, with which the Bank had planned to work, were effectively eliminated. A new coordinating agency, the Executive Agency for Joint Projects (EAJP), was to administer all externally funded housing programmes. This reorganization entirely negated the Bank's institution-building strategy, as the start-up EAJP did not have the legal authority to retain monies produced by cost-recovery and was thus unable to serve as a host for the revolving fund (World Bank, 1986a,b; World Bank consultant, personal communications).

The Manshiet Nasser upgrading component was relatively successful in extending infrastructure. Some 70 000 residents were provided with potable water, sewage and home electricity connections, and benefited from improved roads and refuse collection. Moreover, this systematic commitment of capital seems to have led to substantial private investment and self-help construction (World Bank, 1986a,b).

Still, the ways in which the upgrading actually took place largely negated the Bank's original emphasis on cost-recovery and sustainability. Reduced infrastructure standards, in accordance with the project agreement, were rejected by state utility agencies based in the Cairo governorate; the EAJP was unable to enforce the original terms. Moreover, the Cairo governorate actually went beyond the original agreed upgrading plan, using its own money to provide more comprehensive sewerage services. Importantly, there was no land titling and thus relatively little cost-recovery; the Cairo governorate could not agree with the already upgraded Manshiet Nasser residents over a purchase price. This virtually guaranteed that the upgrading was going to be a one-off project, raising questions as to whether state agencies could afford to maintain the new investments, and illustrating the Bank's failure to institutionalize a more sustainable approach to urban development (World Bank, 1986a,b; El-Messiri, 1989b).

Finally, the Cairo governorate initially had little involvement in project preparation, which was largely carried out by the housing ministry's General Organization for Physical Planning (GOPP) in isolation from the rest of the bureaucracy. Once it did become involved, however, it was dismissive of the Manshiet Nasser upgrading as a minor investment relative to its normal capital expenditures. Not surprisingly, this lack of commitment hampered implementation (World Bank, 1986a,b).

There is probably not enough evidence to demonstrate conclusively that Egyptian government officials deliberately sabotaged the Bank's efforts to make Manshiet Nasser a demonstration of cost-recovery-driven upgrading. Some project consultants did afterwards allege that the state utility agencies had rejected reduced standards, and otherwise obstructed the project because they believed that such upgrading would stimulate further informal urbanization. Moreover, the governorate's unilateral provision of sewerage infrastructure and reluctance to pursue titling in the settlement – the latter will reoccur in the Helwan case – very effectively undermined the project. Conflict between the governorate and the Bank was clearly evident when – following a 1983 reshuffling of governorate personnel – the latter backed an unsuccessful EAJP takeover of the upgrading programme (World Bank, 1986b; Environmental Quality International, quoted by Taher, 1997a).

Helwan Housing and Community Upgrading Project

This was a far more protracted and expensive programme undertaken by USAID in Helwan, an industrial district in the Cairo governorate some 25 miles south of the city centre. Running from August 1978 to August 1988 and costing around US$134 million, the project ended in such public embarrassment for USAID that it never again attempted a housing project in Egypt (USAID, 1988; Taher, 1997b).

The Helwan project was probably compromised from the start by its political context. As with the World Bank project, the Egyptian side originally requested high-standard conventional housing. Not only was this prohibitively expensive, it was obviously intended for middle- to upper-income use. While USAID could not accept such a request, the politics of the US–Egyptian aid relationship meant that neither could they simply reject the scheme. Helwan workers had been highly visible in the notorious January 1977 subsidy riots and other incidents stretching back into the 1960s. The need to provide a visible show of support to Sadat's government, the absence of good alternatives and this background of labour unrest gave Helwan housing a political urgency (USAID consultant, personal communications; Waterbury, 1983; Zetter and Hamza, 1997).

The resulting project – evidently the minimum that would keep the Egyptian government happy – was a single-area demonstration programme. At least nominally, the Helwan project endorsed the USAID preference for aided self-help programmes, emphasizing low-subsidy and cost-recovered housing and upgrading in two discrete components. The first, community upgrading, would take place in existing informal settlements at least partially located on public land. It included electricity, water and sewer networks as well as improved roads, a solid waste-holding site, schools, a vocational centre and community facilities. The upgrading was to be accompanied by titling, ostensibly to facilitate settler investment and home improvements, and also as a means of infrastructure cost-recovery (AID, 1978; Gardner and Van Huyck, 1990; USAID consultant, personal communications).

The second, the Helwan New Community, was a 150-hectare site on which 6697 units of fully serviced core housing were to be built. Intended for industrial workers, Helwan New Community houses were to be auctioned to beneficiaries who would then receive technical assistance and loans for expansion; cost-recovery was built into every phase of the process. The Helwan New Community was initially projected to accommodate 36 000 people, and up to 74 000 when all the units had been fully expanded. Evidently, however, the core model was adopted entirely out of expediency – as the least expensive way to supply a plausible-looking project. From the start, at least one member of USAID staff suspected that the serviced cores could not be built cheaply enough for their low-income buyers (AID, 1978; USAID consultant, personal communications).

The Helwan programme's components also included housing finance and the institutional development of housing agencies. The project sought to a make credits for home improvement available to lower-income Egyptians at reduced levels of subsidy. Following the signature of the project grant agreement, the housing ministry created the EAJP which was given responsibility for the Helwan programme along with the Bank's project (AID, 1978; Gardner and Van Huyck, 1990).

Implementation was plagued by the same problems as with Manshiet Nasser. Some services and infrastructure were provided, but the EAJP was, once again, unable to enforce lower standards. Moreover, there was no land titling. Although the Cairo governorate had received legal authority to do so in 1984, it did not begin a regularization programme until 1986 and insisted that it was obligated to charge what it claimed was the market price for the land. These rates, however, were rejected by the Helwan beneficiaries who realized that the government was not going to demolish communities it had just finished upgrading. In short, they had already been titled de facto by the home-improvement credits. Indeed, there are ample indications from project papers and subsequent research that the Cairo governorate opposed regularization – afraid that it would set precedents for the titling of all informal areas in the governorate as well as giving windfall profits to homesteaders who might sell their newly acquired title (CHF, 1988; El-Messiri, 1989a; Gardner and Van Huyck, 1990; Taher, 1997a).

Moreover, the absence of land sales meant that there was relatively little cost recovery. Even had they gone ahead, the EAJP lacked the legal authority to retain the upgrading revenues and could not have reinvested them in subsequent projects. The home improvement loans – while contributing to the mobilization of private capital in the settlements – did not institutionalize lending to lower-income communities (USAID, 1988; El-Messiri, 1989a; Gardner and Van Huyck, 1990).

Implementation of the Helwan New Community component was protracted and chaotic. As before, USAID and EAJP were unable to insist on lower infrastructure standards. The Egyptian housing ministry later ordered that conventional apartment buildings be constructed in at least three Helwan New Community neighbourhoods. Eventually, USAID and EAJP undertook a 'construction by owner' programme in two of the remainder. Although around 1200 houses were built, with buyers hiring contractors under strict EAJP supervision, there was relatively little self-help. As a demonstration project, the Helwan New Community was a complete failure. Even under 'construction by owner', there were significant subsidies, for example in the form of subsidized construction loans (Gardner and Van Huyck, 1990; Taher, 1997b).

Lastly, USAID failed to achieve significant institutional or governance reforms. While it had originally pressed for the creation of a new agency within the housing ministry, the resulting EAJP had no political base or institutional power with which to carry out USAID's agenda (Gardner and Van Huyck, 1990).

Urban planning

The next category of urban-development interventions comprised three technical assistance programmes, attempted mainly in the 1980s, which were intended to support the Egyptian Government's efforts to plan Cairo's growth. Master plans for the city were mooted in 1956 and 1969. They proposed Cairo's deconcentration and the establishment of satellite cities; the 1969 plan included a ring road. But these were little more than advisory exercises (Abu-Lughod, 1971; Joint Housing and Community Upgrading Team, 1977; Joint Land Policy Team, 1977). From the mid-1970s onwards, the Egyptian government was convinced that the solution to Cairo's growth lay in the construction of brand-new and free-standing desert cities on the edges of the Egyptian Delta – for example the 10th of Ramadan and Sadat cities (Figure 10.2) – which would direct urbanization pressures on the capital away from Egypt's scarce arable areas (Stewart, 1996). By contrast, the donors – while agreeing with the Egyptian desire to protect agricultural land – generally favoured a more modest approach which often included engaging with the informal urbanization process to create semi-formal settlements on desert land within the metropolitan area.

National Urban Policy Study

Undertaken in 1981–82, the National Urban Policy Study (NUPS) was backed by USAID to assess whether the agency should fund the desert cities. Although a country-level study, it included considerable discussion of the capital. While supporting Egypt's objectives of deconcentrating Cairo and protecting arable land from urbanization, the authors of the NUPS nonetheless concluded that the desert-cities programme was unsustainable. The cities lacked a convincing economic rationale, were poorly integrated into

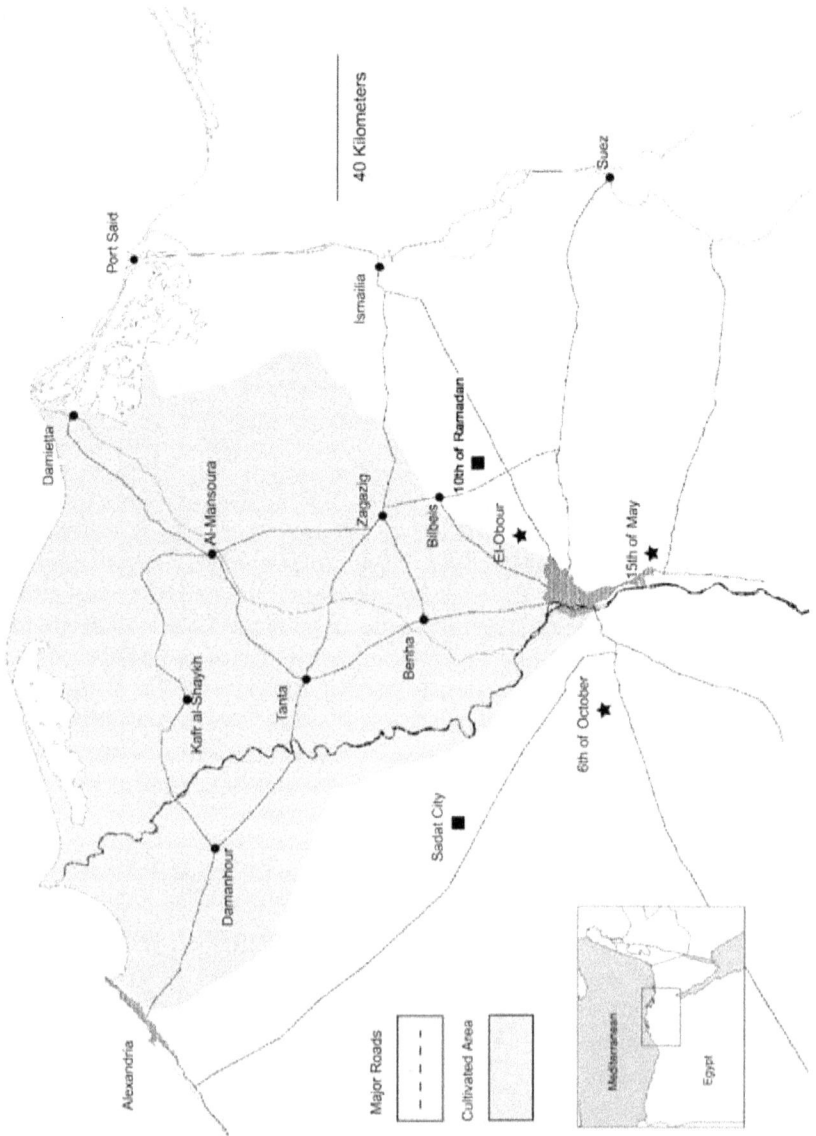

Figure 10.2 Cairo in regional context

the existing national urban system, and had excessively high infrastructure standards. Such a development programme was unlikely to recover its costs, and would probably exhaust national investment funds and slow down Egypt's overall growth. Instead, the NUPS recommended investment in less expensive and better integrated satellite cities on Cairo's desert periphery, for example El-Obour, 6 October and 15 May, as well as desert sites and services development for would-be informal homesteaders (PADCO Inc. et al., 1981,1982; interview with USAID staff).

Perhaps not surprisingly, the NUPS was rejected by the development minister – who, inconveniently, was an important advocate of the new cities strategy – on its submission in 1982. The study was never officially distributed within the Egyptian government or formally acted on (McNair, 1989; Gardner and Van Huyck, 1990).

Extension of Municipal Services

Begun in August 1984 by the World Bank in conjunction with the Cairo and Giza governorates, this was an abortive sites-and-services project to prepare desert areas around Cairo for semi-formal development. It ended prematurely in September 1985 without implementation, because of the reluctance of Egyptian state agencies to make land available to the project and the Cairo governorate's hostility to the sites-and-services concept.

Originally titled the 'Land Assembly' programme, Extension of Municipal Services (EMS) was a pilot project intended to attract informal homesteaders away from Cairo's remaining agricultural areas on to desert land. The planned and serviced lots to be produced by the programme were intended to be more affordable than those in agricultural subdivisions. Homesteaders and builders would then be able to put up shelter at prices that they and their customers could afford; cost-recovery was intended to make the programme self-sustaining (K. Tayler and I. Green, personal communication; interviews with World Bank consultants).

The preliminary phase of EMS required that planners locate and design serviced sites in the Cairo and Giza governorates. These would then need governorate approval. The approved designs would form the basis of a loan to the Egyptian government to fund project implementation. EMS foundered in the first phase, however, over two issues. First, the concept assumed that the government's ownership of most desert land would facilitate site acquisition. But the EMS planners quickly discovered that most such land on the city periphery was under the control of the Egyptian military – which was reluctant to permit its civil development – or had already been allocated to land-development companies, or was otherwise inaccessible. The only available sites were too far into the desert. In the Giza governorate, this effectively precluded further planning. In the Cairo governorate, it made the site eventually selected less attractive to informal homesteaders and entailed infrastructure costs beyond the parameters of the programme. Second, EMS was derailed by governorate opposition to what it viewed as state-sponsored slum-building. The then governor of Cairo – a former senior military officer – described such low-income settlements in tactical terms as 'encircling' the city and threatening it (K. Tayler and I. Green, personal communication; interviews with World Bank consultants).

The Greater Cairo Master Scheme

In August 1981 the Paris planning agency, the Institut d'Aménagement et d'Urbanisme de la Région d'Ile-de-France (IAURIF), began a technical and financial assistance programme with the GOPP in support of the latter's preparation of a new Cairo master plan. The plan was submitted in May 1982 and, like the NUPS, emphasized the deconcentration of Cairo and the protection of agricultural areas through the creation of residential alternatives. To achieve these goals it recommended a series of measures, some of which seemed to be based as much on the replanning of Paris in the 1970s as on conditions in Cairo (GOPP et al., 1982; Elkhishin, 1990).

First, it recommended the division of the metropolitan area into 'homogeneous sectors' – administratively uniform and economically specialized units which would be self-contained with respect to services – in order to limit urban sprawl and traffic-congestion (Figure 10.3). Second, it proposed the creation of 'new settlements', satellite communities outside the built-up area; these resembled the communities proposed by EMS in terms of their morphology, projected growth and infrastructure standards. Third, it advised the establishment of 'development corridors' linking Cairo with other existing and planned urban areas, as well as blocking growth elsewhere. Lastly, it included the building of a ring road which, besides its transportation functions, was probably intended as a physical barrier to Cairo's outward and mostly informal growth. Still, the plan put more emphasis on the other elements for lessening the consumption of arable land (GOPP et al., 1982; GOPP/IAURIF, 1986a,b).

IAURIF/GOPP cooperation continued throughout the mid–1990s, and their work remains the basis of the city's official master plan. Nonetheless, there is little evidence that any of its components – except the ring road, the construction of which started in 1987 and continued through 1999 – has been implemented. There has been no administrative division of the city into homogeneous sectors. Nine years after the plan was officially adopted, its elements had not been communicated through the bureaucracy, which continued to operate according to the earlier master plan of the late 1960s. Moreover, the new settlements element remained unimplemented through the 1980s – apparently because of interministerial rivalries and obstructions of the type that had compromised the implementation of EMS. While some of the proposed sites have been included on a new communities list published by the housing ministry in 1996, they seem to have been transformed into conventional housing projects or upper-income developments (Elkhishin, 1990; Sims, 1990; IAURIF/GOPP, 1991; Ministry of Housing, Utilities and Urban Communities, 1996).

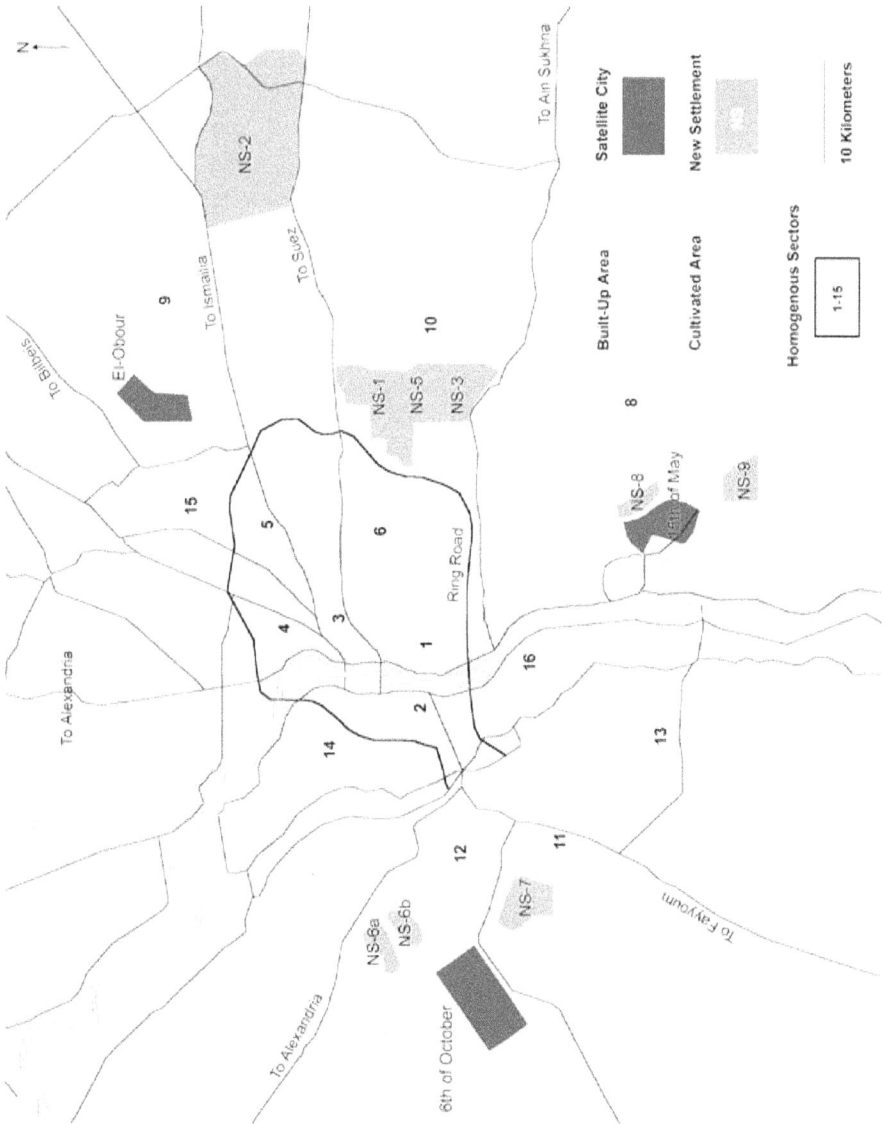

Figure 10.3 Cairo
Urban Planning Project

Greater Cairo Wastewater Project

The Greater Cairo Wastewater Project (GCWWP) was an approximately £1.5 billion programme – funded by an international consortium of donors – to rehabilitate and expand the metropolitan wastewater network (Figure 10.4). Begun in the late 1970s, it continued on the east bank throughout 1999. In a category by itself, it also differs from most of the other projects considered here in that it is generally regarded as a success – having provided wastewater services to millions of Cairenes and ended the sewage floods that had plagued the city since the mid–1960s. USAID, whose remit included the west bank of the Nile, provided about US$900 million in Cairo Sewerage I and II grant packages. These were used to construct several collector systems, serving many of the informal areas in metropolitan Giza, as well as to rehabilitate a wastewater treatment plant and build another. Similarly extensive investments – including a deep spine tunnel, pumping stations and a new treatment plant – have been undertaken on the east bank (where the Egyptian government has also constructed two treatment plants of its own). The British grant package there, however, was significantly more limited, and the works were also funded by European credits as well as a significant Egyptian contribution amounting to about 60 per cent of their cost (AID, 1984; EQI, 1988; ASCG Inc., 1992; Kell et al., 1993; AMBRIC et al., 1995; USAID, undated; AMBRIC[5] staff, personal communications).

Despite this enormous commitment of resources, there nonetheless appear to be several problems with Cairo's wastewater provision and its sustainability. First, it is not always clear to what extent informal communities within the GCWWP service area are actually connected to the network. On the west bank, USAID's assistance included US$140 million for 561 000 local connections to some 2 million Egyptians, probably most of whom were in informal neighbourhoods of the agricultural subdivision type. On the east bank, however, donors did not provide for a similar connection programme. The General Organization for Sanitary Drainage (GOSD) – the state agency responsible for system operations and local connections – is not thought to have much capacity to undertake such hookups. Donor efforts to address this situation, via participatory projects, are dealt with in the final set of case studies (AMBRIC et al., 1991; Miller and Kachinsky, 1993; USAID, undated; AMBRIC staff, personal communications).

Second, especially on the west bank, Cairo's continuing informal growth has produced wastewater flows in excess of the network's original design values. A February 1991 System Load Review, prepared by the project's consultants, estimated that existing treatment plants and pumping stations would be operating at capacity by 1995–97, and recommended further investments of US$1.6 billion – including US$50 million annually for local connections – to 2010. Barring such expansion, unmet demand is likely to increase. A subsequent 1993 Strategic Report predicted that in 1995 the network would serve 72 per cent of the Giza governorate's metropolitan population, but that – without further expansion – this would drop to 58 per cent

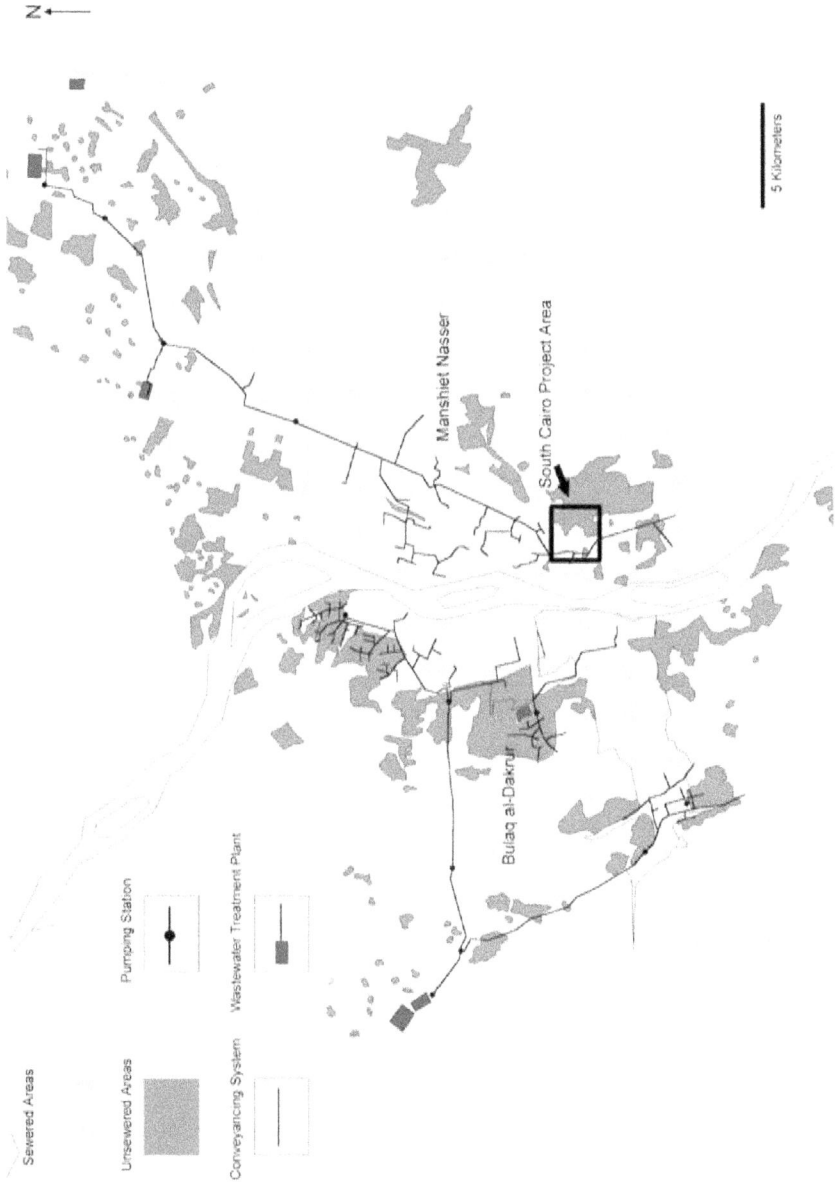

Figure 10.4 Great Cairo Wastewater Scheme

by 2010, because of population increases in unserviced outlying areas (AMBRIC et al., 1991, 1993).

Third, in the mid–1990s USAID declined to fund this proposed 'Cairo Sewerage III' system expansion because the Egyptian government had failed to raise wastewater tariffs to pay for the system's operations and maintenance costs. This is a long-running issue: GOSD did not levy sewage charges until 1985. Since beginning the expansion of the west bank system in the mid–1980s, USAID had pressed for a series of phased tariff increases, intended to lead to complete recovery of these costs. Despite some limited improvements, senior government officials – probably successive Cairo governors and prime ministers – resisted USAID's demands; actual recovery of wastewater expenses from consumers has been at only about 3 per cent (USAID, 1993; interview with USAID official).

Such below-market-cost services have long been seen as an entitlement – part of the putative 'social contract' – intended to guarantee access to the poor. Nonetheless, as critics have noted, they also provide a substantial subsidy to upper-income and institutional consumers. Recent research has indicated that households connected to the city's water and wastewater networks are charged less than a third of what those without such connections pay for such services. In this context, it does not seem entirely unreasonable to charge customers for some portion of the difference to cover, at the very least, operations and maintenance costs (Development Alternatives Inc. et al., 1999a; Hoehn and Krieger, 2000).

Finally, because of GOSD's inability to recover operations and maintenance costs, its dependence on public subsidies for over three-quarters of its budget, and general institutional weakness, there are significant doubts about its ability to maintain the wastewater system. A recent study reported that USAID-provided infrastructure was already showing signs of deterioration and predicted reductions in the quality of wastewater treatment and system failures (Development Alternatives Inc. et al., 1999b).

Participatory urban upgrading

This is the final category of interventions to be considered. Since the mid–1980s, donors in Egypt have attempted a number of programmes explicitly framed in the participatory idiom, whereby project beneficiaries are supposed to be involved in all aspects of the provision process. Most notable has been the Nasriya Upgrading Project in the Upper Egyptian city of Aswan, undertaken by the German aid agency GTZ (German Technical Cooperation). This is considered to have been successful and to have had substantially more beneficiary involvement than the earlier top-down World Bank and USAID projects (Zetter and Hamza, 1997). Despite the unquestionably good intentions of its proponents, however, this upgrading model has not proven to be so easily replicable when applied to the provision of local wastewater connections in Cairo – as suggested by the following two cases.

GTZ in Cairo

Capitalizing on the success of the Nasriya project, GTZ has attempted two participatory upgrading projects in Cairo since the mid–1990s. The first, in one of Manshiet Nasser's neighbourhoods, was temporarily halted in 1998 following the government's announcement that it intended to replan (if not demolish) the entire community. Nonetheless, GTZ persevered and the project – to provide water and wastewater connections as well as street paving – is in implementation.

The second, in the Giza neighbourhood of Bulaq al-Dakrur, is also in implementation but had initially stalled in the preparation phase after GTZ's proposal was rejected by the Giza governor in December 1995. In formulating the programme proposal, GTZ's consultants had difficulties in identifying specific projects around which to mobilize the community. One of Giza's older informal urban-periphery settlements, Bulaq was relatively well served with basic infrastructure. GTZ was limited to recommending objectives such as planning the area's remaining agricultural land, covering over redundant irrigation canals, expanding community facilities, and improving neighbourhood employment opportunities. When the proposal was submitted to the governor of Giza, who was aware of the larger programme being considered for Manshiet Nasser, he insisted that GTZ technical assistance had to be accompanied by 'major capital funding'. Without this, he indicated to the project team, he could not justify its approval politically. Following his departure, however, the project did get under way and has consisted of sanitation and street-front beautification efforts.

South Cairo Wastewater

In February 1996 a British donor reported that, despite significant investments in Cairo's wastewater system, many areas on the east bank remained unserved, and concluded that GOSD lacked the capacity to fill this deficit. In September 1997 a £4.6 million pilot programme was submitted to assist GOSD in installing wastewater connections in two impoverished informal neighbourhoods in the South Cairo district (Figure 10.4). This would be undertaken in cooperation with two nongovernmental organizations (NGOs), the Coptic Evangelical Organization for Social Services (CEOSS) and the Near East Foundation (NEF), which would enter the chosen communities in order to mobilize their participation as a necessary precondition for implementation.

The donor had not received official approval by Spring 1998, apparently because of Egyptian unhappiness with the project's NGO component. Indeed, the Egyptian government is generally reluctant to permit NGOs to undertake social mobilization (White, 1986). Some in the state's network of community development associations, moreover, have opposed the idea of a Christian NGO working in a Muslim community (AbdelRahman,

1999). Tellingly, the donor subsequently resubmitted the proposal minus CEOSS and NEF – allowing the Egyptian side to propose NGOs for the mobilization role.

Although the Egyptian government finally gave its approval in spring 2000, the project – at least as originally formulated – is unlikely ever to reach implementation. Donor staff have become concerned that GOSD does not have the capability even to participate in the project, and is suspicious that it has been seeking to divert their assistance so as to service a more affluent area nearby (anonymous donor, personal communications).

CONCLUSIONS

Despite the diversity of these cases, all suggest that sustainable development in Cairo is not an Egyptian government priority.

First, the Egyptian government has – regardless of the type of programme or donor methodology – consistently adhered to a *narrow definition of urban development as the provision of infrastructure*; this is also probably because construction contracts have long been a key means of allocating patronage (Waterbury, 1976). For example, the upgrading programmes attempted by the World Bank and USAID were successful only as one-off construction projects. Few of their policy-reform and institution-building components were implemented or had a lasting impact. Similarly, the only substantial result of the IAURIF technical cooperation process was the ring road, the idea for which long predated French involvement. This point is further reflected in the success of the international wastewater consortium in installing a city-wide network, but the failure of the Egyptian wastewater sector both in maintaining it and keeping pace with rising demand. The governor of Giza's resistance to GTZ's participatory programmes in the absence of capital inflows suggests that the bias in favour of construction persists.

Second, such consumption of international aid flows takes place *without concern for planning and sustainability*. Again, the initial World Bank and USAID programmes were predicated on what they hoped was to be a self-sustaining process of cost-recovery and reinvestment – demonstrating to the Egyptian government that policy reforms leading to a more extractive approach to shelter provision would allow it to cope with Cairo's steadily expanding population. But in contrast, the housing ministry and the governorates preferred a high-standard and highly subsidized form of housing which the state could not afford to provide in adequate quantities, and thwarted the implementation of any alternative. The failed NUPS, EMS and IAURIF urban-planning efforts, whatever their other deficiencies, were intended to protect Cairo's agricultural periphery from the encroachments of informal urbanization and facilitate the economically sustainable management of the city's growth.

Further, the resistance of successive prime ministers and Cairo governors to reducing wastewater subsidies is likely to have very negative long-term implications for the sustainability of wastewater provision on the east and west banks. Some measure of cost-recovery is necessary, not only so that the hapless GOSD will be able to maintain the expensive investments which donors have made in the Cairo sewerage system, but also so that it might be able to expand the system into underserved informal areas, especially on the east bank.

Third, these problems of sustainability result, in part, from a political economy in which the state *distributes top-down without corresponding taxation or other forms of social extraction.* Yet again, in the World Bank and USAID projects, the state added considerable subsidies to the upgrading process, made little effort to recover capital expenses, and obstructed donor efforts to link supply with demand via cost. In the provision of sewage service, the process was again entirely top-down, with the state not trying to recoup capital or even operations and maintenance costs.

Lastly, top-down distribution without extraction entails an *absence of state accountability to demobilized beneficiaries.* This is the essence of how the distributive authoritarian regime structures Egyptian state–society relations. The Egyptian government's repeated rejection of donor efforts to regularize informal communities, its obstruction of the cost-recovery process and its resistance to semi-formal desert development, are all part of avoiding a formal governance relationship in which the governed, as tax-payers, are entitled to make demands of those who govern them. Instead, state agencies appear to prefer a combination of indifference with a patron–client relationship in which distribution is firmly the prerogative of the state. The British attempt in South Cairo to support a participatory self-help alternative was probably resisted both because it threatened this monopoly on service provision, and because externally financed community mobilization fundamentally contradicts the logic of authoritarian power relations.

In short, no development methodology predicated on social mobilization – essential for sustainable interventions – is likely to be successful in Egypt while the post–1952 political order remains in place.

CHAPTER ELEVEN

The sustainability of community development in El Mezquital, Guatemala City

Emma Grant

The objectives of this chapter are to analyse the sustainability of community development initiatives and processes in El Mezquital, and to identify
the characteristics of those initiatives considered sustainable.[1] El Mezquital
is located in the south of Guatemala City. The settlement originated from
the single most successful land invasion in Guatemala during the 1980s,
and is one of the largest in Central America (3500 families). Data on which
this chapter is based were collected from research carried out from May to
August 1999.

The chapter outlines the history of the community in El Mezquital, and
evaluates the principal interventions of external organizations, including
governmental institutions, international agencies and non-governmental
organizations (NGOs). The evidence suggests that, although these external
organizations have played an important part in community development,
their strategies have often been top-down, non-participatory and non-
transparent. The role of government in the community appears to have
been the least significant of the interventions, and often motivated by
patronage. Thus long-term sustainability remains questionable. Conversely, community-based groups which have generated projects and programmes to meet needs perceived from within the community have been
relatively more sustainable.

Sustainability is conceptualized from two perspectives. First, there is a
focus on the process of achieving sustainability which, although limited in
terms of tangible outputs, has nevertheless been crucial in developing
capacity-building and self-reliance in El Mezquital. Second, as explained in
more detail below, a holistic conceptualization of sustainability is explored
which embraces a diverse portfolio of community needs and aspirations
linked especially to poverty-reduction measures for the present generation
of households.

BACKGROUND[2]

Guatemala is ranked as number 117 by the UN Development Programme's Human Development Index (UNDP, 1997). This is among the

lowest of countries considered to have achieved an intermediate level of development. The country is characterized by inequality in the distribution of resources and by social inequalities. Despite the fact that the GDP per capita of Guatemala is one of the highest in Central America, the country has extremely high levels of poverty: 72 per cent of the rural population and 34 per cent of the urban population are defined as 'extremely poor', meaning that they cannot afford the minimum food requirements (World Bank, 1996).

Guatemala City is characterized by marked inequalities. The middle-income residential areas provide a sharp contrast with the multitude of vulnerable settlements lacking in basic services, having poor-quality housing and presenting hazardous living conditions for the population. On the outskirts of these vulnerable settlements, there are often groups of people who scavenge waste from the settlements for their food and livelihood. Thus, even within such informal settlements, inequality in the distribution of resources and contrast in living environments is evident.

There is little accurate documentation of the vulnerable settlements of Guatemala City and the size of their population. Within Guatemala, the civil war and indigenous rights issues have dominated research until recently, and there is a marked absence of literature documenting issues surrounding low-income informal settlements. Nevertheless, a study by De Alfaro and González (1997) identified 161 areas in Guatemala City as vulnerable, housing a population of approximately 250 000 people, out of a total population of 823 301 in the Metropolitan Area of Guatemala City. Of the 161 vulnerable settlements, 111 have been formed since 1992. Despite the obvious need for programmes to support the development of these areas (basic services, social infrastructure, etc.), 'institutional intervention has decreased' (Gellert and Palma, 1999). The Guatemalan state is 'rolling back', allowing the market to take on the role of principal economic actor while the state withdraws from any tangible role, whether in promoting development or curbing the inequalities and imbalances of the market. The lack of state activity or contribution to community development means that communities must increasingly rely on themselves, and on the assistance of NGOs and partnerships with service providers, to ensure access to basic services and social development.

HISTORY OF EL MEZQUITAL SETTLEMENT

In 1984 a group of approximately 1500 families settled on land surrounding the Colony of El Mezquital, in the south of Guatemala City (zone 12). The origin of the settlers was very diverse geographically (from many different departments of the country) as well as ethnically (Quiché, Mame and mixed-race). The common denominator of all the invading families was poverty. The occupied land belonged, partly, to the reserved area of the Colony of El Mezquital (land set aside for recreational or environmental protection purposes). The rest belonged to a private landowner. The area was declared uninhabitable as it was so close to the ravines and due to the seismic instability in the area.

The first actions of the community centred around defending their land occupation. In addition to police attempts to evict the community, the invaders had to confront threats from hostile local communities whose recreational space had been invaded. These defensive actions led to the consolidation of the settlement which, in turn, strengthened community organization. The creation of the Association of United Residents of El Mezquital (AVAUME), a collaboration of the *juntas directivas* (management boards) of the different subdivisions, gave leadership to the community.

From 1987 to 1992, AVAUME worked in conjunction with the National Reconstruction Committee to develop the settlement, including dividing up and legalizing plots, and improving housing and infrastructure. Other institutions, such as Medicos sin Fronteras (MSF) and the United Nations Children's Fund (UNICEF), supported the community organizations as they worked towards improving the settlement. With time, new development projects were started that required a new type of management, legally entitled to handle funds, so a cooperative was begun in 1990. It was named the Integrated Cooperative of Housing, Esfuerzo and Esperanza (COIVEES). The organization had multiple components: administrative, supervisory, education, water, credit, building materials and housing. In 1995, COIVEES, the *juntas directivas* and UNICEF embarked on a large urbanization project in El Mezquital, relying substantially on community labour and participation. This project, the Programa de Urbanisación de El Mezquital (PROUME), is described below.

At the same time, a number of other community organizations developed, including the Representantes del Programa Integrado de Salud (REPROIN-SAS), a community health-workers' programme founded with UNICEF's support, and Unidas para Vivir Mejor (UPAVIM), a women's group.

OVERVIEW OF COMMUNITY DEVELOPMENT INITIATIVES

Development in El Mezquital has been based on the interaction of different organizations – government institutions, NGOs, international organizations and community organizations. It has occurred on the understanding that living conditions in the settlement cannot be effectively improved by the isolated efforts of either the market, the state, international cooperation or the community.

From the settlement's founding, external organizations have been involved in community development initiatives in the area. Organizations that have worked extensively in El Mezquital from the very beginning are Fundación para el Desarrollo Comunitario (FUNDESCO), MSF, UNICEF and the Catholic Church. In addition, a multitude of Guatemalan NGOs and popular groups have had a strong presence in the settlement at various stages.

Some of the community's most basic achievements, such as the introduction of water service, the first latrines, the creation of the cooperative and the REPROINSAS programme, were dependent on external support.

Government intervention in El Mezquital has been minimal. The National Reconstruction Committee worked in the settlement during the early years when the community was consolidating, but this was a fairly brief intervention that did not focus on community capacity or involve community consultation. Later, a new government body was set up, the Inter-institutional Committee for Precarious Areas (COINAP), with the aim of coordinating the work of the public and private sectors in Guatemala City. COINAP collaborated in a programme with UNICEF and the community to develop the settlement. However, community members were disparaging concerning the contribution made by COINAP.

Among the community and NGOs, UNICEF's Basic Urban Services Programme played an important role. The programme started off as an experiment in El Mezquital in 1986, and was terminated when the urbanization programme of El Mezquital (PROUME, discussed below) came to an end. The initial plan of the Basic Urban Services Programme, which was modified over the years, sought to improve material living conditions as well as working conditions. Among the first priorities of the programme were ownership and suitability of land; housing provision; public services; and social infrastructure (e.g. schools). UNICEF also initiated the Integrated Health Programme which trained community health workers (known as REPROINSAS).

At the end of the 1980s, the National Reconstruction Committee submitted a proposal to the World Bank requesting a loan for a municipal development programme in a vulnerable area. This loan was approved in November 1989, but it was never paid out due to the closure of the World Bank programme in Guatemala. In 1993, the original project was taken up again. Invited by COIVEES and UNICEF, a World Bank evaluation mission visited El Mezquital to ascertain levels of community organization and participation. In 1995, a community improvement programme was initiated, entitled the Programme for the Urbanization of El Mezquital (PROUME), aiming to improve infrastructure, drinking water and housing improvement, as well as creating a main transport road through the settlement with access to the market. It also included the relocation of families who were located in areas that impeded developments.

Other important community initiatives are the development of various community committees and women's groups, and the Integrated Health Programme (REPROINAS) supported by UNICEF.

After 15 years of community work supported by external organizations, almost all the families in El Mezquital have access to water; COIVEES supplies 2537 water meters with good-quality water, 365 days per year, a better service than most residential areas receive in the rest of the city. Ninety-five per cent of families have electricity in their homes, some with electricity meters. The entire population of El Mezquital, 3500 families, have sewers and rainwater drains in their areas.

SUSTAINABILITY

Having outlined the principal programmes and the development of community organizations in El Mezquital, the following sections evaluate the sustainability of these key developments in El Mezquital, and attempt to identify the pertinent characteristics of projects which are considered to be sustainable.

The working definition of sustainability deployed here is based on the definition of the World Commission on Environment and Development (the Brundtland Commission):

Sustainable development is development that meets the needs of the present without compromising the ability of future generations to meet their own needs.

(WCED, 1987).

According to this definition, 'meeting the needs of the present' is an integral part of sustainability, hence poverty reduction is central to the definition. This is important as the initiatives and processes are analysed not merely in terms of their 'durability', but also in terms of their contribution to community development. This view is in line with Marcuse (1998), who argues that:

sustainability is not a goal for a programme – many bad programmes are sustainable – but a constraint: its absence may limit the usefulness of a good programme. If sustainability means the ability not only to formulate and operate a desirable urban programme, but also to see it continue without detracting from other, also desirable goals, then the concept may usefully emphasize the importance of a long-term practicality to the consideration of such programmes.

(Marcuse, 1998: 104).

Sustainability must be understood to encompass the long-term durability of projects – projects should not collapse on withdrawal of external support, but local capacity and interest should be such that projects continue to function when external agencies withdraw support. Moreover, as 'the needs of the present' inherently implies an adequate quality of life for all, some element of social justice will be important in establishing the sustainability of programmes and processes. Without underplaying the importance of the economic framework of a programme, sustainability is perceived to be more holistic than merely financial sustainability.

GOVERNMENT INTERVENTIONS

According to the majority of those interviewed (both within the community and non-community stakeholders), the government played a minimal role in supporting community development. Few interviewees referred to government interventions, and when they did it was almost always in reference to the obstacles they put in the path of community work. As the president of the Administrative Board of COIVEES sums up: 'The government did nothing, absolutely nothing'.

Government intervention or support in El Mezquital, from the beginning to the present day, has indeed been scarce: some initial work through the National Reconstruction Committee was carried out, and local government is responsible for one health centre with a part-time nurse for an area covering 3500 families, and a few schools. When compared with the social infrastructure built through the organized work of the community in conjunction with international agencies, this seems very limited.

COINAP also collaborated to some extent in a community development programme with UNICEF. However, few community interviewees were aware of it having played any role in any interventions. Interviews with community leaders identified several characteristics that reflected their perceptions of government interventions. First, they underestimated community capacity: government officials had little respect for community skills and capacity, and this attitude was directed chiefly at the community leaders and those responsible for the various developments in the settlement. Second, it appears that opportunistic exploitation of the organizational capacity of the community, or attempts to manipulate the community according to specific party-political interests, took place. Third, there was an incapacity to respond to the needs of the population – from the very beginning until now, the community members have been forced to rely on their own solutions to the multiple problems confronting them, with no significant government input. Neither in water provision, nor in general community urbanization, nor in housing construction has the government played a significant role.

Given the definition of sustainable development above, it is difficult to refer to sustainability in a context where interventions have not been characterized by social justice and have not met the needs of the present.

COMMUNITY COMMITTEES

Since 1984 the main community organizations (COIVEES and the *juntas directivas*) have accomplished the large part of their original objectives: legalization of the land (under way), and water, electricity and housing improvements. The *juntas directivas* of the settlement subdivisions were especially committed to legalization of the land, while COIVEES was geared towards housing improvement and provision of water.

The community organizations in El Mezquital achieved the only successful, large land invasion to take place in Guatemala during the 1980s. They successfully lobbied and worked to prevent eviction, and to get basic services, infrastructure and health services; they acquired collective skills in negotiation – with international organizations, NGOs and, to a lesser extent, governmental bodies – and management, and personal skills such as budgeting and public speaking. Many of the initiatives of these community organizations have proven to be sustainable, for example, the introduction of water and sanitation which continues to function and is maintained throughout the settlement (principally by COIVEES). These projects involved extensive community participation, which reflected the priority residents gave to these issues – this is clearly fundamental in the sustainability of the project, both in terms of 'meeting present needs' and also in terms of durability.

However, since the achievement of the main successes in the settlement (the legalization process, electricity, housing, services), the community organizations have not reassessed their current situation and concerns, implying the need for a new prioritization of problems and needs in order to orientate their future actions. For example, most of those interviewed stated that they had no clear idea of the new objectives of the community organizations, although they believed that issues such as housing, education, employment and violence were of high priority. Neither AVAUME nor the *juntas directivas* have been restarted or replaced by other community-based organizations, creating a vacuum which COIVEES, the largest and most consolidated of all the community organizations, cannot fill, as its nature and goals are different. Where the *juntas directivas* have ceased to function, this is in large part because their original mandate has been accomplished (overseeing the legalization of land tenure).

Since the end of the PROUME project, COIVEES has carried out various different kinds of project, including a building block manufacturing enterprise (begun in 1998; this initiative lasted only three months due to a part being broken and stolen, and never replaced); and a waste collection project (which relied on one or two waste collection lorries that unfortunately provided an irregular service). COIVEES functions in part as a service provider (administering water consumption and payment), has a capable, established committee, and shows no signs of disintegrating even without the support of UNICEF in terms of advice and finance. However, without a vision for future developments, it is difficult to see how this community organization will be able to develop plans and proposals to implement any further poverty reduction programmes.

Financial constraints for developing and initiating projects remain critical after the withdrawal of UNICEF. It remains to be seen how successful the community is in negotiation with local government, an area in which they have, to date, shown little capacity. If sustainability is understood to mean continual development, rather than remaining static, COIVEES appears to be sustainable only as a service provider (administering the water projects) unless NGOs or local government change their policy towards the settlement, providing some support for community development projects. The high poverty levels in the community are not conducive to self-financed community projects. Reliance on some external support, whether from government or NGOs, does not in itself make the committee unsustainable: if committees are able successfully to negotiate support for projects, these negotiating skills mean the committees are sustainable. Projects that involve other actors are 'partnership projects', an increasingly popular mechanism for carrying out community development programmes:

> the concept of sustainable urban development has been elaborated far beyond the environmental domain, including other fundamental aspects (political, cultural, etc.) on their own and/or associated with environmental/ecological aspects, and also encompassing a multi-actor approach.
>
> (Werna et al., 1998: 107).

WOMEN'S GROUPS

Integrated Health Programme – REPROINSAS

The Integrated Health Programme began in 1986, driven by the need to confront the serious health problems in the community, and faced by indifference or inefficiency of the relevant government bodies. It was based on a system of microzones or subdivisions, each comprising approximately 50 families, into which the community had divided themselves. In each microzone the families elected one person as a community health worker to represent the Integrated Health Programme. All those elected were women.

The community health workers receive community health training for one year, with the support of UNICEF. They provide healthcare for the sick, and have built up a very good relationship with the community. Their first achievement was in increasing the levels of vaccination within the community. From this auspicious beginning, they set about making other changes within the community, not exclusively in health but in other social areas too, such as literacy schemes. Recently, workers have been trained in HIV/AIDS prevention, as well as legal training for dealing with violence against women, both domestic violence and violence within the community.

The Integrated Health Programme model heralded the beginning of a more complex organization which was replicated in other areas of the city: in 1990 the first Community Pharmacy was founded and the Foundation of Courage and Prosperity (FUNDAESPRO) was established, which provided a network of community health workers across the city, and which rapidly expanded into other vulnerable settlements. At the time of writing, there are between 600 and 700 community health workers in 11 vulnerable settlements in the city, working in psychology, legal advice and literacy, the last in coordination with the National Literacy Commission. The fact that the programme is community based and of high priority has contributed to this scaling-up. Moreover, the community health workers also began to change the perception and status of women through their role in public activities, moving out of the private sphere, and through their major role in community development. This process contributes to the sustainability of the community organization.

At the time of writing, the Integrated Health Programme continues to grow. This is principally thanks to the growing awareness and organization of the women who are part of the programme, and the support of the FUN-DAESPRO network. At the end of the 1980s the Integrated Health Programme and the community health workers started off a complex and profound development process, creating a space for reflection regarding identity and the particular problems faced by women. This gradual process met with resentment and opposition of many men within the community, even of the family members of REPROINSAS themselves. Many REPROIN-SAS mentioned how their training had personal significance for them, as well as contributing to women's empowerment within the community:

> Individually, each one of us has grown, and each one grows together with her children. Now the little girls don't grow up so timid, their mothers work and they too benefit from it, and the little boys too. I am a very different person now to what I used to be. I was really shy, I wouldn't talk to anybody.

> (REPROINSA, focus group, 1999).

The voluntary nature of community health work is significant for its sustainability: it reflects the fact that their work is of high priority. However, it also means that in times of extreme financial hardship, community health work could cease as women are forced to spend more time in income-earning activities. Although some developments have been made to provide income contributions for women (for example, through community pharmacies and shops), the project is not yet financially sustainable without some support from UNICEF to finance training. Nevertheless, as discussed in the definition of sustainability above, the fact that the programme requires support for training does not make it unsustainable: it is rooted in a partnership approach which relies on UNICEF to support this aspect.

Women United for a Better Life

Women United for a Better Life (Unidas para Vivir Mejor, UPAVIM) was an organization which went through a similar process to the REPROINSAS in El Mezquital. This organization was founded in 1988, in order to address the problem of children's health and the situation of women living in extreme poverty and those exposed to domestic violence. UPAVIM started in loaned office space, with three members and a small handicraft workshop. A few years later the group had managed to construct a four-storey building, standing out in the widespread poverty of the settlement.

The creation and growth of UPAVIM showed three important characteristics. First, the search for economic sustainability of the organization's members (all women), which would allow them to confront daily survival. Second, a focus on the subdivision La Esperanza, where the community was in most need, which became a point of identity for the specific community in question. Third, no support was received from the government or from international organizations such as UNICEF or the World Bank, and hence it achieved a degree of financial independence – not total, but certainly critical – which gave the organization a certain sustainability. The main funding comes from UPAVIM's own handicraft workshop and donations from North American religious organizations.

UPAVIM currently has 67 members, more than 50 of whom work in the handicraft workshop. They also have a clinic, nursery, laboratory, Programme for the Healthy Child, dental clinic, women's breast-feeding programme, and a scholarship programme which supports 650 children in their studies. UPAVIM works for the financial independence of women, and the working hours are flexible to accommodate the other chores and needs of the women. The organization has a board of directors in each project, and regular board and general meetings. Every two years there are elections for the committee members of UPAVIM. These factors are important in maintaining a transparent managerial structure, as is the two-yearly changeover in committee members.

Like the Integrated Health Programme, UPAVIM constitutes an environment where women's dignity and self-esteem can develop. The women's earnings from their participation have important implications for the sustainability of the project, and for the change in women's roles within the community: as the president of UPAVIM declared, 'The possibility of earning a salary, albeit small, allows us to make decisions in our homes'. Nevertheless, the North American churches continue to part-finance this institution, meaning that it is not entirely financially sustainable.

In El Mezquital, the Integrated Health Programme and UPAVIM are examples of capacity-building and empowerment of women, a process that takes place at both individual and collective levels. This characteristic increases the commitment of women to the organizations, as they can see the benefits that they themselves derive from the programme. This is critical in contributing to the sustainability of the project.

PROGRAMME FOR THE URBANISATION OF EL MEZQUITAL (PROUME)

PROUME was the outcome of a multi-institutional effort and community input. COIVEES and the *juntas directivas* of El Mezquital and the community themselves were involved in administration and labour for the programme. The World Bank provided the major part of funding. The UNICEF Basic Urban Services Programme provided training and technical assistance for the community organizations managing the implementation of the projects.

PROUME carried out the majority of its target projects, with only a short delay in the two-year timetable initially stipulated. Loans were given for

450 completely new houses to be constructed, out of the 1000 foreseen; two new wells were sunk, extending provision of water to the whole community; pavements, sewers and rainwater drainage were installed in all the subdivisions; and tenants situated in areas needed for development were relocated. In 1997 the FUNDAESPRO clinic was constructed with funds from PROUME. However, PROUME failed to achieve certain objectives, such as construction of a fire station and creation of green areas.

Through PROUME, water and sanitation have been implemented throughout the settlement, and housing developments in some parts. Each household pays for its own water consumption every month, and there have been no significant problems in collection of payments. Projects have been funded, managed and directed by external agencies alongside community organizations, with varying degrees of community participation. In addition to the infrastructural achievements, however, capacity-building and financial independence are critical factors in evaluating the sustainability of the programme – what is the legacy these agencies have left behind now that, for the most part, they have decreased their support to the settlement in a belief that the level of development achieved is adequate?

According to community interviews, projects frequently failed to consider employment initiatives. Despite the fact that, alongside the Basic Urban Services Programme, one of the fundamental components was to be improvements in employment conditions, in fact PROUME restricted itself to the provision of infrastructure. PROUME temporarily improved the employment situation in the community, with up to 1000 people on the payroll at one stage, but it was a short-term project and these employment levels were unsustainable.

In addition, the community felt they were not sufficiently consulted about housing design, productive and employment initiatives, and that donors and officials failed to listen to them. Summing up this contention, one key informant from UNICEF criticized the fundamentally flawed method of consultancy:

> *The people who were consulted were those in the* juntas directivas *and committee members of COIVEES, thirty people in all, out of a community of more than 3500 people.*

The lack of consultation also includes a lack of transparency about the different projects, the changes made along the way, and the destination and allocation of funds.

Finally, PROUME was criticized by community residents for attempting to intervene in processes of internal community organization. When PROUME started, the AVAUME existed only in name, and the different *juntas directivas* (about 10 at that time) were not united. PROUME therefore decided to found another organization to bring them together, the Committee of Management Boards of the Settlement. This decision caused dissension with the old AVAUME, as it constituted the creation of a community organization by an external organization, ignoring the community's historical processes. These deficiencies sparked off opposition to PROUME, and in 1997 a violent protest from within the community led to the immediate closure of the programme. The violent end to PROUME showed that external intervention can destabilize a community organization if it does not take into account the priorities, organizational processes and existing power relations within the community.

In terms of financial stability, there has been no evaluation of household loan repayments from PROUME to date, and it is not clear how or when these repayments will be made, nor what the consequences of non-payment might be. Without a clear plan for repayment, future loans are unlikely to be granted to the settlement.

Although the lack of genuine community consultancy, together with external manipulation of community organizations, may prevent community organizations from learning to design and manage their own programmes, in El Mezquital community organizations have learnt these skills, and capacity-building has taken place. The experience gained by the organizations and community leaders through PROUME has fundamentally changed the community at a level of both physical and social development. The cultural and personal changes experienced by the community are not easily quantifiable, but they have important implications. The struggle of the inhabitants reinforced their group identity, and led to skills development and community organization. A UNICEF consultant who worked there commented that:

> These people will never in all their lives forget their mobilization, participation and the way they worked together like ants in the community. They are conscious that they themselves did this, and in terms of identity this is very valuable, although you cannot measure it. They learnt a lot about how to get people together, how to use participatory techniques, communication and accountancy, and there they still are, it would only take another project and they would be back there organizing people once more.

At the time this research was carried out in 1999, however, no external agency or governmental institution appeared to be interested in developing collaborative projects with the community. The residents of El Mezquital feel they have now been cast aside by the government and international organizations, who perceive that the objectives have been achieved and the area is sufficiently urbanized, overlooking the inequalities within the settlement. One community member expressed this sense of rejection:

> Here, we are really lacking in supportive organizations, and yet El Mezquital is one of the most marginalized areas. Before, they gave us some support, for example the PROUME, but now that that project is finished they have forgotten all about us in El Mezquital.

Without the catalytic effect of other project partners, the residents of El Mezquital appear to be uncertain as to how to instigate further development projects and processes.

CONCLUSIONS

The poverty reduction initiatives described in this chapter focus on a variety of issues including health, housing, water and sanitation, and capacity-building. These projects all aim to reduce some aspect of poverty, where poverty is understood to include not just an income component, but also lack of access to health and education, basic services and adequate housing. According to this framework, since 1984 El Mezquital has successfully improved quality of life in many areas (health, housing, mortality levels), while in other ways it has not advanced and has even deteriorated in part (recreation, levels of consumption, work conditions). There are basic services in most of the settlement, and a certain amount of social infrastructure, yet the residents have not managed to overcome the precariousness of their situation and their poverty.

Experiences such as COIVEES, UNICEF's Basic Urban Services Programme and PROUME are today considered to be 'model' experiences, and are frequently used as a reference for other settlements' developments. Innovative processes of community organization which emerged in El Mezquital, such as COIVEES or the REPROINSAS, have expanded beyond their original purpose: currently, there are more than 700 REPROINSAS in 16 areas of Guatemala City, and the COIVEES model is being tried in two other settlements in Guatemala, El Zarzal and Villa Nueva. In addition, the Guatemalan Slum Improvement Programme, created in 1997, is based on the PROUME model, working with settlements and poor areas in and around the Municipality of Guatemala. In El Mezquital, these experiences generated both individual and collective skills. Nevertheless, fundamental problems remain, such as education, housing, employment and violence, illustrating that while there have been many achievements in the settlement, a lot still remains to be done.

What does this mean in terms of the sustainability of projects? At the infrastructure level, many initiatives have introduced basic services and infrastructure which continue to be maintained and used throughout the community. However, certain interventions have been characterized by a lack of transparency and by top-down processes, and government involvement has been manipulative and clientelistic, leading to a lack of trust in government. The PROUME project introduced important improvements in infrastructure, but ultimately had to be closed down because it failed to respect community structures and, due to its non-transparency and lack of consultation, was believed to be corrupt.

In terms of capacity-building, the development of local organizations and groups has contributed to the transformation of living conditions in the settlement, and has resulted in a legacy of community organization and mobilization. This case study illustrates how the processes of poverty reduction projects have dramatically increased a community's capacity to address its own problems, achieving sustainability through the process of project implementation. The REPROINSAS and UPAVIM organizations have encouraged both skills learning and personal confidence development. In the case of the REPROINSAS, the contribution provided by UNICEF in terms of training is counterbalanced by the voluntary labour of the community health workers: it is a partnership project of mutual dependency.

In other respects, however, sustainable development has not been achieved, as the 'needs of the present' remain unmet. Income-generating opportunities and local labour markets have not been tackled by the interventions, and remain extremely problematic and of high priority for current residents. In addition, there are problems of violence, drug addiction and low health and educational provision that call for a new prioritization of problem-solving within the community in the interests of social justice. It is hoped that the training and experience of community residents will be able to contribute to ongoing development in this area, but without any support from governmental or external agencies, this will be difficult.

To conclude, sustainability represents something more holistic than financial sustainability, reflecting instead a community's desire and capacity to develop. The evaluation of the community organization committees, women's organizations and PROUME suggests that sustainable projects tend to be characterized by respect for established community organizations; community participation to ensure programmes are high priority; capacity training, e.g. in managerial and administrative skills; personal development and satisfaction of community group members; transparent projects; and financial security – access to some form of financial support/resource generation or support in kind.

From apartheid city to sustainable city: the compact city approach as regulative ideal

Koyi Mchunu

Space consumption in general, and urban space in particular, has become a major concern throughout the world. There is a widespread belief that compact urban development contributes to sustainability, where sustainability is regarded as an essential requirement for human survival on planet Earth. Encouraging or even requiring high-density urban development is a major policy after the Agenda 21 proposals (UNCED, 1992), and a central principle of the growth management programmes used by cities around the world.

Sustainable development has become a slogan used worldwide in attempting to promote environmentally sound approaches to spatial and economic change, emphasizing the need for conscious human behaviour to conserve the desirable qualities of the physical environment. Care in the commitment and use of space is one of the most important issues when addressing sustainability.

In this chapter, the discussion focuses on three issues that undermine the compact city approach in South Africa – the current planning framework; multicultural context; and economic factors.[1] Conversely, the main argument is that compact development not only has the potential to improve the quality of the physical environment, but also could serve to promote political stability by reference to an ideal form of living and sense of common destiny.

This is of particular relevance in South Africa, given her recent past and relatively peaceful transition to a more democratic system. However, it is necessary first to situate the current attempts at city compacting in South Africa within the wider international debate on sustainable development.

HISTORICAL BACKGROUND

The compact city approach has been a response to the undesired development in the 1970s and 1980s, especially to the outward movement of growth called urban sprawl. Rapid decentralization in the form of suburbanization has not only meant that rural land is converted to urban uses, but also has increased the costs of providing infrastructure. This has led to compact city approaches as a counter-strategy to reduce sprawl, preserve the countryside and reduce the costs of providing infrastructure. Other advantages have to do with efficiency concerns – the perceived reduction in energy consumption and travelling times. This raised concerns for sustainability, which was popularized after the Brundtland Report, (WCED, 1987).

Various interpretations abound. Some have seen sustainable development as synonymous with carrying capacity (Healey et al., 1993). According to Beatley (1995), sustainable development is the notion that:

> *a given ecosystem or environment can sustain a certain animal population and that beyond that level overpopulation and species collapse will occur.*

Pearce et al. (1990) define sustainable development as managing resource use in such a manner as to be able to meet a set of aspirations of society over a considerable period.

The realization that the environmental impacts of many activities are not limited to the locality in which they occur, but adversely affect sustainability in other areas and regions, has also contributed towards popularizing sustainability. There is a sense in which environmental concerns could act as a source of empowerment for marginalized communities to improve their surroundings, by resisting the siting of land uses regarded as 'not in my back yard' (NIMBY) or 'locally unwanted land use' (LULU) on environmental grounds. The popularity of sustainable development, in this case in the form of compact development, derives from the fact that it cuts across the political divide through a common issue of caring for the environment.

Prescriptions vary, from urban infill and higher densities in existing communities to a call for a greater mixture of uses. Intense urban form and mixed land uses reduce trip lengths and make public transport an active option. Consequently, the compact city must be of a scale and form appropriate for walking, cycling and efficient public transport. Jenks et al. (1996) conclude that the compact city is the most sustainable form.

Some general obstacles to compact development

Evidence from other studies suggests that compact cities have fewer blessings to offer than was expected (Ewing, 1997; Levine, 1998). The perceived advantages of a compact city are idealistic for some (Thomas et al., 1996). Welbank (1996) argues that there is a lack of rational foundation for sustainable development. Rather than rationality, the compact city as sustainable is based on belief. Breheny (1992a) also raises doubts concerning the objective basis of compact city as sustainable. More recent critical assessment suggests that the compact city may be wishful thinking, and a somewhat naïve myth (Gordon et al., 1997; Levine, 1998). The expressed view is that cities are much more complex, and that density does not necessarily translate to the perceived advantages.

In South Africa, concerns have also been raised about the feasibility of the compact city model. The first calls for compaction were made almost 25 years ago (Dewar, 2000). However, it was not until the introduction of new legislation and a planning paradigm to guide urban planning after 1994 that the government committed itself to compaction.[2] Political will has been identified as a critical missing variable (Dewar, 2000). The following section discusses some of the obstacles to the compact city model, namely the planning framework; multiculturalism; and social and economic factors. The following section discusses, among other issues, compact development as a regulative ideal.

THE CASE OF SOUTH AFRICA

Compact city approach in South Africa

South African cities are largely a product of apartheid and modern planning. The emphasis on the separation of land uses in modern planning dovetailed with the cornerstone of apartheid policy of residential segregation according to race.

The development of South Africa's economy resulted in the suburbanization of the white middle classes. This was equally matched by the systematic removal of Africans to the sprawling and infamous townships on the edges of the cities, in order to accommodate apartheid policies of racial residential segregation. Other groups such as Coloureds (refers to people of mixed racial heritage) and Indians were also affected. This has given rise to a low-density sprawl, fragmentation, and separation of people and land uses. The cost of travelling in a hugely subsidized public transport system, distances traversed[3] and times spent have been enormous, especially to those who can least afford the costs.

The idea of the compact city represents one of the emerging orthodoxies concerning the necessity of shaping South African cities to match the necessities of the post-modern, post-fordist phase (Mabin, 1995). The general image, as he rightly notes, is difficult to fault:

> *The objective is to integrate what has been fragmented – to bring home and (potentially) work together, to overcome wide spatial divides, to reduce segregation in racial and perhaps other social-spatial senses.*

> *(Mabin, 1995: 194).*

The sprawling, fragmented and separated form of South African towns and cities is entirely unsustainable (Dewar, 2000: 217). There is increasing national awareness of the need for compaction in the form of an Interim Strategic Framework (1992, Central Witwatersrand Metropolitan Chamber, Gauteng Province); the Draft Municipal Spatial Development Framework (1999, Cape Town, Western Cape Province); and Durban's Spatial Development Framework (1997, Kwa-Zulu Natal Province). All point to the need for some form of compaction in order to improve access to services and amenities, especially for the poorer sectors of the cities.

Current planning framework

The draconian nature of state planning under apartheid was a source of much resistance, and also served to taint the image of planners in South Africa. As a result, the pendulum in planning practice has swung to the extreme opposite, with an overemphasis on community participation, consensus-seeking and negotiation. This is an attempt, perhaps, at compensating for the past; but also South Africa is not immune to emerging international trends in planning theory and practice following the social, economic and political changes in the cities, or what Mabin (1995) calls 'shifts'. The planning framework has, as a result, tended to be less stringent on control measures that are indispensable for compact cities. There is also the issue of lack of understanding and wilful recalcitrance, and vague and unprescriptive strategic plans and policy documents, that has resulted in limits to the means and ability of both government and urban planners to dictate urban development (Schoonraad, 2000: 225–226). The planning profession itself is still in a state of flux, in need of what Muller (1995) calls an enabling paradigm to inform planning practice after the collapse of apartheid. It is as recently as 1996 that Black and White planners merged to form one organization called the South African Planning Institution, and African interests are still not well articulated in planning theory and practice, as the following point illustrates. The general picture emerging is that of an ineffective planning framework, yet stringent control measures and political will (as Dewar, 2000 would have it), are a prerequisite for any serious talk about city compaction.

Planning in a multicultural context

The compact city approach, and town planning in general, need to be sensitized to issues of diversity in a multicultural society such as South Africa. Historically, the needs of Africans have not been accommodated in the urban environment. Two examples illustrate this need – the lack of space for priceless, life-giving, age-old practices such as the ceremonial offering of livestock for traditional celebrations and functions; and space for the initiation process for boys. Lot sizes in most old townships provide adequate space around the house for the ceremonial offering of livestock. However, recent public housing makes no provision for this in the form of front- or back-yard space. The second example concerns the lack of space for the traditional practice of initiation among Xhosa-speaking communities. On reaching a certain age, Xhosa boys must attend a month-long process of initiation before they can take their rightful place as men in the community. As part of this process, the boys must be confined in a secluded area, away from the eyes of the community, in the nearby bushes. Due to lack of appropriately designated/designed spaces for this practice, it continues to be accommodated on fast dwindling pieces of vacant land on the outskirts of the townships.

Equally relevant is Boden's (1989, 1992, 1993) work, which should provide an invaluable source of inspiration for planners and urban designers in South Africa. In short, Boden argues for a method for reconnecting town planning and urban design proposals with their local culture. An acknowledgement and understanding of a 'native point of view' is essential because 'our fractured, pluralistic modern metropolitan societies display minimal consensus regarding perceptions of and meanings attached to the urban environment' (Boden, 1993: 11).

An awareness of such needs and understanding of the use and need for space must inform current attempts to compact the city. Dewar's (2000) idea of meeting these needs on public as opposed to private land is perhaps one way of bringing these issues to the fore for debate and discussion among built environment specialists.

The point is that the built environment profession in general needs to be sensitized to cultural issues in planning. The starting point has to be the education system for planners. Dewar's proposal above is based on the assumption that planners have the prerequisite skills and the will to address these issues. Nothing could be further from the truth – these issues remain unresolved.

Social and economic factors

Two issues are discussed in relation to economic factors. The first concerns higher densities on the edges of most South African cities; the second, the government's macro-economic policy, both of which are in conflict with the compact city approach.

The first point is that the correlation between poverty, residential location and race in South Africa, and the resulting ingenious (that is, economically astute) ways of ameliorating poor economic conditions, have led to the emergence of much higher densities than are provided for on the edges of major South African cities. There is a significant discrepancy between gross layout density, measured in units per hectare, and occupational density, measured in persons per hectare (Schoonraad, 2000: 223). This is a common situation in cities in the developing world, where the poor cannot afford to live in the city due to high property values. Current compact development approaches need to be adapted to reflect this phenomenon.

The second point is that the interplay between the government's macro-economic policy, aimed at attracting foreign investment and stimulating economic growth, and that of local authorities starving for revenue in the form of taxes on land development, has also undermined compaction. This has resulted in what Mabin (1995: 192) regards as a 'built environment shift', where the activities of planners are the ephemeral ones of consumption in the form of waterfront developments, luxury housing and shopping malls. In a context where private developers dictate the nature and form of urban development, and government controls are far less stringent, we cannot expect much other than the status quo.

DISCUSSION

There are very compelling reasons for the adoption of the compact city model. The compact city may be a solution to unsustainable levels of fragmentation, separation, and the sprawling nature of development in South Africa. Equally, there are serious impediments that must be overcome if necessary levels of compaction are to be achieved. Two observations are discussed in relation to the argument presented in this chapter.

First, at the moment it appears that the forces of fragmentation are well organized, with powerful local and international connections, while the newly emerging integrative forces remain relatively weak. The globalization of the economy and the power of multinational corporations have, to a large extent, influenced the national government to adopt market-friendly macro-economic policies. The government's neoliberal macro-economic strategy – growth, employment and redistribution (GEAR) – bears testimony to this fact. Business and not government increasingly determines the nature and location of urban development. The lack of political will to champion the cause for compaction, alluded to earlier, can be attributed to this ascendancy of market forces. Land development tax, largely from commercial developments in areas under their jurisdiction, provide a source of much-needed revenue for cash-strapped local governments. Any development is therefore deemed positive.

Compact development calls for the strict enforcement of government regulation on the location of development. This lack of enforcement of the existing regulations has been alluded to earlier. Essentially, the argument is that the government is failing to address compact development adequately.

Putting the blame at the government's door is, however, not enough, as Putnam (1993) and Flyvbjerg (1998) have aptly demonstrated:

> *two centuries of constitution-writing around the world warn us . . . That designers of new institutions are often writing on water . . . That institutional reforms alter behavior is an hypothesis, not an axiom.*
>
> *(Putnam 1993: 17–18).*

In Flyvbjerg's (1998) native Aalborg, the most powerful part of civil society collaborated in order to shape the city to their interests. The lack of adequate implementation could be understood in terms of the uneven distribution of power in society, in this case in favour of the forces of fragmentation versus integrative forces. In Foucauldian terms, power is also capillary and decentred. It is precisely because power is diffused that there is hope for resistance and struggle. Part of the answer lies in mobilizing the rest of civil society to force the compact city agenda into the public domain similarly to how the environment, gender and minority issues were brought forward. Those with power will continue to shape the city to their own interests, while the rest are kept on the margins of planning and policy decisions. This is the experience of the Aalborg study of Flyvbjerg (1998), and the experience of advocacy planning in South Africa is littered with frustration and despair as the force of police and the army proved mightier than the force of a better argument.

Second, the compact city approach (which has so far been articulated in terms of the public good) corresponds to integrative forces, while the institution of private property (which focuses on individual benefits) can be correlated with the powerful market forces of fragmentation. There are two forces representing two seemingly unreconcilable approaches – integration versus fragmentation. This distinction mirrors the dualism that has peppered the planning literature for several decades, similar to the dualism of arts and sciences, politics and fact and value, and means and ends. These dualisms have served as theoretical justifications for planning practices. Current research, however, suggests that this dichotomy is not only false, but also misleading.[4] The point being made is that in the absence of local, African precedents for compact city living, casting it in terms of 'public good' may be exaggerating.

Lastly, for the compact city to be realized, policies need to be adapted to local conditions – local perceptions and livability in terms of the residents' point of view as opposed to foreign models of the compact city (Shoonraad, 2000). The lack of a model to emulate and criteria for evaluation support this view.

Civil society and city compaction

The compact city approach in South Africa requires not only strong control measures, but also the ability and willingness to enforce these regulations. In the absence of, and/or to complement these regulations, a strong civil society to force the issue of compaction on the public arena is indispensable. Gender and environmental issues provide invaluable lessons in terms of forcing their issues on the public arena. But first the relevant public(s) need to be specified.

Compact city as regulative ideal

In addition to the function of integration and other perceived benefits, the compact city approach could also serve as a regulative ideal, a shared vision of a unified, integrated and harmonious co-existence. South African cities are increasingly polarized along racial and class lines, and the gap between the rich and poor is ever widening (Mabin, 1995: 192). There are violence, homelessness, unemployment, and inner city decline following the suburbanization of mostly commercial activities, and on the other hand a conspicuous consumption ethic in the form of shopping atria, and luxury housing in gated communities or behind high security walls. In short, the ideal of a compact city speaks to the chasm between rich and poor.

The obstacles surrounding the implementation of compact development go further than the concept itself, and in a way reflect the developmental challenges in South Africa. Striving for a compact city focuses our energies towards a common goal that has potential benefits for all. It provides an opportunity to address vital issues such as housing, poverty, unemployment and access to other facilities and services, by framing them around the discourse on the environment. The framing of urban issues in this way allows them to be tackled in a much more inclusive manner than would have been possible otherwise because of different political outlooks. The question of sustainability cuts across the political and racial divide precisely because it also addresses other issues of mutual concern. In this sense, the vision of a compact city represents an ideal city settlement where sharing and caring are the norm. Striving to attain such an ideal city would regulate our actions for the common good.

The lack of a compact city model to emulate, and of criteria for evaluation, suggests that any proposed model of a compact city would be based on an ideal case. In South Africa, a case could be made for a compact city as a regulative ideal to unify divided cities both physically and symbolically.

CONCLUSIONS

There are formidable obstacles to compacting cities in South Africa. The national government lacks the necessary power in the face of dominant market forces that eschew any form state of intervention. The articulation of compact development in terms of an unspecified public interest is equally problematic because it begs the questions of which public is being referred to, and how they are constituted. Recent studies confirm the view that struggle and resistance are more effective means of forcing issues into the public arena for debate and discussion than focusing solely on rules and regulations. Given the physical and social division that characterizes South African society, the relevance of compact development as a regulative ideal of a common vision of unity is even more appealing.

Structural adjustment and water supply in Bolivia: managing diversity, reproducing inequality

Carlos Crespo Flores

INTRODUCTION

Bolivia is a landlocked and rather impoverished developing country, with a population of about 8.5 million of whom about two-thirds live in urban areas (Viceministerio de Servicios Basicos, 1999: 17). Poverty is widespread – some 52 per cent of the urban population live under the poverty line, and 23 per cent live in absolute poverty (CEPAL 2000: 40, 42) – and accompanies an extremely polarized distribution of wealth. These stark conditions provide the backcloth to growing social and economic upheaval within the context of the country's structural adjustment programme, which is exemplified in the specific case study in this chapter – the struggle over water supply.

In April 2000 a popular revolt in Cochabamba, an event not experienced since the 1952 Revolution, forced the Bolivian government to annul the Contract of Concession with the transnational consortium Aguas del Tunari (Tunari Waters), and to modify the Water and Sanitation Law (No. 2029) – two policy decisions implemented within the framework of the country's structural adjustment reform programme.

These two significant policy reversals are the setting for this chapter. The so-called 'Water Wars' highlighted the potential conflicts, in planning vital urban infrastructure, between the sustainable delivery of urban services, the interests of the urban poor and the prevailing political economy of neoliberalism.

Within Bolivia, the Water War implied that a transformation was taking place in the social movements of the country which challenged the orthodox structures of government (Crespo, 2000a). These events also offered a challenge to some of the command strategies deployed by the interests of global capital, mediated through the country's structural adjustment programmes. Crucially, the concern in this context is how the needs of different social groups are managed with respect to equity in the delivery of essential urban services. Here, it is widely argued that neoliberal public policies tend to exclude socially disadvantaged sectors and homogenize cultural differences. The contention in this chapter, however, is that Bolivian neoliberal policies neither exclude nor totally homogenize, but produce a new structure of power, where differences are recognized and

incorporated within a different discourse of consensus about city development. This chapter analyses these propositions from the perspective of the
Bolivian structural adjustment policies, and particularly the Water Supply
and Sanitation Law.

Drawing on the work of Hardt and Negri (2000), the first part of the chapter presents their argument that the current apparatus of command
deployed by global capitalism consists of three distinct moments: one
inclusionary, another differential, and a third managerial. These moments
constitute the framework by which to explore the roles and reactions of the
different stakeholders in the Water War.

The chapter then demonstrates how the new governance system in
Bolivia (designed to support the structural adjustment policies), while pur-
porting to recognize socio-cultural differences in the country, in fact pro-
motes the interests of the capitalist sectors, undermines other groups, and
thus paradoxically frustrates the aim of articulating the country into the
global neoliberal agenda. Conditions of poverty and inequality are reproduced which constitute obstacles to a consensus society, in turn generating
social conflicts such as Cochabamba's Water War.

In the third part the proposed scope of the Water Supply and Sanitation
Law is discussed. The strategy of hierarchical management of two systems
of water management – private capital and social organizations – is presented, and is shown to produce new sources of inequity in access to and
use of water resources, thereby creating the conditions for the Water War.

THREE MOMENTS OF THE GLOBAL CAPITALISM COMMAND

It has increasingly been recognized that the economic system has been
transformed from a national to a new transnational phase (Robinson,
1998/99: 111), summarized as global capitalism (Castells 1997). Neoliberal
economic policies have contributed to the deployment of the forces of globalization, and have become the dominant discourse of global capitalism
(Castells, 1997).

This new world order is both systemic and hierarchical. According to
Hardt and Negri (2000), the general apparatus of global capitalism command consists of three distinct moments: inclusionary, differential and
managerial.

Inclusionary moment

The first moment is what might be termed the magnanimous, liberal face
of global capitalism. It accepts social and cultural diversity within its
boundaries. In its inclusionary moment, global capitalism (called 'Empire'
by Hardt and Negri) is blind to differences. Universal inclusion is achieved
by setting aside differences that are inflexible or unmanageable and thus
might give rise to social conflict (Hardt and Negri, 2000: 199). Differences

can exist as an overlapping consensus across the entire capitalist space. In short, it represents the recognition of stakeholders' equality, rather than different values and perspectives, in the search for consensus.

Differential moment

The second moment involves the affirmation and acceptance of differences. From the cultural perspective, differences are celebrated and contingent. In this way they are thought not to impinge on the overlapping consensus which characterizes inclusionary mechanisms ((Hardt and Negri, 2000: 199–200). For public policy-making, this is a significant contention in that it represents a positive recognition of the existence of different stakeholders, with different demands and needs.

Managerial moment

The third moment is referred to as the management and hierarchization of these differences in a general economy of command (Hardt and Negri, 2000: 199). This presents a new form of governance, based on a non-absolute exclusion, which rules through mechanisms of differential inclusion, making hierarchies (Dumm and Hardt, 2000: 3) and organizing consensus. Global capitalism does not negate or attenuate these differences, but rather affirms them and arranges them in an effective apparatus of command. (Hardt and Negri, 2000: 200). In the context of public policies, this represents a capacity to manage hierarchically the interest and demands of the different stakeholders involved.

In short, economic globalization under a neoliberal regime does not create division, but rather recognizes existing or potential differences among stakeholders or different actors, celebrates them, and manages them within a general economy of command. The triple imperative of global capitalism today incorporates, differentiates, and manages (Hardt and Negri, 2000: 201). By deploying these moments in the context of Bolivia's structural adjustment policies, and in one of the most important policy decisions of the water reforms, the Water Supply and Sanitation Law, we can begin to understand the problems of managing sustainable and equitable city development.

BOLIVIA'S STRUCTURAL ADJUSTMENT POLICIES AS A NEW STRUCTURE OF POWER

Under the conditionality policies of the International Monetary Fund and the World Bank, Bolivia has implemented structural adjustment policies since 1985. One of the components has been the privatization of the strategic national production sectors, particularly mining and oil, and later of public services including telecommunications and basic services.

Structural adjustment in Bolivia has constituted not only an economic reform programme, but also a process of political change – it has generated a new structure of governance with a new power structure based in a market economy and liberal democracy to articulate the country into the framework of global capitalism. Within this neoliberal reform process in Bolivia, we can see the deployment of the three moments of the global capitalist governance.

The first, or inclusionary, moment involves a juridical dimension, because it entails the recognition of citizen equality before the law. Equality in legal terms was established in the modified Bolivian Constitution, 1993 (*Honorable Congreso Boliviano*, 1993: articles 6 and 7). Equality is expressed through the existence of a democratic system; democracy works for the whole Bolivian population.

The second, or differential, moment in Bolivia's neoliberal public policies involves two dimensions. On one hand there is the celebration of differences as essentially socio-cultural. Almost 50 per cent of the population are from indigenous cultures and peasantries, most of them reliant on traditional productive systems. The new structure of command implemented by the structural adjustment programmes recognizes, through the Bolivian Constitution, the multicultural and pluri-lingual character of the country (*Honorable Congreso Boliviano*, 1993: article 1). In short, Bolivia's complex cultural diversity is recognized, including the *mestizaje* process of mixing indigenous and white populations and cultural norms.

On the other hand, the recognition of the 'pluri' and 'multi' features of the country represents, at the same time, the recognition of the existence of two fundamental types of economy, and therefore the existence of two countries (Garcia Linera et al., 2000). There is the *capitalist economy* – considered modern, western, based in private property and oriented to the market, particularly to export, with its political expression through a liberal democracy. In contrast, there is the *subsistence economy* – considered traditional, linked with peasants and indigenous productive systems, although it also includes urban subsistence strategies, particularly in the informal sector. It is oriented to self-sufficiency and the satisfaction of minimal needs. It is based on common values such as reciprocity, mutual aid, solidarity and common good, against the background of rights and customs. It is expressed organizationally as community democracy.

The aim of public policies is to articulate, in a consensual way, cultural and economic diversity through the political system; governability is the key factor. Defined as a state of dynamic equilibrium between social demands and the role of government to respond to those demands (Calderon and Lechner, 1998: 12), Bolivia's governability is connected both to representative democracy (Rojas et al., 1998), and also to a complex process of consensus-seeking (Calderon and Lechner, 1998: 12; Rojas, 1998). Interparty political coalitions have governed since 1985 through a series of pacts which are the product of this 'consensus'.[1] Putting the country's interest over group interests is a common expression of this 'democracy of pacts' (Rojas, 1998). At the same time,

Dialogue Tables have been implemented[2], where different stakeholders negotiate and agree the fundamental agenda of the country's development strategies to be implemented by the government. The agenda of public policies is that citizens, considered equal but socio-culturally different, negotiate in concert without conflicts. The government presents itself as neutral in the face of these diverse actors or stakeholders.

The third moment, hierarchical management of differences, involves the operationalization of the two previous moments. Neoliberal public policies do not exclude, directly or totally. While they imply the articulation of all the social actors or stakeholders in an organized consensus, at the same time these policies prioritize and promote the capitalist and developed sectors of the economy. This has the effect of undermining and controlling the subsistence economy sectors on which the poor in urban and rural areas depend. In short, it represents the management of the two previous moments in an integrated way, at the same time developing a mode of decision-making which is configured as a new structure of power and domination. Table 13.1 reviews the principal features.

Taking first the *economic dimension*, micro-policies support the intervention by local government to support the national agenda of the past three governments of Bolivia, which has been to fight against poverty. But there are tensions here because the decentralization process must distrib-

Table 13.1 Management of diversity in the economy

Dimension	Capitalist economy	Subsistence economy
Economic	Macro-policies: privatization (capitalization, direct transfer or concession) of natural resources exploitation and public services	Micro-policies: poverty alleviation programmes Decentralization
Socio-cultural	Promotion of individualism New relationships, e.g. clientelism Education reform (modernization/westernization)	Recognition of some traditional rights and customs Established relationships: user/consumer Education reform (intercultural and bilingual education)
Political	Representative democracy Accept formal organizations	Popular participation/ decentralization Control/prohibition of informal organizations
Regulatory	Support natural resources exploitation and public services	No regulation, except when it facilitates functioning of capitalist economy
Aims	To articulate to neoliberal global economy	To reduce risks of starvation and social conflicts

ute scarce economic resources from public funds. There is a correlation between poor regions and traditional cultures[3], and the government implements policies to alleviate poverty, with the support of multilateral banks. But subsistence economies are not considered viable (Castells, 1997)[4], and indigenous peasants and the urban poor are not considered part of the strategy of the neoliberal model. And so at the same time there are policies to enable foreign investment to develop some regions considered more profitable.[5] Municipalities with larger populations, generally the more prosperous, receive more public and private investment which attenuates the dichotomy at the core of the country's economy.

At the macro-level, government policies determine the economic direction of the country's development. Under a neoliberal agenda there is an increasingly poor relationship between the different modes of decision-making that have typically characterized the country under the inclusionary and differential moments. Privatization undermines the functioning of other types and strategies of public and social management of resources, services and development (public, municipal, cooperative, community, mutuality and reciprocity).

On the *socio-cultural dimension*, traditional subsistence agriculture, based on rights and customs, is considered marginal to the new economic imperatives. Conversely, agro-industry is oriented to commercial markets and export. Indigenous knowledge is part of the cultural heritage; but when this knowledge is potentially profitable, for example, medicinal plants or native germplasm, multinational companies register the patents as private property rights, with the support of government policies.

On the *political dimension*, the promotion of citizens' participation occurs at the micro-level. But at the level of national economic and political decision-making, the population is rarely consulted and does not effectively participate according to the multi- and pluri-cultural, social and economic structure of the country, except through the formal channels of the political party system (Perelman, 2000). Accordingly, different recognition is given to formally and informally constituted organizations. Currently, Bolivia's political culture is oriented towards institutionalizing a liberal democracy. Any organization outside this aim is considered non-functional and is excluded. Movements and organizations are possible only within the borders defined by the neoliberal model. Against this background, there has been an increase, over the past decade, in forces of repression and surveillance, especially for informal organizations. For example, one of the principal objects of this control has been the *cocaleros* (coca producers), who are thought to be linked to drug trafficking (Law 1008).

One effect of the hierarchical management of differences engendered by the demands of structural adjustment policies is the promotion of the capitalist sectors of the economy, which have deepened social inequality in the country. Thus, as noted in the introduction, in 1997 52 per cent of the urban population were under the poverty line, and 23 per cent live in absolute poverty (CEPAL, 2000: 40, 42). In rural areas poverty is worse: 86 per cent of rural areas are below the poverty line, and 90 per cent are in extreme poverty. Over 94 per cent of rural population does not have access to basic services such as sewerage and electricity, nor do they have adequate housing. At the same time the difference between rich and poor, particularly indigenous populations and peasants, is wide and growing. In 1996 the lowest urban quintile received only 4 per cent of aggregate labour income, while the highest quintile received 56 per cent. Wages for indigenous workers are nearly 40 per cent below those of non-indigenous workers, and average pay for females remains nearly half that of males (World Bank, 1998: 3). The meagre increase in incomes has benefited management, employers, professionals and office workers rather than blue-collar workers.

Structural adjustment, based on the powerful interests of some stakeholders, undermines the social consensus. The growing inequalities and poverty of the subsistence economy sectors appear to be linked to the emergence of conflict and social movements. Of the 7647 social conflicts registered in Bolivia between 1970 and 1998, almost 40 per cent are concentrated in the 13 years corresponding to the period of structural adjustment (1985–98) (Calderon and Szmukler, 1999).

WATER PRIVATIZATION AND MANAGEMENT OF DIFFERENCES

This, then, is the context: socio-economic polarization and increasing poverty under conditions of structural adjustment find particular expression in access to water resources and sanitation in Bolivia. Seventy-eight per cent of the urban population, and only 22 per cent of the rural population, have access to clean water (World Bank/World Resources Institute, 2000: 3). According the Viceministerio de Servicios Basicos, in 1999, while most urban dwellers have access to piped water, about 85 per cent of rural dwellers did not have access to a piped water supply (Viceministerio de Servicios Basicos, 1999: 24). More significant than overall access rates, only about 32 per cent of the poorest quintile of the population have access to a piped water supply, while 93 per cent of the richest quintile do (World Bank, 1999: XXVI). Fifty-one per cent of the urban population and over 82 per cent of rural dwellers are without access to proper sanitation (Viceministerio de Servicios Basicos, 1999: 25).[6]

The privatization of water in Bolivia

Following the recommendations of the first Water World Conference in Dublin in 1992[7], current water policies in developing countries tend to emphasize the extent to which these policies have balanced and incorporated the interests of the stakeholders involved.[8] Such an approach is considered key in the conservation of the resource and the pro-poor orientation of water policies. Donor agencies, particularly the World Bank, promote this perspective, but link it to the transference of the water utilities to the private sector. It is the contradiction in these approaches that is at issue here.

In the case of Bolivia, there are three phases in water privatization (Crespo, 2000b).

Phase 1: planning (1990–93)

During this period the government developed and implemented, with financial and technical support from the World Bank and the InterAmerican Development Bank, the Basic Sanitation National Plan and the tariffs policy for water supply and the sanitation sector. Ironically, in retrospect, the programme was entitled 'Water for All'. It introduced the principle of full cost-recovery, criteria for the economic management of water utilities and, for the first time, indicated the transfer of the water companies to the private sector.

Phase 2: institutionalization (1994–97)

Coincident with the so-called 'Second Generation of the Structural Adjustment', this phase witnessed the approval of the Rules for the Concession of the Water Sector, and the water regulatory system (Water Superintendence) – the latter to guarantee the accountability of the private concessionaires. In addition to privatization, the water companies were to be strengthened financially and institutionally, particularly in three of the most important cities of the country (La Paz, Cochabamba and Santa Cruz).

Phase 3: implementation (1997–2000)

In this phase the concession for the water supply of La Paz was awarded to Aguas del Illimani (Illimani Waters), a consortium headed by the French company Lyonnaise des Eaux (Komives, 1999). The concession of Cochabamba's water company was awarded to the consortium Aguas del Tunari (Tunari Waters), a subsidiary of the English company International Water Ltd, now an affiliate of the American company Bechtel. A juridical framework to institutionalize and legalize the privatization process was necessary, and in October 1999 the Water Supply and Sanitation Law (No. 2029) was approved.

Before the approval of this law, the Cochabamba organization of water irrigation (FEDECOR) and a coalition of NGOs and social organizations established to defend the communities' water rights against the privatization proposals were in negotiation with the government and Parliament over the new Water Resources Law. Little progress had been made because of the profound differences, particularly on the protection of water rights based on rights and customs, the introduction of a market in water, and the role of the regulatory authority.

Nonetheless, the Law was approved via a fast-track process. The reason, according the government, was the pressure exerted by international donors to have a legal framework to enable payment for the water supply projects. In a two-day continuous session, Parliament approved four laws including the Water Supply and Sanitation Law (No. 2029).

In fact, the fast-track approval process was accomplished as a result of an agreement between government political parties and the principal opposition party, the Revolutionary Nationalist Movement. There was no consultation or consensus-building with any of the stakeholders involved in water supply, management and consumption.

Why did the government accelerate the approval of the Water Supply and Sanitation Law, while it was still discussing the general Water Resources Law? The story of pressure from international donors is not sustainable, as later events showed. There were two reasons for this accelerated approval. The first was the need to legalize the award of the concessions, particularly in Cochabamba, which had already been agreed with the Aguas del Tunari without a specific legal framework two weeks before parliamentary approval. Second, there was no agreement in place with social organizations affected by the controversial proposal for the Water Resources Law, in line with the inclusionary and differential moments that characterized consensus-building in the country. Lacking this legal framework, which the government needed to initiate the concession of water sources, and which would have led to protracted debate, the government saw the opportunity to introduce the legislation (Law 2029) through the introduction of a Transitional Article.

The unsurprising outcome of these procedures was Cochabamba's protest against the Law and the Contract of Concession. As Orellana notes: 'if a legal rule is not adhered to and does not support the expectations of social groups, the government will bear the social and political costs of conflicts' (Orellana, 2000: 5).

Hierarchical management of diversity and inequity in the Water Supply and Sanitation Law

What is evident in the process of adopting the Water Supply and Sanitation Law is the hierarchical management of differences (Hardt and Negri, 2000: 199–200), the effects of which were challenged during Cochabamba's Water War.

Inclusionary moment

Article 8 of the Law defines 'Water and Sanitation Providers' (EPSAs) as any 'juridical person, public or private, that supplies one or more of the water and sanitation services', and includes municipal public companies, public–private limited companies, private companies, public services cooperatives, civil associations, indigenous and peasant communities. This includes all sectors involved in water supply, and bestows on them the same rights and duties. Behind this definition is the liberal principle that all are equal before the law, and the principle that all stakeholders involved in a project or activity must be included in the process. Thus, according to the Law, any EPSA could compete to receive a concession for water supply under the same conditions and criteria.

With this approach, the EPSAs constituted an unspecified category where the 'public space' of water supply was articulated without any implicit preference as to provider or power relations among the potential stakeholders. Policies for the provision of water could then imply that a consensus among stakeholders was a prerequisite. The Law placed the same conditions on profit-making private companies as on social organizations supplying water with non-profit aims.

Differential moment

At the same time, the Water Supply and Sanitation Law recognized cultural differences within EPSAs, but with economic and social connotations: the Law recognized the existence of profit-seeking EPSAs (private companies) and others that were not (indigenous/peasant communities, water cooperatives, associations, etc.). Again, what is implicit is the differentiation between the capitalist economy and the subsistence and informal economy, modernity and tradition, or private and community.

Thus, despite the fact that Bolivia celebrates its multicultural characteristics, the Water Supply and Sanitation Law translated this differentiation into a conflict, rather than cohesion between the two basic systems of water supply. The Law operationalized these differences through the division between *concession* and *non-concession* or *licence* areas. The criteria for this distinction were demographic, but also economic, particularly in areas where water could be supplied profitably. Localities where there was a possibility of guaranteeing profits were the object of private concessions, while zones considered financially unattractive – the rest of the country – were subject to a system of much less attractive licences.

Managerial moment

The distinction between concession and licence/non-concession zones (private and public/communal) involved a hierarchical management of these differences, where the concession zones mean the profitable sector (Table 13.2).

Elaborating on Table 13.2, the principal features of differentiation of legal rights are as follows.

- Theoretically, in concession zones all EPSAs could compete to win a concession. The practical question is whether non-profit social organizations of water supply could compete equally with national

Table 13.2   Concessionary and non-concessionary zones

Type of organization	Type of zone	To whom	Period of service provision	Period for extraction from water source	Legal categories	Exclusivity
EPSA	Concessionary zone: more than 10 000 population and profitable service	Private companies, large cooperatives and public companies	Up to 40 years	Up to 40 years	Concession	Limited to sole concessionaire
EPSA	Non-concessionary zones: non-profitable service, fewer than 10 000 inhabitants	Small cooperatives, water committees, peasant/indigenous systems and municipal companies	5 years	Water source access not guaranteed	Licence	No

Source: Solón and Orellana (2000).

private and transnational companies to obtain a concession (Solón, 2000: 3); this was unlikely, as the eventual outcomes confirm. Moreover, the Law was oriented to facilitate transference to the private sector. To obtain a concession, it was necessary to present financial guarantees to undertake and adhere to the contractual requirements, and to present investment programmes and financial profitability criteria; these requirements favour private companies, not social organizations (Crespo, 2000b: 8; Solón, 2000: 4).

▪ The licence/non-concession zones, unprofitable areas where water rights were limited, were considered secondary to the main aim of the Law. But the Law contained regulations not only on water supply and sanitation, but also on access to water sources (Orellana 2000: 2)[9], which had a particularly punitive effect on local communities' access to water. In terms of the relationship between the source and the supply of water, the Law recognized the potentially profitable matter of water sources. In this case, the company gaining the concession had the right to expropriate water sources, land and infrastructure through a mechanism called *servidumbres*[10] (Crespo, 2000b).

▪ Another distinction was that in concession areas, the concessions for supply and source are up to 40 years (Article 29); the licences for services in licence areas are just 5 years (Article 44). This means that the licence guaranteed operators little in the way of providing the service, access to sources, and still less, ownership. The Law failed to assure rural and indigenous communities rights to the property of water sources they were currently using, in many cases since well before their rights and customs were established in law. As the leader of irrigators said: 'we, who are owners of these sources, and have worked our wells, *tajamares*[11], and lakes, we will receive just a licence for five years, in this way we are going to lose our ownership' (Omar Fernandez, Conosour XII/99). In other words, the security given to concession companies in line with the argument to guarantee the expansion of water supply to growing urban populations was not given to non-profit licensees.

▪ Another important difference was that a licence did not guarantee exclusivity to social organization service providers (Article 44). This means that if a concessionaire company wanted to include a non-concession area in its plans to expand the service, because of its potential profitability, this was permitted under the Law, under the argument of non-exclusivity. Conversely, in concession zones the concessionaire had exclusivity of service provision

▪ If water service provision, under the licence regime, turned out to be profitable, the Regulator could transfer it to a concession regime, awarding the service to a private company. In other words, the non-profitable EPSAs (Entidades prestudoras de Servico – water associations, rural municipal services, and local cooperatives) opened the door to private entrepreneur EPSAs (Solón, 2000: 3).

- Although the Law was portrayed as accepting all stakeholders, at the same time it declared that the State 'will encourage private sector participation in the Water Supply and Sanitation service' (Article 19). The alternative mode of rights and customs, based on the traditional system of water access and use, was subordinated to the privatization process.

What were the implications of the Law's management of diversity for water resource management and for access and use by the poorest sectors?

The management of diversity of the Water Supply and Sanitation Law was hierarchical, because it prioritized and enabled the transfer of utilities concessions to the private sector. It was inequitable because it reduced the rights of social organizations to provide water, and to gain access to and use of water resources. The Law did not have a pro-poor approach, as the donors and multilateral lending agencies contend (Komives, 1999).

The Law did not enable a consensus of interests to emerge among the stakeholders involved in water supply, because it was oriented to promote the development of only one of the stakeholder sectors, the private sector linked to multinational water companies.

The Law considered the opportunities for social and community organizations to supply water, including organizations based on traditional rights and customs, reciprocity and common good; but only in so far as they could be viable in terms of neoliberal economic aims. These organizations of the poor were included as beneficiaries in so called pro-poor poverty alleviation programmes, but only to the extent that they were maintained in a subsistence situation, with minimum rights and financial opportunities in water resource extraction and distribution, while on the other hand the financially most significant water supply opportunities were destined for privatized concessionaires.

The concession of water utilities was geared up only for large, profitable cities. But in non-profitable areas the functioning of municipal companies and other alternative water supply arrangements, almost without regulation, would be the rule, as part of micro-policies for poverty alleviation. But even in these cases, the Law allowed transfer to the private sector of alternative systems of water supply, based in social organizations such as small water cooperatives, committees and associations, as part of concessions, where profitability could be shown. This was established in Cochabamba's contract of concession.

The Law did not guarantee water supply to the poorest urban areas because they were considered to lack the capacity to afford the full costs of the service, thus reproducing inequality in access to the services.

CONCLUSIONS

Bolivia's new governance system, resulting from the structural adjustment policies, although in theory recognizing socio-cultural and economic diversity in its organizational and productive forms, in practice promoted capitalist economy sectors, undermining the subsistence economy sectors. These were considered unviable in the overall aim of entering the country into the global economy of private capital.

One criticism of the consensus discourse (Flyvbjerg, 2000) is that, like the stakeholder approach, it does not offer an appropriate understanding of the relations of power involved in the implementation of public policies. The stakeholder approach assumes that all actors are in the same position to engage in dialogue and to achieve consensus. In reality, this does not recognize that, in relation to dominant power, the consensus-seeking tendency of the stakeholder model denies asymmetries among the stakeholders involved. As Tully points out, markets and bureaucracies are not democratic if we understand that democracy implies dialogue (Tully, 1999). Most definitely, Bolivia is not a consensus society, and structural adjustment has not achieved a basis to generate consensus. On the contrary, the solutions implemented by Bolivia's neoliberal economic policies to control, in a differential and hierarchical way, the interests of stakeholders, have reproduced social and cultural inequality. These policies are promoting the emergence of a new landscape of social conflicts, such as the Water War in Cochabamba. In such an environment it is not possible to implement a society of consensus.

The scope of the new juridical framework, enacted through, for example, the Water Supply and Sanitation Law (No. 2029), is part of this new economy of power implemented through neoliberal reforms which manage the interest of water stakeholders within hierarchical criteria. Private interests are prioritized over the social organization of water supply, associated with the interests of the urban poor and the subsistence sectors of the economy. Cochabamba's Water War puts this strategy in question. It highlights the need for the democratic participation of civil society in water management, with equitable access to and use of water resources and services, and with respect to social and community-based organizations and interests dependent on rights and customs.

CHAPTER FOURTEEN

Linking theory and practice in development processes: the case of urban sanitation

Kevin Tayler

BACKGROUND – THE PROBLEM OF URBAN SANITATION

Rapid urbanization in the developing world is creating a growing demand for housing, infrastructure and services. Infrastructure deficiencies are often greatest in informal settlements, which are provided with few, if any, services at the time that they are first occupied. Given the fact that dense urban settlements are likely to suffer more than rural areas from the adverse effects of poor sanitation and drainage, there is a pressing need to deal with wastes in a hygienic and environmentally friendly way. Yet the World Bank estimates that approaching 26 per cent of the World's urban population, over 400 million people, lack access to even the simplest latrines (World Bank, 2000a: 140). The story is not just about the absence of facilities. Where sanitation services are provided, they may be unpleasant or unhygienic because of poorly designed technology, poor operation and maintenance, a failure to provide enough facilities to meet the needs of all the population, or some combination of the three. Poor and vulnerable groups may be excluded from the facilities that do exist. Even where action to solve local sanitation problems is taken, it may be at the expense of the wider environment.

Progress in improving urban sanitation has been limited. Large projects and programmes, often funded by international agencies, have had some success but they have rarely been scaled-up to make a city-wide impact. The local, more-or-less ad hoc, interventions favoured by many municipalities and local communities have similarly failed to match the overall demand for sanitation. The result is that the absolute number of people without access to adequate sanitation continues to grow in many countries and regions.

THE STRATEGIC SANITATION APPROACH – ONE POSSIBLE RESPONSE

In the 1980s, attempts to address the problem of inadequate sanitation focused on the development of 'appropriate', low-cost technologies. It soon became clear that, while the need for appropriate technologies could not be ignored, technology is only one aspect of a much larger picture. Changes are also needed in the ways in which the various stakeholders think about sanitation, and the systems and procedures through which sanitation services are provided. Without these changes, new technologies are likely to be used in one-off, externally funded projects rather than the sustainable programmes required for real development. There is a need to go beyond new technologies to an approach that considers social, financial, managerial and technical issues in an integrated way. This must be 'owned' by local stakeholders, since without this local ownership there can be no operational sustainability.

In recent years, a number of 'new' approaches to urban sanitation have been proposed in an attempt to respond to this need. These vary in detail, but most originated in international agencies and Northern research institutions, and are concerned with systems and procedures rather than technologies. Some approaches focus on one or two basic principles, while others incorporate a range of principles and concepts. An example of the latter is the Strategic Sanitation Approach (SSA), developed by the UNDP-World Bank Water and Sanitation Programme, now the Water and Sanitation Programme or WSP (Wright, 1997).

The SSA's two fundamental principles represent World Bank orthodoxy. The first is that sanitation initiatives should be responsive to demand, providing what people want and are willing to pay for. Without this emphasis on cost-recovery, it will not be possible to ensure the sound finances required to ensure sustained operation of sanitation services. This focus on sound finances underlines the SSA's implicit concern that operation and maintenance should be given as much attention as provision when planning sanitation services.

The SSA's second fundamental principle is its emphasis on appropriate incentives, which can be either positive or negative. An example of a positive incentive would be a bonus paid to sludge tanker operatives on every load of septic tank sludge delivered to a recognized treatment site; while a fine for dumping litter in a sewer or drain is an example of a negative incentive. Wright originally referred to the three Rs, rewards, rules and referees, required to ensure that rules are enforced firmly and fairly. More recently he has noted the need for a fourth R, the *resolution of conflicts*.

To take into account local circumstances, including user preferences, the SSA argues for the adoption of different approaches to sanitation in different areas. It refers to this as horizontal unbundling of technologies. Management responsibilities may similarly be horizontally unbundled, with different organizations taking responsibility for managing sanitation facilities in different zones within a city. As few people are familiar with the term unbundling, it is perhaps better to refer to diversity between the approaches used in different areas and division of management responsibilities for different areas. The SSA also recognizes that different management arrangements may be appropriate at different levels of a hierarchically structured system. It refers to this as vertical unbundling, although devolution has a similar meaning and is a more widely recognized term. The assumption is that various forms of unbundling make it easier to proceed in small steps requiring manageable levels of investment.

The term unbundling was originally used in the context of attempts to bring about increased private sector involvement in infrastructure provision, but can also be used in relation to the involvement of civil society groups and organizations in both provision and management. The SSA recognizes that such groups and organizations are most likely to be involved with provision at the local level. There are clear links with the theme of governance here. The SSA is, in effect, proposing governance arrangements involving strong partnerships between government, the private sector and civil society. By expanding the number of stakeholders involved in sanitation provision and management, it aims to increase the resource base and allow limited government resources to be used in a more focused and effective way.

The goal of good governance is also implicitly recognized in the SSA's insistence on the need to look at cities as a whole, as this implies a need to move beyond externally funded, one-off initiatives to a locally owned continuous process. Similarly, the SSA's call for a wide view of sanitation, encompassing stormwater drainage, solid waste management, sullage disposal and the disposal of human excreta, requires improved coordination between different service providers and is thus implicitly dependent on improved urban management. Its proposed division of towns and cities into zones, each with its own sanitation services, fits well with efforts to promote decentralized administrative arrangements that bring government closer to the people it serves.

Field testing the SSA in West Africa

The SSA principles and concepts were first tested and refined in projects in West Africa, in particular Kumasi in Ghana and Ouagadougou in Burkina Faso in the early 1990s. These projects included a strong emphasis on determining willingness to pay for services, using sophisticated contingent valuation surveys. Whittington et al. (1992) describe the process followed in Kumasi and the conclusions drawn from it. Unbundling was seen primarily in terms of the opportunities it gave for increasing private sector participation in a more competitive approach to local service provision. The West African projects appear to have been intended to prove the validity of the SSA, rather than to develop and prove the principles. Saywell and Hunt (1999) provide an overview of the results achieved in Kumasi, and their findings suggest that the process there did not move beyond the pilot project stage to achieve lasting benefits across the city as a whole.

RESEARCH ON THE PRACTICAL DEVELOPMENT OF THE APPROACH

The Dhaka workshop

Following the early West African initiatives, the South Asia division of the WSP (WSP-SA) held a regional workshop on the SSA in Dhaka, Bangladesh in order to promote greater awareness of strategic principles within the region. Several case studies of South Asian initiatives, each of which incorporated at least some aspects of the SSA, were commissioned prior to the workshop. For instance, the approach to the division of responsibilities between government and local communities adopted by the Orangi Pilot Project in Karachi, Pakistan had much in common with the SSA's emphasis on unbundling. Various initiatives, including the Orangi Pilot Project and the Mumbai-based NGO Society for the Promotion of Area Resource Centres (SPARC), had implemented local sanitation programmes based on the principle that users should pay in full for local sanitation services. However, the workshop confirmed that no major initiative in the region had incorporated anything like a comprehensive attempt to apply strategic principles. The activities that were closest to the SSA approach had been started by NGOs and, even where successful, had rarely been adopted by the municipal authorities.

Summary details of research

In the light of these findings, a proposal was prepared for a research study to explore the issues surrounding the practical implementation of strategic sanitation principles and concepts. This research was led by GHK Research and Training, a UK-based consultancy company. The team also included the Water, Engineering and Development Centre (WEDC) at Loughborough University, also in the UK, and WSP-SA. The research set out to answer to basic questions regarding the SSA:

- Are the key SSA principles and concepts valid as they stand, or do they need some modification in the light of experience?
- How can a strategic approach to sanitation provision, encompassing planning, implementation and ongoing management, be developed in practice?

The research involved short studies of a number of projects and programmes that were thought to illustrate SSA principles, and detailed studies on specific areas of relevance to aspects of the SSA. This chapter is mainly concerned with a third aspect of the research, a pilot strategic sanitation planning exercise which the research team initiated, supported and monitored in the Indian town of Bharatpur. Bharatpur has a population of about 200 000 and is situated in Rajasthan about 200 km south of Delhi. The exercise centred on the Bharatpur Municipal Council, but also involved other stakeholders from both government and non-government sectors. The aim was to attempt the implementation of a strategic process, and to record the successes achieved and any barriers to full implementation. It was expected that this would provide at least some answers to the two questions posed above.

THE BHARATPUR PILOT PROCESS

Background on Bharatpur

Bharatpur centres on a large fort which is surrounded by a wide moat, the Sujan Ganga. The original town was contained within an outer moat, most of which remains, although parts of it have been filled. In the past 50 years development has extended beyond the outer moat. Apart from the central fort area, the whole town is very flat. The Sujan Ganga originally received fresh water via a channel from outside the town, but it is now heavily polluted, as is the outer moat.

The town includes a number of types of development, including planned housing, unplanned areas and so-called 'slums'. At present, most of the higher-income areas are served by WCs, which discharge to open drains via septic tanks. Many lower-income households still rely on 'dry' toilets from which conservancy workers, commonly called scavengers or sweepers, remove faeces daily. Others rely on communal toilets or WCs discharging to double leach pits and provided under the Indian Government's Integrated Low Cost Sanitation (ILCS) programme. The state Public Health Engineering Department (PHED) produced plans for sewering the town in the 1970s, but had not been successful in implementing these plans at the start of the pilot project process, partly at least because the Rajasthan State Government had not provided funds to implement the scheme. Regardless of this, experience in similar towns in South Asia raised doubts about the institutional and financial capacity of towns such as Bharatpur to manage sewerage on a long-term basis

The planning process

The immediate aim of the pilot process was to involve local stakeholders in the development of a sanitation plan for the town, following strategic sanitation principles as far as possible. The intention was that the plan would then provide the basis for future action, where necessary being used to attract funding from state and national governments and external agencies. The research team would monitor the process, assess the relevance to it of the SSA principles, and use its findings to develop a guide to strategic sanitation planning.

To start the process, a research team member spent two months in Bharatpur in May and June 1998, during which period the idea of producing a strategic plan was introduced and the various local stakeholders were encouraged to come together to produce the plan. Following this, WSP-SA staff made intermittent support visits, and the team member who had made the first two-month input continued to provide inputs at critical periods during the process.

Two areas of concern quickly became apparent. Government officials tended to focus on the environmental aspects of poor sanitation and, in particular, on the effect of untreated wastewater discharges on water quality in the Sujan Ganga. Their concern was partly aesthetic and partly economic. Bharatpur is close to a major bird sanctuary, which receives many visitors. Improvements in Bharatpur's environment could well encourage visitors to the bird sanctuary to spend more time and money in the town. The NGOs, on the other hand, were more concerned about the options for improving the condition of the urban poor.

The first external input culminated in a planning workshop at which the various stakeholders agreed priorities and identified a number of tasks to be undertaken in order to move towards the production of a strategic plan for Bharatpur. These tasks included the following.

- Actions to improve the information base – for instance, the commissioning of a comprehensive topographical survey of the town in order to provide a basis for understanding and, if necessary, redesigning its drainage system.
- A review of existing services and programmes – including existing solid waste collection services and the ILCS.
- The implementation of immediate improvements where possible, in particular improved maintenance procedures for existing drains.
- Social and technical mapping of typical low-income settlements, envisaged as a town-wide activity that would provide information on the physical and social characteristics of various settlements and help identify the areas of greatest need.
- A study of sanitation finances, with a particular focus on the collection of user contributions for facilities provided under the ILCS programme.

A Sanitation Coordination Committee was formed to coordinate these activities. This included key municipal officials and representatives of the two NGOs that had actively engaged with the process before and during the planning workshop. It met regularly, and played an active role in linking the various stakeholders. Some stakeholders, in particular the state PHED and the NGO Sulabh International, which was responsible for implementation of the ILCS in Bharatpur, initially stayed aloof from the process. Over time, Sulabh became somewhat more involved but the PHED remained outside the process, partly because it equated sanitation with expensive investment in sewerage, an option that was quickly discarded by other stakeholders; and partly because of the centralized nature of decision-making within the PHED. Local PHED officials were reluctant to become involved in the strategic planning process in the absence of specific instructions to participate from the PHED head office in Jaipur, the state capital.

The rate of progress achieved varied between tasks. Completion of topographical mapping, at a scale of 1:500, with financial assistance from WSP-SA, took around one year from start to finish. As part of this work, main drainage routes were identified and longitudinal profiles of main drains were prepared. Progress in cleaning main drains was slow, partly because of difficulties in knowing how the drainage system worked in the absence of an overall drainage plan. A solid waste management study for the whole town was carried out by ACORD, one of the two active NGOs. Lupin, the second NGO, initially focused on community mobilization and later became involved in activities relating to household sanitation and local drainage. Efforts to engage with financial issues, particularly cost recovery, were less successful, for reasons that will be explored later.

As the process progressed, it became clear that financial and institutional constraints, including a lack of planning experience among local stakeholders, would make it difficult to move directly into a town-wide action plan. Rather, it was decided to implement demonstration initiatives that could be used to illustrate the possibility of strategic planning. Two wards with poor sanitation conditions and a high concentration of poor people were chosen for this purpose, and the two NGOs concentrated their efforts in these wards. In one ward the focus was on local solid waste management, while in the second efforts were made to mobilize community members to keep tertiary drains clean and desilt them as and when necessary. Parallel actions by the Bharatpur Municipal Corporation to ensure the adequacy of higher-order services and facilities, secondary solid waste collection in the first ward and secondary drainage in the second, were also identified. In both wards, residents identified the absence of latrines as another major concern, and it was decided that the next phase of Sulabh's ILCS work should start in these two wards. Possibilities for improving hygiene education were also considered at this stage.

The various activities and proposals were brought together to produce a draft Strategic Sanitation Plan for Bharatpur. The focus and contents of this plan were agreed by the Sanitation Committee, and work then continued to develop outline costings for the various plan components prior to finalizing the plan. As finally produced, the plan included a brief statement setting out its overall goal, a framework consisting of the rules and principles underlying the plan, and more detailed statements relating to five key areas – solid waste management, drainage, the low-cost latrine programme, hygiene promotion and sanitation finance. For each of these, the plan identified the current situation, medium-term (three-year) objectives, annual activities and targets, responsibilities for implementation and resource requirements.

Direct external WSP-SA and research team involvement with the process ceased with the completion of the plan, although WSP-SA expressed its intention to use Bharatpur as the location to pilot a number of training modules relating to various aspects of sanitation planning over the coming months. A workshop on participatory appraisal methods, using one of the two pilot wards for fieldwork, was held in February 2000. The plan was formally accepted in April 2000, at which time the Sanitation Committee was reconstituted as it emerged that it had previously had no status under standard government rules and procedures. The NGO Lupin, which had previously been a major stakeholder, lost its influence at this point and the committee became a much more conventional government body.

In June 2000, a *Guide to Strategic Planning for Municipal Sanitation* was produced by the research team and widely distributed to practitioners, researchers and representatives of international agencies (GHK, 2000). This set out a modified set of strategic concepts and principles, based on the findings of the research, together with guidance on the processes to be followed in developing and implementing strategic initiatives at the state, municipal and local levels. Perhaps the most important point made in the guide is the need to focus on process, concentrating not only on overall goals, but also on the immediate actions that can be taken to move towards those goals.

Copies of this guide were distributed at a follow-up workshop on the process, held in Jaipur in September 2000. The hope was that this would lead to further strategic initiatives in Rajasthan but, for reasons that will become clear, this intention was not realized.

RESEARCH FINDINGS RELATING TO THE KEY STRATEGIC PRINCIPLES

Demand

An early finding of the Bharatpur process was that, in the absence of suitable incentives, the various institutional stakeholders had limited interest in demand and cost recovery. Thus, for example, the ILCS should theoretically be demand-responsive and incorporate a degree of cost recovery from 'beneficiaries'. In practice, it seems that the process is very supply-driven and virtually no attempt is made to recover costs, partly because the Rajasthan State Government makes little attempt to recover its contribution, which is theoretically a loan to the municipality.

Complex demand assessment exercises have little relevance in such situations, because they assume that willingness to charge for services will follow once it is established that users are willing to pay more for those services. In practice, reluctance to charge for sanitation services in Bharatpur appeared to be based on a series of barely rationalized and deeply held assumptions that were unlikely to be changed by demand assessment exercises carried out by outsiders. The first need was therefore to change assumptions and raise willingness to charge, rather than to demonstrate willingness to pay.

Regardless of this, the experience with complex issues such as drainage suggested that demand cannot be explored in isolation from what can realistically and effectively be supplied. In this respect, the SSA's emphasis on demand as an alternative to supply-driven approaches appears misguided. The issue is not whether to focus on supply or demand, but rather how to respond to demand that has been informed in the light of what can realistically and usefully be supplied. Failure to consider the supply side may lead to frustrated demand, which may further undermine attempts to develop effective approaches to service provision.

Incentives

An equally important finding concerned the failure of existing systems to provide incentives for municipal officials and other stakeholders to plan and act strategically. Municipal officials in Bharatpur were used to responding to pressures from higher levels of government, politicians and interest groups in an essentially ad hoc way. These pressures arose in part from the centralized nature of government systems in Rajasthan, and could be seen as perverse incentives that actually discouraged the development of a planning culture. Those plans that existed, such as the PHED's sewerage plan, lacked credibility, partly because they were supply-driven and paid little attention to issues of affordability and cost recovery.

The introduction of a strategic planning approach under such circumstances is always likely to be difficult. In Bharatpur, the research team was the catalyst for the adoption of a strategic approach, and one incentive for local stakeholders to engage with this process was the hope that the World Bank's involvement through WSP-SA might lead to funds being made available to implement major improvement schemes identified in the plan. This mechanism is not generally replicable, even if it is desirable. Widespread application of strategic principles will be possible only if these principles are backed by appropriate incentives at the national and/or state levels. The SSA's concern with incentives is thus very important, but the focus must be on higher levels of government rather than the municipal level. This is perhaps the most important finding of the research. It ties in with Tendler's finding that improvements in local government are likely to arise from a three-way dynamic among local government, civil society and an active central government (Tendler, 1997).

The need to encourage higher levels of government to introduce and maintain incentives is illustrated by the case of the Bharatpur Sanitation Coordination Committee. While all stakeholders in Bharatpur accepted the value of the committee, this acceptance was passive rather than active, and the drive to maintain the effectiveness of the committee came largely from research team members. It is unlikely that the committee will continue to function without external support unless the need for such committees is mandated by the state government. In this respect, Zaidi's findings in Pakistan are relevant. Local authorities have a wide range of functions, some mandatory and some optional. Zaidi reported that local authorities found it difficult to fulfil their mandated roles, and rarely if ever attempted those that were optional (Zaidi, 1996). The experience in Bharatpur suggests that the same is likely to be true in India.

Hygiene education offers a specific example of the potential role of higher levels of government in creating effective incentives. It might be carried out more effectively if the state government amended its standard terms and conditions to include provision for hygiene education in all ILCS contracts, together with clear guidelines to local stakeholders on how they might provide it.

Unbundling

The research revealed that SSA's focus on unbundling represents one side of a more complex relationship. Organizations such as the World Bank, which deal with large, complex projects, should indeed be concerned to avoid monolithic management structures. However, the situation in Bharatpur was somewhat different in that a number of organizations were already involved in aspects of sanitation provision and were failing to coordinate with one another. This suggests that concern with unbundling must be balanced with awareness of the need for effective coordination between the various stakeholder groups. The latter is perhaps the greater problem in the context of India. This need for coordination is doubly important when attempts are made to take a wide view of sanitation, involving excreta, sullage, solid waste and stormwater disposal, as was done in Bharatpur.

On process, small steps and overall objectives

In retrospect, it is clear that the defining features of the Bharatpur approach were its emphasis on process and the central position given to the small-steps concept. The process involved three broad stages – understand problems; develop solutions; and plan city-wide. In situations characterized by limited resources, this approach allows action to be matched to resources. The initial emphasis on understanding problems helps to ensure that decisions are made on the basis of information rather than assumptions. Unfortunately, it proved hard to 'sell' the small steps concept to local stakeholders. In his opening address to the final Jaipur workshop, the State Secretary for Urban Development gave strong support to the small-steps approach taken in Bharatpur, but some of the other participants saw small steps as a synonym for ad hoc, and argued strongly for a more comprehensive master plan approach for networked systems such as drainage. The lesson here is that it is important to consider the ways in which immediate small-steps improvements will fit into some sort of overall plan. In this respect, the SSA concern with cities as a whole should be seen as an objective as much as a principle. Sound finances can similarly be seen as an overall objective. In the short term, the emphasis may well have to be on the 'art of the possible', improving existing financial arrangements where possible rather than seeking to implement radical change, while keeping in mind the need for sound finances so as to provide an overall check that a sanitation process is indeed strategic. As with the planning process, the key point is to keep the overall objective in mind while taking the limited steps imposed by financial and institutional constraints.

CONCLUSIONS AND THEIR IMPLICATIONS FOR SUSTAINABLE CITIES

Validity of the key SSA principles and concepts

In this final section we return to the questions posed at the start of the chapter. First, what are the findings regarding the validity of the key SSA principles and concepts? The basic strategic principles derived from the research project are similar to those identified by Wright (1997). To be strategic, sanitation initiatives must respond to informed demand; involve all the stakeholders, devolving and dividing responsibilities where appropriate; match action to available resources in a small-steps approach; and take a wide view of sanitation that considers it in an integrated way. Where our approach differs from that of Wright and, arguably, of many international agencies, is in its stress on grounding plans firmly in understanding of the existing situation. Conventional 'engineered' responses to development problems often start from the assumption that nothing exists already, so that it is possible to start with a blank sheet. The Strategic Sanitation research revealed that this is very rarely the case. People have usually taken some action to solve their sanitation problems, and their efforts may represent a considerable sunk investment which planners ignore at their peril. While this might seem too obvious to need mentioning, it can easily be ignored when principles and concepts are applied in a formulaic manner. The implication is that principles and concepts should be used to inform flexible processes, rather than being applied in a formulaic way. Thus, for example, attempts to transfer rigid prescriptions as to who should do what in an unbundled approach to sanitation from one country to another should be avoided. The basic social and institutional factors in the second country may be very different from those in the first.

Strategic planning in practice

The second question, relating to the development of strategic approaches in practice, presents greater difficulties. Wright (1997) suggests that the SSA is possible only if adaptable and flexible institutional systems already exist. By implication, these institutional systems should be ready to promote and support strategic principles. At the beginning of the process, Bharatpur fell short of these requirements in several important respects. First, local government organizations in India are bureaucracies and the people who work within them respond to rules, regulations and instructions that are generally handed down from higher levels of government. Their willingness and capacity to take independent action is often limited. An example of this is provided by the contrast between the research team's unsuccessful attempts to persuade the Bharatpur Municipal Corporation to carry out a review of work completed earlier under the low-cost Sanitation Scheme, and its quick response to a request from the state government to carry out a similar survey. The quality of the survey was not good, but it was done. Second, very few of the stakeholders had *practical* experience of working in a strategic way. Thus, for example, the need for participatory training was identified largely because it became clear that the local NGOs knew how to form community groups, but had little idea about what to do next. Similarly, government engineers and municipal officials found it difficult to know what to do to respond to sanitation-related needs in a strategic way. Because they were used to responding to problems as they arise, rather than planning proactively, they lacked a planning culture.

The Bharatpur process responded to these constraints by taking a small-steps approach at the local level, aiming to promote incremental improvements that built on the awareness and capacity of the various stakeholders and which have the potential to be integrated later into an overall strategic plan. However, this approach proved unsustainable in the long term, in the absence of appropriate incentives at the state level and a lack of capacity among the various stakeholders. The experience suggests the need for increased attention to developing the supportive context required to underpin planning at the municipal level. Special attention must be paid to the development of effective incentives and capacity for strategic planning and action. It is also important to recognize that different stakeholders have different priorities and concerns which, at times, will be mutually exclusive. In Bharatpur, efforts to introduce improved solid waste collection services in one ward foundered because private 'sweepers' working in the ward saw the initiative as a threat to their livelihoods, and the NGO working in the ward was unable to convince them otherwise. The experience confirms the need to develop capacity to deal with Wright's fourth R, the resolution of conflicts.

Attempts to introduce appropriate incentives will clearly be problematic unless higher levels of government see the need for change. The fact that this is often not the case is perhaps the greatest obstacle to sustainable urban development. Experience suggests that the Bharatpur process was not unique in its dependence on external ideas and inputs. There is no magic formula for dealing with this dilemma. Development will continue to depend on external inputs, and it is worth remembering that new ideas will be adopted only if they make sense in terms of the intended user's own rationale (Dudley, 1993). This suggests that development theorists and practitioners should examine their basic assumptions in order to establish whether they are likely to be comprehensible to local stakeholders and, where necessary, to work with local stakeholders to develop new ways of thinking about development. Without such actions, sustainable urban development is likely to remain a chimera. Beyond this, there is a need for shared action to develop a concern with strategic planning. This action may take various forms. The research team is currently working on initiatives to share the findings of the research through a series of workshops, the publication of the strategic sanitation planning guide, and the development of training courses in collaboration with South Asian training institutions.

Contributors

Cormac Davey is a planner from Oxford Brookes University, with professional interests in urban poverty, institutional development and land tenure. He has worked for NGOs in Oxford, Mexico and India. Currently he is a Physical Planner and Urban Development Adviser for the Department for International Development (DFID), UK. He worked as Project Adviser to the Government of Lesotho, assisting with public sector capacity-building in land and housing. He has recently coordinated the development of DFID's new urban strategy, Meeting the Challenge of Poverty in Urban Areas: Strategies for Achieving the International Development Targets.

W Judson Dorman is researching at the Department of Political Studies at the School of Oriental and African Studies, University of London. He is currently completing his PhD on state–society relations in Egypt with special reference to informal urbanization in Cairo.

Carlos Crespo Flores, a Bolivian sociologist, is currently Lecturer and Co-ordinator of the Environmental Centre for Post-Graduate Studies at San Simon University, Cochabamba, Bolivia. He has received a Fellowship from the European Union under the ALFA-IBIS Programme. His research interests focus on the conjuncture of natural resources, privatization policies and social movements. The chapter in this book is drawn from PhD research at Oxford Brookes University, UK on these themes, related to the privatization of urban water supply in Bolivia.

Emma Grant is based at the Faculty of the Built Environment, South Bank University, London. She works as a researcher and consultant on urban environment and health issues among low-income populations, with a particular focus on Latin America. Her current research is on social capital and violence, and its links to health and governance.

Dr Al-Moataz Hassan studied at the University Ain Shams in Egypt, University of Wales (Aberystwyth), UK, and the School of Planning, Oxford Brookes University, UK, where he gained his PhD. He is currently a Visiting Fellow at the School of Planning of Oxford Brookes University and a Lecturer at the Faculty of Engineering at the United Arab Emirates University. He has extensive experience with consultancies and international agencies including

UNDP and DFID. His teaching and research interests include urban development, environmental planning and management, environmental impact assessment, public participation, environmental policy making and sustainable urban environment in the less-developed countries.

Dr Paul Jenkins is Director of the Centre for Environment and Human Settlements in the School of Planning and Housing, Edinburgh. An architect/planner, he has worked in central and local government, NGOs, the private sector, and international and community-based organizations. His work has focused on urban development and housing; policy and practice; architecture and construction; training and research – based in Latin America and Southern Africa. Current interests include policy advocacy and professional practice related to low-income groups, through widening participation and community empowerment.

Dr José Júlio Lima is Brazilian. He studied architecture at Pará Federal University, Brazil; engineering at Fukui University, Japan; and urban design at Oxford Brookes University, UK, where he also gained his PhD. After working in local planning agencies in Brazil, he has been a senior lecturer at Pará Federal University since 1994. His current research interests are in urban regulatory instruments and systems in the developing world, urban management and social sustainability in urban design.

Dr Gordon McGranahan is Senior Researcher at the Human Settlements Programme of the International Institute for Environment and Development (IIED), London, where he heads the research programme on urban development. Until 2000 he headed the Urban Environment Programme at the Stockholm Environment Institute. With a PhD from Wisconsin-Madison, he has written widely on urban environment issues including *Citizens at Risk: From Urban Sanitation to Sustainable Cities* (with Jacobi, Songsore, Sujadi and Kjellén), Earthscan, 2001.

Koyi Mchunu is South African and has studied social anthropology, history and law at Natal University, South Africa, and city and regional planning at Cornell University, USA. He is Lecturer in Planning in the Department of Town and Regional Planning at the Cape Technikon, Cape Town, but is currently on research study leave at Oxford Brookes University, UK. In addition to environmental issues, his research interests include planning theory, local economic development and multiculturalism.

Andrés Ortiz-Gómez is a lecturer in urban planning at the Universidad Javeriana in Bogotá, Colombia. He trained as an architect in Columbia, engaging in a wide range of projects and research which included land tenure forms in Bogatá and the public–private interaction in provision of housing for the urban poor. He has recently completed an MSc in Urban Planning for Developing Countries at Oxford Brookes University, UK.

David Sanderson is currently Technical and Policy Adviser at CARE International UK. He trained as an architect before taking an MSc in Development Practices at Oxford Brookes University, UK. He has worked for 10 years in development- and emergency-related activities in Asia, Africa and Latin America

Dr David Satterthwaite is Director of the Human Settlements Programme of the International Institute for Environment and Development (IIED), London, and Editor of the journal *Environment and Urbanisation*. A development planner by training with a PhD from the London School of Economics, he edited the *Earthscan Reader on Sustainable Cities* (Earthscan, 1998) and co-authored (with Jorge Hardoy and Diana Mitlin) *Environmental Problems in an Urbanising World: Supporting Local Solutions to City Problems in Africa, Asia and Latin America* (Earthscan, 2001).

Dr Harry Smith is a Research Fellow at the Centre for Environment and Human Settlements in the School of Planning and Housing (CEHS), Edinburgh. He trained in architecture in Spain and planning in the UK, where he was in professional practice; recent activities include research on housing in Costa Rica; teaching in the CEHS; and the management of community self-build projects in Scotland. Current research interests include planning for sustainable urban development, housing policy, participation in planning and housing focusing on low-income groups in the developing world.

Kevin Tayler is a chartered civil engineer specializing in urban services provision with an emphasis on water and sanitation. He has extensive international experience and is currently a freelance consultant after almost 20 years with the GHK International consultancy. From 1996 to 2000 he was managing Director of GHK Research and Training. The main focus of his work is bridging the theory–practice gap, believing that development is a practical discipline in which sound theory must flow from analysis of real situations.

Professor Rodney White studied at the Universities of Oxford, UK, Pennsylvania State, USA and Bristol, UK. He is currently Professor of Geography and Director of the Institute for Environmental Studies at the University of Toronto, Canada. He is an infrastructure planner with extensive experience, especially in Africa, where he has been working on self-help housing, rural road, and urban and rural water supply projects. Recent books include *North, South and the Environmental Crisis* (University of Toronto Press, 1993) and *Urban Environmental Management* (John Wiley, 1994). *Building the Ecological City* is in press with Woodhead Publishing. In 1997 he co-chaired a research group which produced *Coping with Natural Hazards in Canada: Scientific, Government and Insurance Industry Perspectives*. In 2000–01 he was an Associate Fellow of the Environmental Change Institute at the University of Oxford.

Professor Roger Zetter holds degrees from Cambridge, Nottingham and Sussex Universities in the UK. He is a planner, and Deputy Head of the School of Planning at Oxford Brookes University, UK, where he is also director of the DATEs (Developing and Transitional Economies) research cluster and the MSc programme in Urban Planning in the Developing World. His research, teaching and publishing interests are in urban sector aid policies, land markets and shelter provision in the developing world, especially in the context of Africa. He also has extensive research and consultancy experience on refugees, asylum-seeking and forced migration. He is currently editing two other books – *Designing Sustainable Cities in the Developing World* (Ashgate), and *From Welfare to Market Economy: Policy Shifts in Urban Development* (Earthscan), both due for publication in 2003.

Notes

CHAPTER 1

1. Secretary General of the Stockholm Conference and former executive director to the United Nations Environment Programme (UNEP).
2. Carrying capacity has no universally accepted definition (Jacobs, 1997). However, the underlying notion is that of a threshold in the relationship between human activities and the environment. The environmental capacity in this sense means the amount of use the area or resource is able to sustain without irreversible or otherwise unacceptable loss or damage (Jacobs, 1997; Aplin et al., 1999).

CHAPTER 3

1. There are also two other areas of disagreement, which are beyond the scope of this chapter, that have been discussed elsewhere. The first is disagreement over the extent to which the concept of sustainability can be usefully taken to include non-environmental goals such as poverty alleviation (McGranahan et al., 1996; Marcuse, 1998). The second, related to this, is the scale of the urban poor's contribution to environmental degradation; many green agenda authors assume that urban poverty in general, or the urban poor in particular, contribute much to environmental degradation. But, in general, levels of consumption and waste generation among low-income urban households are very low, so it is difficult to see how this is the case. Green agenda proponents often confuse high levels of environmental risk, which most low-income groups face, with large contributions to environmental degradation, which are far more associated with higher-income groups and larger industrial or commercial concerns (Hardoy et al., 1992b; Hartmann, 1998; Satterthwaite, 1998).
2. This chapter is a revised version of McGranahan and Satterthwaite (2000). The authors are grateful to Cedric Pugh for his comments on an earlier draft.
3. Obviously, not all urban environmental innovation happens in democratic societies, as can be seen in the fact that much of the environmental innovation in Curitiba (Brazil) preceded the return to democracy in Brazil. The brown agenda is likely to be more strongly associated with local democracy than the green agenda, especially where the green agenda serves the interests of higher-income or otherwise politically powerful groups. In addition, the low consumption and waste-generation levels of most low-income urban dwellers also serve to keep down the ecological impact of the urban centres in which they live – which means care is needed to avoid potential conflicts between reducing consumption as part of the green agenda and the increased consumption implied by poverty reduction. But as various examples given in this chapter

suggest, the levels of consumption required to meet the health needs of deprived groups tend to be very small relative to the levels of consumption in excess of health needs already going to more affluent groups.

CHAPTER 5

1. 107 schools × 1300 students = 139 100 students
   5–17-year-olds make up 25 per cent of the Colombian population
   139 100 × 4 = 556 400 inhabitants
   556 400/50 per cent out of 158 000 new inhabitants per year = 7 years

CHAPTER 6

1. The author worked (as part of a DFID-funded programme) in Lesotho from October 1997 to October 1999 with DLHUD.
2. See World Bank, 1995 a, b and Wegelin et al., 1996.
3. During August 1998 South Africa and Botswana, representing the Southern Africa Development Community, intervened in the internal affairs of Lesotho in order to maintain the elected government of the day, the Lesotho Congress for Democracy Party, whose governance was being undermined by political instability caused by those in opposition to the May 1998 election results. The Link Manager and consultants were absent from Lesotho between July 1998 and April 1999.
4. Significantly, during this time the Link Manager left the project, leaving it without a recognized expert on change management and institutional development.
5. In July 1999 the World Bank launched the Comprehensive Development Framework – representing a new process approach to doing business for the World Bank and its members – which helps countries become the leaders and owners of their own participatory development actions. Together with the IMF, they have agreed that country-owned poverty reduction strategies should provide the basis for all World Bank (International Development Assistance) and IMF concessional lending, as well as debt relief under the Highly Indebted Poor Countries. In effect, the Poverty Reduction Strategy Programme translates the principles of the Comprehensive Development Framework into practical plans for action. City development strategies complement these approaches at city and town levels.

CHAPTER 9

1. An exception was the US International Co-operation Administration's programme for family-based self-help and mutual aid projects in several Latin American Countries in the late 1950s.
2. As part of the US government's drive to ensure political 'stability' in the region in the aftermath of the Cuban revolution.
3. A strategy based on squatter settlement upgrading to contain crises, and sites and services to meet current and future needs (UNCHS, 1987: 195).
4. The implementation of this Habitat Agenda, as well as of Local Agenda 21, is monitored and evaluated by two UNCHS programmes: the Best Practices and

Local Leadership Programme and the Urban Indicators Programme which, combined, form the Global Urban Observatory. In 2000 UNCHS developed two new but related flagship programmes – Secure Tenure and Governance.

5. The UNCHS Community Development Programme comprised the Training Programme in Community Participation and the Community Management Programme, both with Danida support. The objective of the Training Programme (1984–94) was 'to make community participation an institutional element of urban low-income housing development programmes and, thus, of national strategies' (Danida, 1994: 1). It comprised projects in Bolivia, Sri Lanka and Zambia. The objective of the Community Management Programme (which began in 1991) was 'to strengthen the capacity of low-income communities to plan, operate and maintain needed facilities, services and housing improvements' (Danida, 1994: 1). It was implemented in four countries: Costa Rica, Ecuador, Ghana and Uganda.

6. In 1994 it was also supported by over 10 bilateral external support agencies, making it the largest global multi-agency technical assistance programme in urban development in the world (Cohen and Leitmann, 1994; Wegelin, 1994).

7. Stren (1993) and Post (1997) have noted the lack of a precise and commonly shared definition of 'urban management', and have discussed the implications of this lack of definition for policy-making.

8. There have also been some minor bilateral aid activities in the shelter sector, the only others of any significance being Swedish and Finnish assistance to urban management in Beira and Nacala, respectively. UNICEF has also been active in rural and some peri-urban water supply projects.

9. UNDP fought for the dominant programme position in the sector in Mozambique and essentially lost as the World Bank continued to operate with only passing reference to UN activities in the country – see detail in Jenkins (1998). UNCHS in this period was also going through its major restructuring and had lost considerable influence within the international agency community.

10. Source: official Mozambique web page, www.mozambique.mz (absolute poverty is defined as per capita expenditure of less than US$0.5 per day).

11. Over a total population of some 19 million, this means an 85 per cent increase, or 2.5 per cent a year (UNCHS, 1996a). The approximately 1 million residents are expected to rise to some 1.6 million by 2010 – more than an additional 100 000 households (Metropolitan Maputo Structure Plan, 1999 – unpublished consultancy document, see also *Cities* 17(3): 139–150).

12. For instance the USA exerted political pressure to withhold food aid in 1983–94 until Mozambique agreed to enter into the N'Komati Accord with South Africa, which paved the way for an agreement with the IMF and the Paris Club (for more detail see Jenkins, 1998).

13. The main conclusion of an evaluation of PROFAC's activities in several settlements was that no significant differences could be found between project settlements and non-project settlements as a result of PROFAC's intervention (UNCHS, 1998).

14. This is further developed by Jenkins and Smith (2001a).

15. In relation to the former, UNCHS (1987) referred to 'government' in general, but when dealing with civil society it was much more specific and referred basically to community-based organizations.

16. Governments' roles were to 'move away from producing, financing and maintaining housing, and towards improving housing market efficiency and the housing conditions of the poor' (World Bank, 1993: 7).

17. The former, focusing mostly on state organizations, involved housing; the latter was involved with central and local states throughout Central America, as well as with community organizations (in a theoretical ratio of 2 to 1).

CHAPTER 10

1. This chapter draws on doctoral thesis research in Cairo which was, in part, supported by a grant from the University of London Central Research Fund. I would also like to thank Nigel James, David Sims and Graham Toon for their help with the maps, Lesley Downing for her considerable editorial assistance, as well as Marjorie and Sara Rich Dorman for proofreading, suggestions and moral support. Obviously, any errors of fact, interpretation and mapping are mine alone.
2. The state is defined here as comprising the institutions of power, whereas the notion of regime refers to the form of rule – particularly with respect to relations between social groups and state organs. Lastly, much of the empirical material in this chapter is discussed in terms of the category of government, defined as 'the specific occupants of public office' (Chazan et al., 1992).
3. Less than 4 per cent of Egypt's surface is arable (Ikram, 1980).
4. Although the government announced plans to demolish 12 informal areas in Cairo and proposed to upgrade 67 others, relatively few areas have been cleared (Arandel and El Batran, 1997; IDSC, undated). Large-scale, Egyptian-financed upgrading has been confined to a single showpiece project in Giza (interview with Giza governorate official; Tadros, 1996).
5. AMBRIC (American British Consultants) is the engineering consortium that has managed the project since its early phases.

CHAPTER 11

1. The author would like to thank the Instituto Centro Americano de la Salud, Guatemala for their role in the fieldwork for this study, and in particular Andres Cabanas, whose research report contributed to the context description in this chapter.
2. This chapter constitutes part of a larger research project which aimed to identify the positive and negative experiences of the 'development process' in El Mezquital, and to disseminate this information within a society where the space for discussion and debate has been very restricted, and where poverty, marginality and precariousness are increasing rather than declining. The research also aimed to document and synthesize the nature of community organization in El Mezquital; to analyse the interventions and impact of external organizations – international, governmental and non-governmental; and evaluate the successes and failures of the case of El Mezquital in tackling poverty, where poverty is understood to refer broadly to inadequate quality of life and unmet basic needs.

CHAPTER 12

1. See Dewar (2000) and Schoonraad (2000) for a detailed discussion on some of the challenges to the compact city approach.
2. The Development Facilitation Act (1995) and the Local Government Transition Act Second Amendment (1996).
3. In worst cases, distances over 60 kilometres away have been recorded (Dewar, 200: 210).
4. See Hoch (1984) for an argument against dualism; and Milroy (1991); Beauregard (1998); Sandercock (1998) on the problem with 'public interest'.

CHAPTER 13

1. Pacto por la Democracia (Democracy Pact), 1985–89; Acuerdo Patriotico (Patriotic Coalition), 1989–93; Pacto de la Gobernabilidad y la Democracia (Pact of Governability and Democracy), 1993–97; Compromiso por Bolivia (Compromise for Bolivia), 1997–2001.
2. There is a National Dialogue Law in process of approval by Parliament.
3. North of Potosi and South of Cochabamba provinces, and some Amazon indigenous groups, are in this situation.
4. Castells (1997) refers to African countries that have not articulated the global capitalism dynamic, which largely ignores them and develops programmes such as poverty alleviation to avoid starvation.
5. The Department of Santa Cruz is the best example, where agro-industry is promoted and supported by policies.
6. World Bank figures vary slightly: 62.9 and 17.5 per cent of urban and rural populations, respectively, have access to sanitation services (World Bank/World Resources Institute, 2000: 3).
7. One of the propositions approved by the International Conference on Water and the Environment in Dublin (1992) was the importance of participation in the conservation of water under a stakeholder approach.
8. Stakeholders are those actors whose interests are affected by interventions of a project or strategy; these vary from project to project. It is contended that, through a consensus of the common interests of the different actors involved in development processes, public policies will reflect the interests of all those affected by these policies (World Bank, 1995c).
9. The concession in La Paz and Cochabamba included the water sources.
10. In the case of Cochabamba's water contract, the company could use water sources belonging to small municipalities from the metropolitan area.
11. Small surface water sources served by rivers.

References

AbdelRahman, M. (1999) Civil society against itself: Egyptian NGOs in the neoliberal era, paper presented at the Third EURAMES Conference, Ghent, September 1999.

Abt Associates et al. (1982) *Informal Housing in Egypt*, report submitted to US Agency for International Development, Washington, DC, pp. 25–48, 61–62.

Abu-Lughod, J. (1971) *Cairo: 1001 Years of the City Victorious*, Princeton University Press, Princeton, NJ, pp. 221–237.

AID (1978) *Project Paper: Egypt – Housing and Community Upgrading*, Agency for International Development, Cairo.

AID (1984) *Project Paper: Cairo Sewerage II*, Agency for International Development, Cairo.

Alcaldía Mayor de Bogotá (1998) Por la Bogotá que Queremos, *Plan de Desarrollo 1998–2000*, www.alcaldiabogota.gov.co

Alcaldía Mayor de Bogotá (1999) *Plan de Ordenamiento Territorial. Documento Técnico de Soporte*, Departamento Administrativo de Planeación Distrital (DAPD), Bogotá.

AMBRIC et al. (1991) *Greater Cairo Wastewater Project: System Load Review*, report by AMBRIC (American British Consultants) for the Ministry of Reconstruction, New Communities, Housing and Utilities – Organization for the Execution of the Greater Cairo Wastewater Project (Arab Republic of Egypt), February 1991, Vol. 1, p. 19.

AMBRIC et al. (1993) *Greater Cairo Wastewater Project: West Bank Project – West Bank Strategic Plan, Final Report*, report by AMBRIC (American British Consultants) for the Ministry of Reconstruction, New Communities, Housing and Utilities – Organization for the Execution of the Greater Cairo Wastewater Project (Arab Republic of Egypt), October 1993, p. 3/20.

AMBRIC et al. (1995) *Greater Cairo Wastewater Project: Review Statement – Second Quarter 1995*, report by AMBRIC (American British Consultants) for the Ministry of Housing and Utilities – Organization for the Execution of the Greater Cairo Wastewater Project, General Organization for Sanitary Drainage, Second Quarter 1995.

Anderson, L. (1997) Prospects for liberalism in North Africa: identities and interests in preindustrial welfare states, in: Entelis, J. (ed.), *Islam, Democracy and the State in North Africa*, Indiana University Press, Bloomington, IN, pp. 127–140.

Aplin, G., Beggs, P., Brierly, G., Cleugh, H., Curson, P., Mitchell, P., Pitman, A. and Rich, D. (1999) *Global Environmental Crises: An Australian Pespective*, Oxford University Press, Melbourne, Australia.

Arandel, C. and El Batran, M. (1997) *The Informal Housing Development Process in Egypt*, DPU Working Paper No. 82, Development Planning Unit, The Bartlett – University College London, p. 30.

ASCG Inc. (1992) *Cairo Sewerage II – West Bank: 1991 Interim Evaluation Summary Report*, report to US Agency for International Development, Office of Urban Administration and Development, Portland, 19 March 1992, pp. 2–4.

Badash, A.A. (1996) *Our Urban Future: New Paradigms for Equity and Sustainability*, Zed Books, London.

Bahl, R. and Linn, J. (1992) *Urban Public Finance in Developing Countries*, Oxford University Press/World Bank, New York.

Bahr, J. and Mertins, G. (1992) The Latin American City, *Colloquium Geographicum*, 22: 65–75.

Barton, C., Bernstein, J., Leitmann, J. and Eigen, J. (1994) *Towards Environmental Strategies for Cities; Policy Considerations for Urban Environmental Management in Developing Countries*, UNDP, UNCHS and World Bank Urban Management Program No. 18, World Bank, Washington, DC.

Batley, R. (1983) *Power through Bureaucracy, Urban Political Analysis in Brazil*, Gower, Aldershot.

Bava, S. (1995) Dilemas da Gestão Municipal Democrática, in: Valladares, L. and Coelho, M. (eds), *Governabilidade e Pobreza no Brasil*, Civilização Brasileira, Rio de Janeiro, pp. 161–190.

Beatley, T. (1995) Planning and sustainability: the elements of a new improved paradigm?, *Journal of Planning Literature*, 4: 383–395.

Beauregard, R. (1998) Writing the Planner, *Journal of Planning Education and Research*, 18: 93–101.

Boden, R. (1989) *The Urban Designer As Interpretant – A Case Study From A Developing Country*, PhD thesis, University of Washington, Seattle, WA.

Boden, R. (1992) The influence of traditional values and historical symbols on urban design, *Journal of Architectural and Planning Research*, 9(4): 287–299.

Boden, R. (1993) Cultural anthropology in relation to urban design and planning, *Journal of South African Town and Regional Planning*, 35.

Bradley, D., Stephens, C., Cairncross, S. and Harpham, T. (1991) *A Review of Environmental Health Impacts in Developing Country Cities*, Urban Management Program Discussion Paper No. 6, World Bank, UNDP and UNCHS (Habitat), Washington, DC.

Breheny, M. (1992a) The contradictions of the Compact City, in: Breheny, M. (ed.), *The Compact City*, Pion, London.

Breheny, M.J. (ed.) (1992b) *Sustainable Development and Urban Form*, Pion, London.

Brennan, E. (1993) Urban land and housing issues facing the third world, in: Kasarda, J. and Parnell, A. (eds), *Third World Cities: Problems, Policies and Prospects*, Sage, London.

Bryner, G. (1999) Agenda 21: myth or reality, in: Vig, N. and Axelord, R. (eds), *The Global Environment: Institutions, Law, and Policy*, Earthscan, London.

Burgess, R. (1992) Helping some to help themselves: third world housing policies and development strategies, in: Mathéy, K. (ed.) *Beyond Self-Help Housing*, Mansell Publishing, London/New York, pp. 75–91.

Burgess, R. (1998) Urban violence: the next agenda? *Newsletter, Cendep*, Oxford Brookes University, Oxford, UK.

Burgess, R., Carmona, M. and Kolstee, T. (eds) (1997) *The Challenge of Sustainable Cities: Neoliberalism and Urban Strategies in Developing Countries*, Zed Books, London.

Burgess, R., Carmona, M. and Kolstee, T. (1998) *Neoliberalismo y Estrategias Urbanas. Flasco*, Facultad Latinoamericana de Ciencias Urbanas, Costa Rica.

Caldeira, T. (1996) *Building up Walls: The New Pattern of Spatial Segregation in Sao Paulo*. Blackwell, Oxford/Unesco, pp. 55–72.

Calderon, F. and Lechner, N. (1998) *Más allá del Estado, más allá del Mercado: la democracia*, Plural Editores, La Paz.

Calderon, F. and Szmukler, A. (1999) *La Política en las Calles*, CERES-Plural Editores, La Paz.

Caldwell, L. (1996) *International Environmental Policy: From the Twentieth to the Twenty-First Century*, Duke University Press, Durham, NC.

Cámara de Comercio de Bogotá (1996) *Estudio Prospectivo de Seguridad*, Misión Siglo XIX, Bogotá.

Cammack, P., Pool, D. and Tordoff, W. (1993) *Third World Politics, A Comparative Introduction*, Macmillan, London.

Carney, D. (1998) Implementing the sustainable rural livelihoods approach, in: Carney, D. (ed.), *Sustainable Rural Livelihoods: What Contribution Can We Make?* DFID, London, pp. 3–26.

Castells, M. (1997) *The Rise of the Network Society, The Information Age: Economy, Society and Culture*, Vol. I, Blackwell, Oxford, UK.

CEPAL (2000) *Panorama Social de America Latina*, Naciones Unidas, Santiago.

Chambers, R. and Conway, G. (1992) *Sustainable Rural Livelihoods: Practical Concepts for the 21st Century*, Discussion Paper No. 296, Institute for Development Studies, Brighton, UK.

Chazan, N. et al. (1992) *Politics and Society in Contemporary Africa*, 2nd edn, Lynne Rienner, Boulder, CO, pp. 39–40.

CHF (1988) *Project Completion Report: Housing and Community Upgrading for Low Income Egyptians*, USAID/Arab Republic of Egypt – Ministry of Housing and Public Utilities, Cooperative Housing Foundation, Cairo, 26 August 1988, pp. 27–38.

COGEP (1992) *Diagnóstico do Plano Diretor de Belém*, Prefeitura Municipal de Belém.

Cohen, M.A. and Leitmann, J.L. (1994) Will the World Bank's real new urban policy please stand up? *Habitat International*, 18(4): 117–126.

Cointreau, S. (1982) *Environmental Management of Urban Solid Waste in Developing Countries*, Urban Development Technical Paper No. 5, World Bank, Washington, DC.

Connolly, P. (1999) Mexico City: our common future?, *Environment and Urbanization*, 11(1): 53–78.

Cooper, G. (1999) Carbon dioxide permits prepare for take-off, *Environmental Finance*, December/January, 16–17.

Cooper, G. (2000) Shell steps off the gas, *Environmental Finance*, February, 14–15.

Crespo, C. (2000a) *La Coordinadora como movimiento social y Crisis de Dispositivos de Poder*, paper presented at 'Agua y Conflictos', UMSSS–Cochabamba, May 2000. A version of this paper was published in *Ecología Política* 20 (segundosemestre) under the title 'La guerra del agua en Cochabamba: movimientos socilaes y crisis de dispositivos de poder'.

Crespo, C. (2000b) Democracia y equidad en la ley de agua potable y alcantarillado sanitario no 2029, in: Crespo, C. (ed.), *Agua: Conflicto y Poder. Seis ensayos sobre la Guerra del Agua*, CERES, Cochabamba.

Dahiya, B. and Pugh, C. (2000) The localization of Agenda 21and the Sustainable Cities Programme, in: Pugh, C. (ed.), *Sustainable Cities in Developing Countries*, Earthscan, London.

Damián, A. (1992) Ciudad de México: servicios urbanos en los noventas, *Vivienda*, 3(1): 29–40.

Danida (1994) *Evaluation of DANIDA/UNCHS Training Programme in Community Participation*, Danida, Copenhagen.

De Alfaro, G. and González, L. (1997) *Estudio cuantitativo de las áreas urbano-marginales del AMCG*, COINAP/UNICEF, Guatemala.

DAPD (2000) *Plan de Desarrollo Territorial*, Acuerdo 7 de 1979, Acuerdo 6 de 1990, Departamento Administrativo de Planeación Distrital, Bogotá.

DNP (1999) *Datos de Población*, Departamento Nacional de Planeación, www.dnp.gov.co

Development Alternatives Inc. et al. (1999a) *Policy Reform in Egypt's Water and Wastewater Sector: Decentralization and Private Sector Participation*, report prepared for the US Agency for International Development, p. 4.

Development Alternatives Inc. et al. (1999b) *Assessment of the Managerial Capacity of the Cairo General Organization for Sanitary Drainage*, report prepared for the US Agency for International Development, p. ii.

Dewar, D. (2000) The relevance of the compact city approach: the management of urban growth in South African cities, in: Jenks, M. and Burgess, R. (eds), *Compact Cities: Sustainable Urban Forms for Developing Countries*, Spon Press, London.

DFID (2001) *Meeting the Challenge of Poverty in Urban Areas: Strategies for Achieving the International Development Targets*, Department for International Development, London.

Díaz, D.B., López Follegatti, J.L. and Hordijk, M. (1996) Innovative urban environmental management in Ilo, Peru, *Environment and Urbanization*, 8(1): 21–34.

Douglass, M. (1989) The environmental sustainability of development – coordination, incentives and political will in land use planning for the Jakarta metropolis, *Third World Planning Review*, 11(2): 211–238.

Downing, T.E. (1999) Household food security in the third world, in: Potter, T. and Colman, B. (eds), *Handbook of Weather, Climate and Water*, McGraw-Hill, New York.

Downing, T.E., Oolsthorn, A.A. and Tol, R.S.J. (eds) (1999) *Climate, Change and Risk*, Routledge, London.

Drakakis-Smith, D.Y (1986) *Urbanization in the Developing World*, Croom Helm, New Hampshire, USA.

Drakakis-Smith, D. (1996) Third world cities: sustainable urban development, in: *International Perspectives in Urban Studies 4*, Jessica Kingsley, London.

Dudley, E. (1993) *The Critical Villager: Beyond Community Participation*, Routledge, London/New York.

Dumm, T. and Hardt, M. (2000) Sovereignity, multitudes, absolute democracy: a discussion between Michael Hardt and Thomas Dumm about Hardt and Negri's Empire, *Theory and Event*, 4(3): 1–6.

Economist Intelligence Unit (1997) *Lesotho Country Profile* 1996–1997, *The Economist*, London.

Edralin, J. (1997) New local governance and capacity-building: a strategy approach. examples from Africa, Asia and Latin America, *Regional Development Studies*, 3, 109–149.

Elkin, T. and McLaren, D. with Hillman, M. (1991) *Reviving the City towards Sustainable Development*, Friends of the Earth, London.

Elkhishin, K. (1990) Planning for growth in the Cairo region: a strategic management approach modelled on the Paris experience, PhD thesis, University of Pennsylvania, PA, pp. 128, 150–151, 177.

El-Messiri, S. (1989a) *Regularization of Land Title for Informal Communities in Cairo: An Analysis and Proposed Approach*, Cooperative Housing Foundation for USAID, Cairo, pp. 3–19.

El-Messiri, S. (1989b) *Recovering Development Costs for Community Upgrading: An Analysis of the Experience in Egypt*, Cooperative Housing Foundation for USAID, Cairo, p. 6.

Engelman, R. (1998) Population, consumption and equity, *Tiempo: Global Warming and the Third World*, 30: 3–10.

EQI (1988) Evaluation of Cairo Sewerage I Rehabilitation, report by Environmental Quality International to US Agency for International Development, February 1988.

ERF (2000) Economic Trends in the MENA Region 2000: Fiscal Performance in the MENA Region, Economic Research Forum for the Arab Countries, Iran and Turkey, www.erf.org.eg/html/body_mena.asp

Ewing, R. (1997) Is Los Angeles-style sprawl desirable? *Journal of the American Planning Association* 63(1).

Faber, G. (1996) International trade and environmental policy, in: Blowers, A. and Glasbergen, P. (eds), *Environmental Policy in an International Context*, No. 3, Open University of Netherlands/Arnold, UK.

Fernandes, E. and Varley, A. (1998) *Illegal Cities: Land and Urban Change in Developing Countries*, Zed Books, London.

Flyvbjerg, B. (1998) *Rationality and Power: Democracy in Practice*, University of Chicago Press, Chicago, IL.

Flyvbjerg, B. (2000) Ideal history, real rationality: Habermas versus Foucault and Nietzsche. Paper presented to the Political Studies Association, UK, 50th annual Conference, London.

Forondo, M.E.F. (1998) Chimbote's Agenda 21: initiatives to support its development and implementation, *Environment and Urbanization*, 10(2): 129–147.

Garcia Linera, A. et al. (2000) *El retorno de la Bolivia Plebeya*, Muela del Diablo Editores, La Paz, Bolivia.

Garcia, M. and Zamudio, J. (1997) *Descentralización en Bogotá Bajo la Lupa (1992–1996)*, CINEP, Bogotá.

Gardner, D. and Van Huyck, A. (1990) *The Helwan Housing and Community Upgrading Project for Low-income Egyptians: The Lessons Learned*, report to US Agency for International Development, Cairo.

Garner, R. (2000) *Environmental Politics: Britain, Europe and the Global Environment*, Contemporary Political Series, Macmillan, London.

Gaye, M. and Diallo, F. (1997) Community participation in the management of the urban environment in Rufisque (Senegal), *Environment and Urbanization*, 9(1): 9–29.

Gellert, G. and Palma, S.I.P. (1999) *Precariedad urbana, desarrollo comunitario y mujeres en el Area Metropolitana de Guatemala*, FLACSO, Guatemala.

GHK (2000) *Strategic Sanitation for Municipal Sanitation: A Guide*, GHK Research and Training, www.ghkint.com

Gilbert, A. (1993) Third world cities: the changing national settlement system, *Urban Studies*, 30(4/5): 721–740.

Gilbert, A. (ed.) (1996) *The Mega City in Latin America*, United Nations University, Tokyo.

Gilbert, A. (1998) *The Latin American City*, Latin America Bureau, London.

Gilbert, R., Stevenson, D., Girardet, H. and Stren, R.E. (1996) *Making Cities Work: The Role of Local Authorities in the Urban Environment*, Earthscan, London.

GOPP/IAURIF (1986a) *Greater Cairo Region – Long Range Urban Development Scheme: Guide Plan – Implementation of the Homogeneous Sectors*, Ministry of Development, New Communities and Land Reclamation, General Organization for Physical Planning/Institut d'Aménagement et d'Urbanisme de la Région d'Ile-de-France, Chapter 1.

GOPP/IAURIF (1986b) *Greater Cairo Region – Long Range Urban Development Scheme: East Cairo Urban Development Plan (Master Plans)*, Ministry of Development, New Communities and Land Reclamation, Section 2.4.3.

GOPP et al. (1982) *Greater Cairo Region – Long Range Urban Development Scheme: Master Scheme*, General Organization for Physical Planning, Ministry of Development, State Ministry for Housing and Land Reclamation, Chapter 2.

Gordon, P. et al. (1997) Are compact cities a desirable goal? *Journal of the American Planning Association*, 63(1).

Government of Lesotho (2000) *Lesotho: Interim Poverty Reduction Strategy Paper*, Ministry of Development Planning, Kingdom of Lesotho.

Grieg-Gran, M. (1998) *The Waste Hierarchy: Recycling and Solid Waste Management in Developing Countries*, report prepared for Department for International Development, IIED, London.

Gross et al., (1995) in: Frankenberger, T., *Household Livelihood Security: a Unifying Conceptual Framework for CARE Programming*, CARE USA, Atlanta.

Grubb, M., Vrolijk, C. and Brack, D. (1999) *The Kyoto Protocol: A Guide and Assessment*, Royal Institute of International Affairs, London.

Habraken, N.J. (1972) *Supports: An Alternative to Mass Housing*, Architectural Press, London.

Hall, P. (1992) *Urban and Regional Planning*, 3rd edn, Routledge, London.

Hamdi, N. and Goethert, R. (1989) The support paradigm for housing and its impact on practice: the case in Sri Lanka, *Habitat International*, 13(4): 19–28.

Hamdi, N., Harpham, T., Manchosette, M. and Payne, G. (1998) *The Urban Development Agenda*, EC Approach Paper, Urban Development Series, Working Paper No. 4, European Commission, Brussels.

Hamza, M. and Zetter, R. (1998) Structural adjustment, urban systems and disaster vulnerability in developing countries, *Cities*, 15: 291–299.

Handoussa, H. (1991a) The impact of foreign aid on Egypt's economic development, 1952–1986, in: Lele, U. and Nabi, I. (eds), *Transitions in Development: The Role of Aid and Commercial Flows*, International Center for Economic Growth, San Francisco, pp. 195–224.

Handoussa, H. (1991b) Crisis and challenge: prospects for the 1990s, in: Handoussa, H. and Potter, G. (eds), *Employment and Structural Adjustment: Egypt in the 1980s*, American University in Cairo Press, Cairo, pp. 3–21.

Hardoy, J.E., Mitlin D. and Satterthwaite, D. (1992a) *Environmental Problems in Third World Cities*, Earthscan, London.

Hardoy, J.E., Mitlin, D. and Satterthwaite, D. (1992b) The future city, in: Holmberg, J. (ed.), *Policies for a Small Planet*, Earthscan, London, pp. 124–156.

Hardt, M. and Negri, A. (2000) *Empire*, Harvard University Press, Cambridge, MA/London.

Harik, I. (1997) *Economic Policy Reform in Egypt*, University Press of Florida, Gainesville, FL, pp. 86–108, 156–178.

Harris, N. (1994) Structural Adjustment and Cities, Development Planning Unit Working Paper no. 63, University College, London.

Harris, N. (1995) Bombay in a global economy: structural adjustment and the role of cities, *Cities*, 12(3): 175–184.

Harris, N. and Fabricus, I. (eds) (1996) *Cities and Structural Adjustment*, University College London Development Planning Unit/Overseas Development Administration, London.

Harriss, J. (1989) Urban poverty and urban poverty alleviation, *Cities*, 6(3): 186–194.

Hartmann, B. (1998) Population, environment and security: a new trinity, *Environment and Urbanization*, 10(2): 113–127.

Harvey, L.D.D. (2000) *Climate and Global Environmental Change*, Prentice-Hall, London.

Hassan, M.M. (1998) Urban expansion in a fast growing third world city: Dhaka, Bangladesh, PhD thesis, Oxford Brookes University, Oxford, UK.

Haughton, G. (1999) Environmental justice and the sustainable city, *Journal of Planning Education and Research*, 18(3): 233–243.

Haughton, G. and Hunter, C. (1994) *Sustainable Cities*, Regional Studies Association, Cromwell Press, UK.

Healey, P. et al. (1993) Planning, plans and sustainable development, *Regional Studies*, 27(8).

Heissler, K. (1998) B is for begging, beating and butterflies, *Orbit* 70: 10–12 VSO, London.

Hettne, B. (1990) *Development Theory and Three Worlds*, Longman Scientific and Technical, UK.

Hewitt, T. (1992) Developing countries 1945–1990, in: Allen, T. and Thomas, A. (eds), *Poverty and Development in the 1990s*, Oxford University Press/Open University, Oxford/Milton Keynes, UK.

Hoch, C. (1984) Doing good and being right: the pragmatic connection in planning theory, *Journal of American Planning Association*, Summer: 335–345.

Hoehn, J. and Krieger, D. (2000) An economic analysis of water and wastewater investments in Cairo, Egypt, *Evaluation Review*, 24(6): 579–608.

Holdgate, M., Kassas, M. and White, G. (eds) (1982) *The World Environment: 1972–1982*, United Nations Environment Programme (UNEP).

Hoshino, C. (1997) Emerging trends and prospects in local and regional development planning, *Regional Development Dialogue*, 3: 147–181.

Houghton, J. (1994) *Global Warming: The Complete Briefing*, Lion Publishing, Oxford, UK.

Houghton, J.T., Jenkins, G.J. and Ephraums, J.J. (eds) (1990) *Climate Change: The IPCC Scientific Assessment*, Cambridge University Press, Cambridge, UK.

Houghton, J.T., Callander, B.A. and Varney, S.K. (eds) (1992) *Climate Change 1992: The Supplementary Report to the IPCC Scientific Assessment*, Cambridge University Press, Cambridge, UK.

Houghton, J.T., Meiro Filho, L.G., Callander, B.A., Harris, N., Kattenberg, A. and Maskell, K. (eds) (1996) *Climate Change 1995: The Science of Climate Change*, Cambridge University Press, Cambridge, UK.

IAURIF/GOPP (1991) *Greater Cairo Region Master Scheme: Implementation Assessment, Updating Proposals*, Ministry of Development, New Communities, Housing and Public Utilities, Institut d'Aménagement et d'Urbanisme de la Région d'Ile-de-France/General Organization for Physical Planning, pp. 13–16.

Ibrahim, S. (1996) *Egypt, Islam and Democracy: Twelve Critical Essays*, American University in Cairo Press, Cairo, pp. 87–8.

IDSC (undated) *Report on High-Density Random Areas in Certain Governorates of the Republic* (in Arabic), Information Decision Support Center, Prime Minister's Office, Cairo, Vol. 3, pp. 2, 4–5.

Ikram, K. (1980) *Egypt: Economic Management in a Time of Transition*, Johns Hopkins University Press, Baltimore, pp. 3–8.

Ino, T. et al. (1989) *Local Administration and Center–Local Relations in Egypt*, MES Series No. 25, Institute of Developing Economies, Tokyo, pp. 105–113.

Ismail, S. (1996) The politics of space in urban Cairo: informal communities and the state, *Arab Studies Journal*, 4: 119–132.

Jacobi, P.R. (1994) Households and environment in the city of Sao Paulo: problems, perceptions and solutions, *Environment and Urbanization*, 6(2): 87–110.

Jacobs, M. (1997) *Making Sense of Environmental Capacity*, report for the CPRE, Department of Geography, London School of Economics, sponsored by Johnson Wax Ltd.

Jeffrey, P. (2000) Lives saved in Caracas slum, *ReliefWeb Earthquakes Situation Report* No. 36, www.reliefweb.int

Jenkins, P. (1998) National and international shelter policy initiatives in Mozambique: housing the urban poor at the periphery, PhD thesis, Heriot-Watt University, Edinburgh.

Jenkins, P. (1999) Mozambique: housing and land markets in Maputo, Research Paper No. 72, Edinburgh College of Art/Heriot-Watt University, School of Planning and Housing, Edinburgh.

Jenkins, P. (2000) Urban management, urban poverty and urban governance: planning and land management in Maputo, Mozambique, *Environment and Urbanisation* 12(1): 137–152.

Jenkins, P. (2001a) Emerging urban residential land markets in post-Socialist Mozambique: the impact on the poor and alternatives to improve land access and urban development. An action-research project in peri-urban areas of Maputo, Research Paper No. 75, Edinburgh College of Art/Heriot-Watt University, School of Planning and Housing.

Jenkins, P. (2001b) When the state and market are weak – the role of civil society in shelter at the periphery. The experience of peri-urban communities in Maputo, Mozambique, in: Carley, M., Jenkins P. and Smith H. (eds) *Urban Development and Civil Society: The Role of Communities in Sustainable Cities*, Earthscan, London, pp. 33–50.

Jenkins, P. (2001c) Relationships between the state and civil society and their importance for sustainable urban development, in: Carley, M., Jenkins P. and Smith H. (eds) *Urban Development and Civil Society: The Role of Communities in Sustainable Cities*, Earthscan, London, pp. 175–191.

Jenkins, P. (forthcoming) The Image of the City in Mozambique, in: Bryceson and Potts, (eds) *African Urban Economies: Viability, Vitality or Vitiation of Major Cities in East and Southern Africa?* James Currey, Oxford.

Jenkins, P. and Smith, H. (2001a) The state, the market and community – an analytical framework for community self development, in: Carley, M., Jenkins P. and Smith H. (eds), *Urban Development and Civil Society: The Role of Communities in Sustainable Cities*, Earthscan, London, pp. 16–30.

Jenkins, P. and Smith, H. (2001b) An institutional approach to the analysis of state capacity in housing systems in the developing world: case studies in South Africa and Costa Rica, *Housing Studies*, 16(4): 485–507.

Jenks, M., Burton, E. and Williams, K. (1996) *The Compact City, A Sustainable Form?* Spon, London.

Joint Housing and Community Upgrading Team (1977) *Housing and Community Upgrading for Low-Income Egyptians*, Cairo, pp. 25, 51–83.

Joint Housing Team (1976) *Immediate Action Proposals for Housing in Egypt*, Vol. 1, Cairo, pp. v–viii, 15–47, 61–72.

Joint Land Policy Team (1977) *Urban Land Use in Egypt*, Vol. 2, Cairo, pp. 46–48.

Jones, G.A. and Ward, P.M. (1994) The World Bank's new urban management programme: paradigm shift or policy continuity? *Habitat International*, 16(3): 33–51.

Kell, A. et al. (1993) Project objectives, organization and implementation, *Proceedings of the Institution of Civil Engineers*, Special Issue, Paper 10228, 8–17.

Kelly, P.F. (1998) The politics of urban–rural relationships: land conversion in the Philippines, *Environment and Urbanization*, 10(1): 35–54.

Koenig, D. (1995) Sustainable development: linking global environmental change to technology cooperation, in: Dwivedi, O.P. and Vajpeyi, D. (eds), *Environmental Politics in The Third World: A Comparative Analysis*, Mansell Publishing, UK.

Komives, K. (1999) *Designing Pro-poor Water and Sewerage Concessions: Early Lessons from Bolivia*, World Bank Policy Research Papers, World Bank, Washington, DC.

Kreimer, A., Munasinghe, M. and Preece, M. (1992) Reducing environmental vulnerability and managing disasters in urban areas, in: Kreimer, A. and Munasinghe, M. (eds), *Environmental Management and Urban Vulnerability*, World Bank Discussion Paper No. 168, World Bank, Washington, DC.

Latesteijn, H. and Schoonenboom, J. (1996) Policy scenarios for sustainable development, in: Blowers, A. and Glasbergen, P. (eds), *Environmental Policy in an International Context 3*, Open University of the Netherlands, Arnold, UK.

Leguizamón, L. (1997) *Manual de la Administración Local en el Distrito Capital*, Librería Ethos, Bogotá.

Leitmann, J. (1994) The World Bank and the brown agenda: evolution of a revolution, *Third World Planning Review*, 16(2): 117–127.

Leitmann, J. (1999) *Sustaining Cities: Environment Planning and Management in Urban Design*, McGraw-Hill, New York.

Levine (1998) Rethinking accessibility and jobs housing balance, *Journal of the American Planning Association*, 64(2).

Linz, J. (1970) An authoritarian regime: Spain, in: Allardt, E. and Rokkan, S. (eds), *Mass Society: Studies in Political Sociology*, Free Press, New York, pp. 251–283.

Londoño, J.L. (1992) *Bogota: Problemas y Soluciones*, Departamento Nacional de Planeación, Bogotá.

López Follegatti, J. (1999) Ilo: a city in transformation, *Environment and Urbanization*, 11(2): 181–202.

Luciani, G. (1987) Allocation vs production states: a theoretical framework, in: Beblawi, H. and Luciani, G. (eds), *The Rentier State*, Croom Helm, London, pp. 63–82.

Mabin, A. (1995) On the problems and prospects of overcoming segregation and fragmentation in Southern Africa's cities in the postmodern era, in: Watson, S. and Gibson, K. (eds), *Postmodern Cities and Spaces*, Blackwell, Oxford, UK.

Malpezzi, S.J., Tipple, A.G. and Willis, K.G. (1990) *Costs and Benefits of Rent Control: a Case Study of Kumasi*, World Bank Discussion Paper No. 74, World Bank, Washington, DC.

de la Macorra, C.M. (1998) Innovative community projects and their role in the urban development of Mexico City, PhD thesis, Oxford Brookes University, Oxford, UK.

Marcuse, P. (1998) Sustainability is not enough, *Environment and Urbanization*, 10(2): 103–111.

Marvin, S. and Guy, S. (1999) Beyond the Myth of the New Environmental Localization, in Atkinson, A., Davila, J., Fernandes, E. and Mattingly, M. (eds) The Challenge of Environmental Management in Urban Areas, Ashgate Publishing Ltd, UK, Athenaeum Press Ltd, USA.

Maxwell, D. (1996) *Household Livelihood Security in an Urban Context; Conceptual Framework for the Dar es Salaam Urban Livelihood Security Assessment*, CARE, USA.

Maxwell, D. (1999) Livelihoods and vulnerability: how different is the urban case?, paper presented to the 1999 meeting of the Society for Applied Anthropology, Tucson, AZ, April 20–25.

Mayfield, J. (1996) *Local Government in Egypt: Structure, Process and the Challenge of Reform*, American University in Cairo Press, Cairo, p. 42.

McGranahan, G. (1991) *Environmental Problems and the Urban Household in Third World Countries*, Stockholm Environment Institute, Stockholm.

McGranahan, G. and Satterthwaite, D. (2000) Environmental health or ecological sustainability? Reconciling the brown and green agendas in urban development, in: Pugh, C. (ed.), *Sustainable Cities in Developing Countries*, Earthscan, London, pp. 73–90.

McGranahan, G., Songsore, J. and Kjellén, M. (1996) Sustainability, poverty and urban environmental transitions, in: Pugh, C. (ed.), *Sustainability, the Environment and Urbanization*, Earthscan, London, pp. 103–134.

Mchunu, K. (2002) Being a man the Xhosa way: planning in the context of a multi-cultural South Africa, presented at Sixth Australasian Urban and Planning History Conference, Southern Crossings, University of Auckland, NZ, February 2002.

McNair, M. (1989) Egypt: profusion of plans, poverty of programs – a consultant's experience, in: May, R. (ed.), *The Urbanization Revolution*, Plenum Press, New York, pp. 151–169.

Meirelles, H. (1998) *Direito Municipal Brasileiro* 10th edition, updated by Monteiro, I. and Prendes, Co., Malheiros, São Paulo.

Menegat, R. (ed.) (1998) *Atlas Ambiental de Porto Alegre*, Universidade Federal do Rio Grande do Sul, Prefeitura Municipal de Porto Alegre and Instituto Nacional de Pesquisas Espaciais, Porto Alegre.

Miller, G. and Kachinsky, R. (1993) West Bank Scheme, *Proceedings of the Institution of Civil Engineers*, Special Issue, Paper 10231, 56–59.

Milroy, B. (1991) Into postmodern weightlessness, *Journal of Planning Education Research*, 10(3): 181–187.

Ministerio de Desarrollo Económico (1995) *Ciudades y Ciudadanía, La Política del Salto Social*, Ministerio de Desarrollo Económico, Bogotá.

Ministry for Housing and Land Reclamation (undated) *Greater Cairo Region Master Plan*, Cairo.

Ministry of Housing, Utilities and Urban Communities (1996) *1976–1996, Twenty Years of Development: We Build for People, New Communities in Egypt*, Official brochure, Cairo.

Ministry of Urban Affairs and Employment (1999) Agenda 21 report: Promoting sustainable human settlement development, presented at 17th Session of the UN Commission on Human Settlements, Nairobi, May 1999, Government of India.

Miranda, L. and Hordijk, M. (1998) Let us build cities for life: the national campaign of local Agenda 21s in Peru, *Environment and Urbanization*, 10(2): 69–102.

Mitlin, D. and Satterthwaite, D. (1996) Sustainable Development in Cities, in: Pugh, C. (ed.), *Sustainability, the Environment and Urbanization*, Earthscan, London.

Mohan, R. (1994) *Understanding the Developing Metropolis: Lessons from the City Studies of Bogotá and Cali, Colombia*, World Bank/Oxford University Press, New York/Oxford.

Montenegro, F. (1999) *Bogotá Zona Norte*, Departamento Administrativo de Planeación Distrital, Bogotá.

Mueller, C.C. (1995) Environmental problems inherent to a development style: degradation and poverty in Brazil, *Environment and Urbanization*, 7(2): 67–84.

Muller, J. (1995) A Post-Apartheid Planning Paradigm, paper presented at the Toward and Beyond 2000: The Future of Planning and Planning Education Conference, June, East London, South Africa.

Muller, M.S. (ed.) (1997) *The Collection of Household Excreta: The Operation of Services in Urban Low-income Neighbourhoods*, WASTE and ENSIC, Gouda.

Nickson, A. (1995) *Local Government in Latin America*, Lynne Rienner, London.

Oldham, L. et al. (1987) Informal communities in Cairo: the basis of a typology, *Cairo Papers in Social Science*, 10(4).

Oman, C. and Wignaraja, G. (1991) *The Postwar Evolution of Development Thinking*, Macmillan/OECD, London.

Orangi Pilot Project (1995) NGO profile: Orangi Pilot Project, *Environment and Urbanization*, 7(2): 227–236.

Orellana, R. (2000) *Desde la revuelta cochabambina hacia la modificación de la Ley de Agua Potable y Alcantarillado Sanitario*, Santa Cruz (mimeo).

PADCO Inc. et al. (1981) *Working Paper on Second Round Alternatives for the National Urban Policy Study*, prepared by the Planning and Design Cooperative for the Advisory Committee for Reconstruction, Ministry of Development, Arab Republic of Egypt.

PADCO Inc. et al. (1982) *The National Urban Policy Study*, Vol. 1, Final Report, prepared by the Planning and Design Cooperative for the Advisory Committee for Reconstruction, Ministry of Development, Arab Republic of Egypt, pp. xviii–xxx, 12–13, 85–7, 101, 447–448.

Payne, G. (ed.) (2000) *Making Common Ground: Public–private Partnerships in Land for Housing*, Intermediate Technology Publications, London.

Pearce, D. et al. (1990) *Sustainable Development: Economy and Environment in the Third World*, Elgar, Aldershot, UK.

Perelman, J. (2000) *El revival entreguista*, La Paz (mimeo).

Pergolis, J. (1998) *Bogotá Fragmentada: Cultura y espacio Urbano a Finales del siglo XX*, T.M. Editores, Universidad Piloto de Colombia, Bogotá.

Post, J. (1997) Urban management in an unruly setting, *Third World Planning Review*, 19(4): 347–366.

Postel, S. (1992) *The Last Oasis; Facing Water Scarcity*, Worldwatch Environmental Alert Series, Earthscan, London.

Prefeitura Municipal de Belém (1993) *Plano Diretor 1991–2010*, Belém, Diário Oficial do Município.

Pugh, C. (1994) 'The idea of enablement in housing sector development: The political economy of housing for developing countries', Cities, 11:6, pp. 357–371.

Pugh, C. (1995a) International structural adjustment and its sectoral and spatial impacts, *Urban Studies*, 32(2): 261–285.

Pugh, C. (1995b) 'The role of the World Bank in housing' in Aldrich, B. and Sandhu, R. (eds) *Housing the Urban Poor, Policy and Practice in Developing Countries*, Zed Press, London pp 37–92.

Pugh, C. (ed.) (1996) *Sustainability, The Environment and Urbanization*, Earthscan, London.

Pugh, C. (1997) The changing roles of self-help in housing and urban policies, 1950–1996: experience in developing countries, *Third World Planning Review*, 19(1): 91–109.

Pugh, C. (ed.) (2000) *Sustainable Cities in Developing Countries*, Earthscan, London.

Putnam, R. (1993) *Making Democracy Work: Civic Tradition in Modern Italy*, Princeton University Press, Princeton, NJ.

Ribeiro, L. and Lago, L. (1995) Restructuring in large Brazilian cities, *International Journal of Urban and Regional Research*, 19: 369–382.

Robinson, W. (1998/99) Latin America and global capitalism, *Race and Class*, 40(2/3): 111–131.

Rojas, E. (1995) *The IDB in Low-cost Housing: The First Three Decades*, IDB Strategic Planning and Operation Policy Department, Washington, DC.

Rojas, G. (1998) Concertación y gobernabilidad en Bolivia, in: Rojas, G. et al. (eds), *Concertación y legitimidad en América Latina*, Friedrich Ebert Stiftung/CESU/ILDIS, La Paz.

Rojas, G. et al. (1998) *Concertación y legitimidad en América Latina*, Friedrich Ebert Stiftung/CESU/ILDIS, La Paz, Bolivia.

Roussillion, A. (1998) Republican Egypt reinterpreted: revolution and beyond, in: Daly, M. (ed.), *The Cambridge History of Egypt*, Vol. 2, *Modern Egypt, from 1517 to the End of the Twentieth Century*, Cambridge University Press, Cambridge, UK, pp. 334–393.

Ruel, M., Haddad, L. and Garrett, J. (1999) Some urban facts of life: implications for research and policy, *World Development*, 27(11): 1917–1938.

Sage, C. (1996) The scope for North–South co-operation, in: Blowers, A. and Glasbergen, P. (eds), *Environmental Policy in an International Context 3*, Open University of the Netherlands, Arnold, UK.

Sandercock, L. (1993) *Towards Cosmopolis: Planning for Multicultural Cities*, John Wiley, Chichester.

Sanderson, D. (1999a) HLS in Urban Settlements, *CARE UK Urban Briefing Note*, February, p.l.

Sanderson, D. (1999b) Implementing action planning to reduce urban risk, Delhi, *Open House International*, 24(3): 33–39.

Sandor, R. (1999) Voluntary carbon deals break records, *Environmental Finance*, November: 11–12.

Satterthwaite, D. (1995) The underestimation of poverty and its health consequences, *Third World Planning Review*, 17(4): iii–xii.

Satterthwaite, D. (1998) Cities and sustainable development: what progress since Our Common Future?, in: Softing, G.B., Benneh, G., Hindar, K., Walloe, L. and Wijkman, A. (eds), *The Brundtland Commission's Report – 10 years*, Scandinavian University Press, Oslo, pp. 27–39.

Satterthwaite, D. (2001) *The scale and nature of urban poverty in low and middle income nations*, paper prepared for CARE Zambia urban conference, Lusaka, February 2001.

Saywell, D. and Hunt, C. (1999) *Sanitation Programmes Revisited*, WELL Study Task No. 161, London School of Hygiene and Tropical Medicine, UK and Water, Engineering and Development Centre (WEDC), Loughborough University, UK.

Schoonraad, M.D. (2000) Cultural and institutional obstacles to compact cities in South Africa, in: Jenks, M. and Burgess, R. (eds), *Compact Cities: Sustainable Urban Forms for Developing Countries*, Spon Press, London.

Schusterman, R. and Hardoy, A. (1997) Reconstructing social capital in a poor urban settlement: the Integrated Improvement Programme, Barrio San Jorge, *Environment and Urbanization*, 9(1): 91–119.

SED (1998) *Plan Sectorial de Educación 1998–2000 de Santa fe de Bogotá*, Secretaria de Educación del Distrito, Bogotá.

SEFIN/PMB (1991a) *Planta Genérica de Valores*, Secretaria de Finanças Prefeitura Municipal de Belém (mimeo).

SEFIN/PMB (1991b*) Planta de Setores Fiscais*, Secretaria de Finanças Prefeitura Municipal de Belém (mimeo).

SEFIN/PMB (1998a) *Evolução da Receita Arrecadada no Período de 1996 a 1998*, – Secretaria de Finanças Prefeitura Municipal de Belém (mimeo).

SEFIN/PMB (1998b) *Índices de Inadimplêncioa e IPTU por Faixa de Alíquota*, Secretaria de Finanças Prefeitura Municipal de Belém (mimeo).

Selman, P. (1996) *Local Sustainability: managing and planning ecologically sound places*, Paul Chapman Publishing Ltd, London.

Sharma, A. and Gupta, M. (1998) *TDR Project: Reducing Urban Risk, India*, SEEDS report, Delhi.

Sherif, Y. et al. (1996) *Elements of the Egyptian Partnership Experience in Urban Development*, Local Initiative Facility for Urban Environment (LIFE Programme), Cairo, p. 21.

Sims, D. (1990) Development Benefits of the Cairo Ring Road and Associated Bridges: Final Report, Submitted to USAID/Egypt, Cairo, 20 August .

Sims, D. (1998) *Telal Zeinhum Participatory Urban Upgrading Project: Project Concept and Pre-Appraisal Report*, prepared for Kreditanstalt für Wiederaufbau/ Cairo Governorate, Cairo.

Sims, D. (ed.) (2000) *Residential Informality in Greater Cairo: Typologies, Representative Areas, Quantification, Valuation, and Causal Factors*, prepared for the Institute for Liberty and Democracy, Cairo.

Singerman, D. (1996) *Avenues of Participation: Family, Politics, and Networks in Urban Quarters of Cairo*, Princeton University Press, Princeton, pp. 244–268.

Smit, J., Ratta, A. and Nasr, J. (1996) *Urban Agriculture: Food, Jobs and Sustainable Cities*, Publication Series for Habitat II, Vol. 1, UNDP, New York.

Smith, H. (1999) Networks and spaces of negotiation in low-income housing: the case of Costa Rica, PhD thesis, Heriot-Watt University, Edinburgh, UK.

Smith, H. and Valverde, J.M. (2001) When community development becomes a political bargaining tool: the case for structural change in low-income housing provision in Costa Rica, in: Carley, M., Jenkins, P. and Smith, H. (eds), *Urban Development and Civil Society: The Role of Communities in Sustainable Cities*, Earthscan, London, pp. 121–138.

Smith, K. and Lee, Y. (1993) Urbanization and environmental risk transition, in: Kasarda, J. and Parnell, A. (eds), *Third World Cities: Problems, Policies and Prospects*, SAGE Publications, London.

Solón, P. (2000) Las nuevas políticas de Saneamiento Básico: Privatización y Concesión de los Servicios de agua Potable y Alcantarillado, paper presented at *Gestion integral del agua en Cochabamba*, Cochabamba, February 2000. www.aguabolivia.org

Solón, P. and Orellana, R. (2000) Cambios en la Ley de Agua Potable . . . quienes ganan?, *Suplemento Ventana de La Razon* 16/IV, La Paz.

Souza, D. (1992) Intervenção Estatal no Município: o caso de Belém na década de 80. Master's thesis, NAEA Universidade Federal do Pará, Brazil.

Spence, R., Wells, J. and Dudley, E. (1993) *Jobs from Housing: Employment, Building Materials and Enabling Strategies for Urban Development*, ICT Publications/ODA, London.

Stewart, D. (1996) Cities in the desert: the Egyptian new-town program, *Annals of the Association of American Geographers*, 86(3): pp. 459–480.

Streeten, P. (1984) Basic needs: some unsettled questions, *World Development*, 12(9): 973–978.

Stren, R. (1993) Urban management in development assistance: an elusive concept, *Cities*, May: 125–138.

Stren, R.E. and White, R.R. (eds) (1989) *African Cities in Crisis*, Westview Press, Boulder, CO.

Stretton, H. (1978) *Urban Planning in Rich and Poor Countries*, Oxford University Press, Oxford, UK.

Sullivan, E. (1983) Should Cairo be governed? in: Lobban, R. (ed.), *Urban Research Strategies for Egypt, Cairo Papers in Social Science* No. 6:2, pp. 9–14.

Tadros, M. (1996) Dump to model district, *Al-Ahram Weekly*, 24–30 October: 12.

Taher, N. (1997a) *Socio-Political and Economic Costs of a Donor-Led Housing Programme: The Case of Rashed–Greater Cairo*, DPU Working Paper No. 84, Development Planning Unit, The Bartlett – University College London.

Taher, N. (1997b) Foreign aid and power relations: the government of Egypt, USAID and housing in Helwan, PhD thesis, London School of Economics and Political Science, London, pp. 208–241.

Tekçe, B. et al. (1994) *A Place to Live: Families and Child Health in a Cairo Neighborhood*, American University in Cairo Press, Cairo, pp. 1–61.

Tendler, J. (1997) *Good Governance in the Tropics,* Johns Hopkins University Press, Baltimore, MD/London.

Thomas, L. et al. (1996) A New Compact City Form: Concepts in Practice, in: Jenks, M. et al. (eds) *The Compact City: A Sustainable Urban Form?* E & FN Spon, London.

Timmerman, P. and White, R.R. (1997) Megahydropolis: coastal cities in the context of global environmental change, *Global Environmental Change*, 7(3): 205–234.

Tolba, M. (ed.) (1988) *Evolving Environmental Perception: From Stockholm to Nairobi*, UN Environment Programme (UNEP), Butterworth, London.

Tolba, M. and El-Khouly, O. (eds) (1992) *The World Environment 1972–1992: Two Decades of Challenge*, UN Environment Programme (UNEP)/Chapman & Hall, London.

Townroe, P.M. (1996) The changing structure of the city economy, in: Harris, N. and Fabricus, I. (eds), *Cities and Structural Adjustment*, University College London Development Planning Unit/Overseas Development Administration, London, pp. 13–28.

Tully, J. (1999) The agonic freedom of citizens, *Economy and Society*, 28(2): 161–182.

Turner, J.F.C. (1982) Issues in self-help and self-managed housing, in: Ward, P.M. (ed.), *Self-help Housing: A Critique*, Mansell, London, pp. 99–113.

Turner, J.F.C. (1988a) Introductory perspective, in: Turner, B. (ed.), *Building Community: A Third World Case Book*, Community Books, London, pp. 13–16.

Turner, J.F.C. (1988b) Issues and conclusions, in: Turner, B. (ed.), *Building Community: A Third World Case Book*, Community Books, London, pp. 169–181.

UN (1996) *Habitat Agenda and Istanbul Declaration*, UN Department of Public Information, New York.

UNCED (1992) *Earth Summit: Agenda 21 – The United Nations Programme of Action from Rio*, UN Conference on Environment and Development, New York.

UNCHS (1984) *The Construction Industry in Developing Countries, Vol. 1, Contributions to Economic Growth*, UNCHS, Nairobi.

UNCHS (1987) *Global Report on Human Settlements 1986*, Oxford University Press, Oxford/New York.

UNCHS (1988) *Refuse Collection Vehicles for Developing Countries*, HS/138/88E, UNCHS (Habitat), Nairobi.

UNCHS (1989) *A New Agenda for Human Settlements*, UNCHS (Habitat), Nairobi.

UNCHS (1990) *The Global Strategy for Shelter to the Year 2000*, UNCHS (Habitat), Nairobi.

UNCHS (1991) *Human Settlements and Sustainable Development*, UNCHS (Habitat), Nairobi.

UNCHS (1993) Underemployment, unemployment and shelter provision, *Habitat News*, 15(2): 9–12.

UNCHS (1996a) *An Urbanizing World: Global Report on Human Settlements, 1996*, Oxford University Press, Oxford/New York.

UNCHS (1996b) *The Habitat Agenda: Goals and Principles, Commitments and Global Plan of Action*, UN Conference on Human Settlements (Habitat II), UNCHS, Nairobi.

UNCHS (1998) *Participación Comunal/Autogestión Comunitaria y Gobierno Facilitador, Costa Rica: Informe Nacional de Investigación Fase II*, UNCHS (Habitat), Nairobi.

UNDP (1991) Cities, People and Poverty: Urban Development Cooperation for the 1990s, a UNDP Strategy Paper, the United Nations Development Programme, New York.

UNDP (1993) *UNDP and Organizations of Civil Society*, United Nations Development Programme, New York.

UNDP (1997) *Human Development Report 1997*, United Nations Development Programme, Oxford University Press, New York.

UNDP Lesotho (1997) *Assessment of Urban Poverty*, United Nations Development Programme, Lesotho.

UNDP (1998) *Los Contrastes del Desarrollo Humano*, United Nations Development Programme, Guatemala.

UNEP (1999) *Global Environment Outlook 2000*, United Nations Environment Programme, Earthscan, London.

USAID (1988) *Audit of Helwan Housing and Community Upgrading in Egypt, Project No. 263–0066*, Audit Report No. 6–263–89–1, US Agency for International Development/Regional Inspector General/Audit, Cairo.

USAID (1993) *Using Capital Project to Promote Development and US Commercial Interests*, AID Evaluation Technical Report No. 19, US Agency for International Development, Center for Development Information and Evaluation, Washington, DC, p. 53.

USAID (undated) Cairo Sewerage Project: Embaba Unsewered Area, internal report, US Agency for International Development, Washington, DC.

Vandewalle, D. (1998) *Libya Since Independence: Oil and State-Building*, Cornell University Press, Ithaca, NY, pp. 17–38.

Vélasquez, L.S. (1998) Agenda 21: a form of joint environmental management in Manizales, Colombia, *Environment and Urbanization*, 10(2): 9–36.

Viceministerio de Servicios Basicos (1999) *Descentralizacion de los Servicios Basicos en Bolivia*, La Paz.

Victor, D.G. (2001) *The Collapse of the Kyoto Protocol and the Struggle to Stop Global Warming*, Princeton University Press, Princeton, NJ/Oxford, UK.

Wackernagel, M. and Rees, W.E. (1996) *Our Ecological Footprint: Reducing Human Impact on the Earth*, New Society Publishers, Gabriola Island, BC.

Wakely, P., Ramirez, R. and Mumtaz, B. (1992) *The Formulation of National Shelter Strategies. Six Case Studies: Nicaragua, Costa Rica, Uganda, Zimbabwe, Philippines, Indonesia*, Development Planning Unit, The Bartlett – University College London.

Waterbury, J. (1976) Corruption, political stability and development: comparative evidence from Egypt and Morocco, *Government and Opposition*, 11: 426–445.

Waterbury, J. (1983) *The Egypt of Nasser and Sadat: The Political Economy of Two Regimes*, Princeton University Press, Princeton, NJ, pp. 3–40, 229, 231, 329.

Waterbury, J. (1985) The soft state and the open door: Egypt's experience with economic liberalization, 1974–1984, *Comparative Politics*, 18(1): 65–83.

Waterbury, J. (1993) *Exposed to Innumerable Delusions: Public Enterprise and State Power in Egypt, India, Mexico and Turkey*, Cambridge University Press, Cambridge, pp. 76–82.

WCED (1987) *Our Common Future*, The Brundtland Report, World Commission on Environment and Development/Oxford University Press, Oxford, UK.

Webber, M. (1968) *Explorations into Urban Structure*, 3rd edn, University of Pennsylvania Press, Philadelphia, PA.

Webster, A. (1990) Introduction to the Sociology of Development, Palgrave Macmillan, London.

Wegelin, E.A. (1994) Everything you always wanted to know about the urban management programme (but were afraid to ask), *Habitat International*, 18(4): 127–137.

Wegelin, E., Vanderschueren, F. and Wekwete, K. (1996) *Programme Options for Urban Poverty Reduction: A Framework for Action at the Municipal Level*, World Bank, Washington, DC.

Weiss, D. and Wurzel, U. (1998) *The Economics and Politics of Transition to an Open Market Economy – Egypt*, Development Centre Studies, OECD Development Centre, Paris, pp. 41–103.

Welbank, M. (1996) The search for a sustainable urban form, in: Jenkins, M. et al. (eds), *The Compact City: A Sustainable Form*? Spon Press, London.

Welford, R. (1996) Business and environmental policies, in: Blowers, A. and Glasbergen, P. (eds), *Environmental Policy in an International Context 3*, Open University of the Netherlands, Arnold, UK.

Werna, E., Harpham, T., Blue, I. and Goldstein, G. (1998) *Healthy City Projects in Developing Countries: An International Approach to Local Problems*, Earthscan, London.

White, L. (1986) Urban community organizations and local government: exploring relationships and roles, *Public Administration and Development* 6: 239–253.

White, R.R. (1993) *North, South and the Environmental Crisis*, University of Toronto Press, Toronto.

White, R.R. (1994) *Urban Environmental Management: Environmental Change and Urban Design*, John Wiley and Sons, Chichester, UK.

Whittington, D., Lauria, D., Wright, C.K., Hughes, J. and Swarna, V. (1992) *Household Demand for Improved Sanitation Services: A Case Study of Kumasi, Ghana*, UNDP-World Bank Water and Sanitation Programme, Washington, DC.

WHO (1992) *Our Planet, Our Health*, Report of the WHO Commission on Health and Environment, World Health Organization, Geneva.

WHO (1996) Creating healthy cities in the 21st century, Background Paper prepared for the *Dialogue on Health in Human Settlements* for Habitat II World Health Organization, Geneva, reprinted in: Satterthwaite, D. (ed.) (1999) *Sustainable Cities: A Reader*, Earthscan, London, pp. 137–172.

WHO/UNICEF (1993) *Water Supply and Sanitation Sector Monitoring Report 1993*, WHO/UNICEF Joint Monitoring Programme, Geneva.

World Bank (1986a) Project completion report – Egypt: first urban development project, Europe, Middle East, and North Africa Regional Office, in: *Project Performance Audit Report: Egypt First Urban Development Project* [for official use only], No. 6561, Operations Evaluation Department, World Bank, Washington, DC, pp. 33–89.

World Bank (1986b) *Project Performance Audit Report: Egypt First Urban Development Project* [for official use only], No. 6561, Operations Evaluation Department, World Bank, Washington, DC.

World Bank (1991) *Urban Policy and Economic Development: An Agenda for the 1990s*, Policy Paper, World Bank, Washington, DC.

World Bank (1993) *Housing: Enabling Markets to Work*, Policy Paper, World Bank, Washington, DC.

World Bank (1995a) *Poverty Reduction and the World Bank; Progress in fiscal 1994*, World Bank, Washington, DC.

World Bank (1995b) *Urban Policy and Economic Development: An Agenda for the 1990s*, World Bank, Washington, DC.

World Bank (1995c) Bolivia: evaluation of Bank Assistance Strategy, in: *Country Assistance Review*, www.worldbank.org

World Bank (1996) World Bank Latin American and Caribbean Studies: Proceedings from the Annual World Bank Conference on Development in Latin America and the Caribbean, Bogotá, Colombia, World Bank, Washington, DC.

World Bank (1998) *Memorandum of the President of the International Development Association and the International Finance Corporation to the Executive Directors on a Country Assistance Strategy of The World Bank Group for the Republic of Bolivia*, www.worldbank.org

World Bank (1999) *Bolivia: Public Expenditure Review*, World Bank, Washington, DC.

World Bank (2000a) *Entering the 21st Century: World Development Report 1999/2000*, Oxford University Press, New York.

World Bank (2000b) *Global Urban and Local Government Strategy*, World Bank, Washington, DC.

World Bank (2001) *World Development Report 2000/2001*, World Bank, Washington, DC.

World Bank/World Resources Institute (2000) *Bolivia at a Glance*, World Bank, Agriculture and Natural Resources Department, Washington, DC.

Wright, A. (1997) *Towards a Strategic Sanitation Approach: Improving the Sustainability of Urban Sanitation in Developing Countries*, IBRD/World Bank, Washington, DC.

Yearley, S. (1996) *Sociology, Environmentalism, Globalization: Reinventing the Globe*, Sage Publications, London.

Zaghloul, M. (1994) The structure and dynamics of the informal urban growth: the Cairo urban region, 1976–1986, PhD thesis, Harvard University, Cambridge, MA, pp. 6–7.

Zaidi, A. (1996) Urban local government in Pakistan – expecting too much from too little? *Economic and Political Weekly*, Vol. XXXI no. 44 Nov. 2: 2948–2953.

Zetter, R. and Hamza, M. (1997) The impact of foreign technical assistance on urban development projects in Egypt, *Habitat International*, 21(2): 153–166.

Zetter, R. and Hamza, M. (1998) Egypt: the state, foreign aid and community participation in urban shelter projects, *International Planning Studies*, 3(2): 185–205.

Zetter, R. and Hassan Al-Moataz, K. (2002) Urban economy or environmental policy? The case of Egypt, *Journal of Environmental Policy*, 4: 169–184.

Index

www.ingramcontent.com/pod-product-compliance
Lightning Source LLC
Chambersburg PA
CBHW041255040426
42334CB00028BA/3025